POSTMORTEM REPORT

TOMISLAV SUNIC

POSTMORTEM REPORT

Cultural Examinations from Postmodernity

Second Edition
Foreword by Kevin MacDonald

ARKTOS
LONDON 2017

Copyright © 2017 by Arktos Media Ltd.

All rights reserved. No part of this book may be reproduced or utilized in any form or by any means (whether electronic or mechanical), including photocopying, recording or by any information storage and retrieval system, without permission in writing from the publisher.

Printed in the United Kingdom.

ISBN	978-1-912079-77-3 (Paperback)
	978-1-912079-75-9 (Ebook)
EDITING	Martin Locker
COVER AND LAYOUT	Tor Westman

www.arktos.com

// CONTENTS

FOREWORD	ix
NOTE ON THE TEXT	xiv

PART I: Religion — 1

Marx, Moses, and the Pagans in the Secular City	2
Monotheism vs. Polytheism	21

PART II: Cultural Pessimism — 30

History and Decadence: Spengler's Cultural Pessimism Today	31
"Gemeinschaft and Gesellschaft": A Sociological View of the Decay of Modern Society	42
Emile Cioran and the Culture of Death	50
The Right Stuff (Drugs and Democracy)	61

PART III: Race / The Third Reich — 66

The Beauty and the Beast: Race and Racism in Europe	67
Art in the Third Reich: 1933–1945	95
The Destruction of Ethnic Germans and German Prisoners of War in Yugoslavia, 1945–1953	102

PART IV: Liberalism and Democracy — 111

Democracy Revisited: The Ancients and the Moderns	112
Liberalism or Democracy? Carl Schmitt and Apolitical Democracy	125
The Liberal Double-Talk and Its Lexical and Legal Consequences	137
Historical Dynamics of Liberalism: From Total Market to Total State	146

PART V: Multiculturalism and Communism   **161**

America in the Eyes of Eastern Europe	162
The Decline and Splendor of Nationalism	170
Woodrow Wilson's Defeat in Yugoslavia: The End of a Multicultural Utopia	180
A Global Village or the Rights of the Peoples?	189

ENDNOTES   **197**

INDEX   **214**

FOREWORD

This collection of articles and essays, previously published in a variety of journals and delving into topics ranging from race to literary criticism to philosophy of history, is most welcome. Tom Sunic is an important intellectual — all the more so because there are so few intellectuals, especially in Europe, who are willing to dissent from the standard views of the left that have dominated intellectual discourse on issues related to race, multiculturalism, and World War II.

There are several qualities of his writing and his personal talents that I think are noteworthy. As an American, I greatly appreciate his European view of things. Every time I read one of his essays, I am introduced to a large number of authors who are unfamiliar to American audiences. Like most Americans, one of my (several) vices is that I am restricted to the English language. Sunic has read widely in French and German, and Croatian. This is a huge advantage in developing a broad perspective on European history and culture as a whole. So many intellectuals are confined to one little area — I think because they are afraid to be criticized by resident experts if they cross-disciplinary boundaries. The towering egos of so many intellectuals and their desires to defend their little territory against interlopers are huge barriers to progress.

Add to that his personal experience: The vast majority of Americans, myself included, have no experience of anything remotely resembling the brutal history of Europe's recent past. Sunic grew up in Croatia under Communism and is personally acquainted with some of the darkest phenomena of the twentieth century. His family was persecuted by the communists and he clearly has a deep sense of the tragic aftermath of

World War II when the communists slaughtered many thousands of Croat nationalists as well as nationalists in other Eastern European countries that came under communist domination. He discusses "The Aristocide of Bleiburg and other communist killing fields" — the point being that the communists murdered a considerable percentage of the Croatian elite. Indeed, he proposes that the murderous actions of the communists probably had a dysgenic effect on the population as a whole. As he points out, this murderous hostility toward the intelligent, the talented, and the physically gifted is the common denominator of the political left. Armed with theories of radical environmentalism ("the thesis that the social-economic environment engenders miracles") — what some have called "left creationism," and impervious to scientific facts and logic, Communism has had devastating effects wherever it has come to power. Sunic is what has been called a "race realist" — someone who is not reticent in discussing the importance of race in human affairs based on scientific evidence and common sense. From ancient times, people have understood the importance of good breeding, and their perceptions of physical beauty and health have been adaptive in an evolutionary sense. The misshapen faces of gargoyles, on the one hand, and the ideal human forms in much of Western art tell the story of normal, healthy attitudes for much of our history. And it says much that the triumph of the left in World War II resulted also in the triumph of the abstractions and down-right ugliness of modern art. This is art that becomes established as high culture not because it naturally pleases the eye but because it pleases a corrupt, hostile, hyper-intellectualized, ethnically alien and politically motivated cultural establishment.

As Sunic reminds us, the defeat of National Socialism had devastating effects on the culture of the West — transforming it into a culture of suicide. In one of his most interesting essays, he shows that the art in Germany during the National Socialist period had strong classical themes. Whatever its faults — and they were many — the record shows that one strand of National Socialism was to preserve the traditional culture of Europe.

With historical hindsight, it is not too much to suggest that, unless there is a change of direction, the destruction of National Socialism represents the death knell of the West. This is because the culture of the post-World War II West idealized White people with no allegiance to their people or their traditional culture, with no understanding of their own history. The books were burned and whatever was left of the old culture was anathematized.

Sunic writes that "the whole purpose of classicism and neoclassicism, particularly in plastic art, but also in philosophy and literature suggested that Europeans had to abide by the cosmic rules of racial form and order. Whatever and whoever departs from order brings in decadence and death." The obvious implication is that to abandon this aesthetic is to accept death. The culture of the West has become the culture of Western suicide, and indeed there can be little doubt that that is exactly where we are headed.

Sunic goes where very few post-WWII intellectuals dare to tread: The idea that people of other racial backgrounds look up to Whites and behave accordingly. There is an envy and a desire to mimic Whites: "The Western heritage, regardless of whether it is despised or loved by non-Europeans, is viewed either consciously or subconsciously as the ideal type and role model for all."

This envy is also an aspect of the peril of European peoples. The ideology of the victors of World War II has placed Europeans in a situation where their official ideology has as its central feature the moral imperative of cultural and demographic suicide. The racial resentment against the Western "Other" that has often resulted in mimicry and emulation can also lead to violent retribution when the balance of power has shifted. Whites who fail to see all the signs of festering hostility among non-Whites who have been welcomed into Western countries under the aegis of wildly optimistic ideologies promulgated by hostile elites are simply not paying attention. It was the festering hostility of a large, deeply aggrieved Jewish population in the Soviet Union that led to the darkest horrors of the 20th century.

Sunic understands the importance of race, but he does not think of the White race as a genetically homogeneous group. Far from it. He rightly emphasizes that central Europe has been a melting pot of different racial subgroups. Sunic points out that even during the Third Reich, the Germans did not think of themselves as a pure Nordic race but as a mixture of European racial sub-types. They recruited many different racial sub-types into high positions in the military, including a great many Slavs. As Sunic notes, the result was that the Wehrmacht and Waffen SS did not represent a very narrow racial type but included a great many Slavs and other peoples. The result was what he calls a "united European" fighting force. This departs quite radically from the received wisdom, and should have a major effect on how we think about World War II.

Sunic also brings up things about World War II that most of us are somewhat aware of but which are very painful to read about. The psychopathic slaughters of civilians perpetrated in Dresden and other German cities at a time when the outcome of the war had been decided are a monument to the viciousness of the allies. The same can be said about the brutal treatment of German soldiers and civilians after the war, at least some of which was the result of Jewish influence. Indeed, it is apparent that if powerful Jews like Henry Morgenthau, Jr. (Secretary of the Treasury in the Roosevelt Administration) had had their way, many millions more Germans would have been murdered.

Sunic is one of those rare Western intellectuals who is willing to discuss Jewish influence openly and honestly. The real winners of World War II were not the allies, including even the Soviet Union whose domination over Eastern Europe ultimately lasted less than 50 years. The real winners were the Jews.

Jewish power increased dramatically after World War II. Israel was established in 1948 over the strong objections of the non-Jewish foreign policy establishment of the United States. Israel is now a regional power that is using its military capability and alliances with the United States to increase its territory.

After World War II, anti-Jewish attitudes declined rapidly in the United States and throughout the West. There was a corresponding upsurge of Jewish wealth, political power, and cultural influence in the media, the arts, and the academic world. And a major facet of Jewish cultural power is that even by the 1940s Jewish influence became a taboo topic for anyone wishing to avoid social ostracism and penury.

Sunic presents a rational, unbiased assessment of Jewish influence that is refreshingly free of the usual inhibitions without resorting to wild accusations and unverifiable assertions. In other words, Jewish influence should be discussed in the dispassionate manner of a social scientist just as it is with every other identifiable group. As Sunic points out, the only people who are allowed to discuss Jewish influence at all in the mainstream media are Jews. On the other hand, many Jews have achieved a great deal of influence as historians and critics of Western culture. The implicit attitude seems to be that Jewish history and Jewish influence are topics to be discussed, if at all, only within the Jewish community. It is a dialogue among Jews that non-Jews have no part in. This is an inherently unfair situation, which has always had a tendency to lead to paranoia among non-Jews. Europeans who have any allegiance to their people and culture cannot stand by and accept this state of affairs. We are approaching an endgame situation in the West. In the United States, people of non-European descent will be the majority in just a few short decades, and the same will happen throughout Europe and other societies established by Europeans since the dawn of the Age of Discovery. At that point, the centuries old hostilities and resentments of non-White peoples toward Whites that Sunic discusses will come to the fore, and the culture and Europe will be irretrievably lost. We must confront this impending disaster with a sense of psychological intensity and desperation. Reading Tom Sunic's essays will certainly provide the background for understanding how we got here and perhaps also for finding our way toward the future.

Prof. Kevin MacDonald
Long Beach California September 23, 2009

NOTE ON THE TEXT

The essays presented in this volume have been collected from a number of original sources. These sources are as follows: *Marx, Moses, and the Pagans in the Secular City* first appeared in *CLIO: A Journal of Literature, History, and the Philosophy of History*, Vol. 24, No. 2, Winter 1995; *Monotheism vs. Polytheism* in *Chronicles (A Magazine of American Culture)*, in April 1996; *History and Decadence: Spengler's Cultural Pessimism Today* in *CLIO*, Vol. 19, No. 1, pp. 51–62, Fall 1989; *"Gemeinschaft and Gesellschaft": A Sociological View of the Decay of Modern Society* in *Mankind Quarterly*, Vol. 34, No. 3, 1994; *Emile Cioran and the Culture of Death* in *Planet Cioran*, in 2004; *The Right Stuff (Drugs and Democracy)* in *Chronicles of American Culture*, in 1996; *The Beauty and the Beast: Race and Racism in Europe* in *The Occidental Observer*, as a five-part series, between 9 August and 22 September 2009; *Art in the Third Reich: 1933–1945* in *Autonom*, as a three-part series, between 19 and 24 November 2006; *The Destruction of Ethnic Germans and German Prisoners of War in Yugoslavia, 1945–1953* in the *Institute of Historical Review* website, in June 2002; *Democracy Revisited: The Ancients and the Moderns* in *The Occidental Quarterly*, Vol. 3, No. 2; *Liberalism or Democracy? Carl Schmitt and Apolitical Democracy* in *This World (An Annual of Religious and Public Life)*, Vol. 28, 1993; *The Liberal Double-Talk and Its Lexical Consequences Historical Dynamics of Liberalism: From Total Market to Total State* in *Empresas Políticas*. No. 10/11, 1st/2nd Semester 2008; *America in the Eyes of Eastern Europe* in *World and I Magazine*, November 2001, Vol. 16, No. 11, pp. 292; *The Decline and Splendor of Nationalism* in *Chronicles of American Culture*, January 1992; *Woodrow Wilson's Defeat in Yugoslavia:*

The End of a Multicultural Utopia in the *Journal of Libertarian Studies*, Vol. 11, No. 1, Fall 1994; *A Global Village or the Rights of the Peoples?* in *Chronicles*, January 1991.

The texts were written using the American spelling system and, save for occasional punctuation and typographical corrections, have been left unaltered.

PART I
RELIGION

MARX, MOSES, AND THE PAGANS IN THE SECULAR CITY

With the conversion of the Roman Emperor Constantine to Christianity, the period of pagan Europe began to approach its end. During the next millennium the entire European continent came under the sway of the Gospel — sometimes by peaceful persuasion, frequently by forceful conversion. Those who were yesterday the persecuted of the ancient Rome became, in turn, the persecutors of the Christian Rome. Those who were previously bemoaning their fate at the hands of Nero, Diocletian, or Caligula did not hesitate to apply "creative" violence against infidel pagans. Although violence was nominally prohibited by the Christian texts, it was fully used against those who did not fit into the category of God's "chosen children". During the reign of Constantine, the persecution against the pagans took the proportions "in a fashion analogous to that whereby the old faiths had formerly persecuted the new, but in an even fiercer spirit." By the edict of A.D. 346, followed ten years later by the edict of Milan, pagan temples and the worship of pagan deities came to be stigmatized as *magnum crimen*. The death penalty was inflicted upon all those found guilty of participating in ancient sacrifices or worshipping pagan idols. "With Theodosius, the administration embarked upon a systematic effort to abolish the various surviving forms of paganism through the disestablishment, disendowment, and proscription of surviving cults."[1] The period of the dark ages began.

Christian and inter-Christian violence, *ad majorem dei gloriam*, did not let up until the beginning of the eighteenth century. Along with Gothic spires of breathtaking beauty, the Christian authorities built pyres that swallowed nameless thousands. Seen in hindsight, Christian intolerance against heretics, Jews, and pagans may be compared to the twentieth-century Bolshevik intolerance against class opponents in Russia and Eastern Europe — with one exception: it lasted longer. During the twilight of imperial Rome, Christian fanaticism prompted the pagan philosopher Celsus to write: "They [Christians] will not argue about what they believe — they always bring in their, 'Do not examine, but believe'..." Obedience, prayer, and the avoidance of critical thinking were held by Christians as the most expedient tools to eternal bliss. Celsus described Christians as individuals prone to factionalism and a primitive way of thinking, who, in addition, demonstrate a remarkable disdain for life.[2] A similar tone against Christians was used in the nineteenth century by Friedrich Nietzsche, who, in his virulent style, depicted Christians as individuals capable of displaying both self-hatred and hatred towards others, i.e., "hatred against those who think differently, and the will to persecute."[3] Undoubtedly, early Christians must have genuinely believed that the end of history loomed large on the horizon and, with their historical optimism, as well as their violence against the "infidels", they probably deserved the name of the Bolsheviks of antiquity.

As suggested by many authors, the break-up of the Roman Empire did not result only from the onslaught of barbarians, but because Rome was already "ruined from within by Christian sects, conscientious objectors, enemies of the official cult, the persecuted, persecutors, criminal elements of all sorts, and total chaos." Paradoxically, even the Jewish God Yahveh was to experience a sinister fate: "he would be converted, he would become Roman, cosmopolitan, ecumenical, gentile, goyim, globalist, and finally anti-Semite."(!)[4] It is no wonder that, in the following centuries, Christian churches in Europe had difficulties in trying to reconcile their universalist vocation with the rise of nationalist extremism.

Pagan Residues in the Secular City

Although Christianity gradually removed the last vestiges of Roman polytheism, it also substituted itself as the legitimate heir of Rome. Indeed,

Christianity did not cancel out paganism in its entirety; it inherited from Rome many features that it had previously scorned as anti-Christian. The official pagan cults were dead but pagan spirit remained indomitable, and for centuries it kept resurfacing in astounding forms and in multiple fashions: during the period of Renaissance, during Romanticism, before the Second World War, and today, when Christian Churches increasingly recognize that their secular sheep are straying away from their lone shepherds. Finally, ethnic folklore seems to be a prime example of the survival of paganism, although in the secular city folklore has been largely reduced to a perishable commodity of culinary or tourist attraction.[5] Over the centuries, ethnic folklore has been subject to transformations, adaptations, and the demands and constraint of its own epoch; yet it has continued to carry its original archetype of a tribal founding myth. Just as paganism has always remained stronger in the villages, so has folklore traditionally been best protected among the peasant classes in Europe. In the early nineteenth century, folklore began to play a decisive role in shaping the national consciousness of European peoples, i.e., "in a community anxious to have its own origins and based on a history that is more often reconstructed than real."[6]

The pagan content was removed, but the pagan structure remained pretty much the same. Under the mantle and aura of Christian saints, Christianity soon created its own pantheon of deities. Moreover, even the message of Christ adopted its special meaning according to place, historical epoch, and *genius loci* of each European people. In Portugal, Catholicism manifests itself differently than in Mozambique; and rural Poles continue to worship many of the same ancient Slavic deities that are carefully interwoven into the Roman Catholic liturgy. All over contemporary Europe, the erasable imprint of polytheist beliefs continues to surface. The Yule celebration represents one of the most glaring examples of the tenacity of pagan residues.[7] Furthermore, many former pagan temples and sites of worship have been turned into sacred places of the Catholic Church. Lourdes in France, Medjugorje in Croatia, sacred rivers, or mountains, do they not all point to the imprint of pre-Christian pagan Europe? The cult of mother goddess, once upon a time intensely practiced by Celts, particularly near rivers, can be still observed today in France where many small chapels are built near fountains and sources of water.[8] And finally, who could dispute the fact that we are all brainchildren of pagan Greeks and Latins? Thinkers, such as Virgil, Tacitus, Heraclitus, are as modern today as they were during the dawn of European civilization.

Modern Pagan Conservatives

There is ample evidence that pagan sensibilities can flourish in the social sciences, literature, and arts, not just as a form of exotic narrative but also as a mental framework and a tool of conceptual analysis. Numerous names come to mind when we discuss the revival of Indo-European polytheism. In the first half of the twentieth century, pagan thinkers usually appeared under the mask of those who styled themselves as "revolutionary conservatives", "aristocratic nihilist", "elitists" — in short all those who did not wish to substitute Marx for Jesus, but who rejected both Marx and Jesus.[9] Friedrich Nietzsche and Martin Heidegger in philosophy, Carl Gustav Jung in psychology, Georges Dumézil and Mircea Eliade in anthropology, Vilfredo Pareto and Oswald Spengler in political science, let alone dozens of poets such as Ezra Pound or Charles Baudelaire — these are just some of the names that can be associated with the legacy of pagan conservatism. All these individuals had in common the will to surpass the legacy of Christian Europe, and all of them yearned to include in their spiritual baggage the world of pre-Christian Celts, Slavs, and Germans. In an age that is heavily laced with the Biblical message, many modern pagan thinkers, for their criticism of Biblical monotheism, have been attacked and stigmatized either as unrepentant atheists or as spiritual standard-bearers of Fascism. Particularly Nietzsche, Heidegger, and more recently Alain de Benoist came under attack for allegedly espousing the philosophy that, for their contemporary detractors, recalled the earlier National Socialist attempts to "dechristianize" and "repaganize" Germany.[10] These appear as unwarranted attacks. Jean Markale observes that "Naziism and Stalinism were, in a sense, also religions because of the acts that they triggered. They were also religions insofar as they implied a certain Gospel, in an etymological sense of the word ... Real paganism, by contrast, is always oriented towards the realm of sublimation. Paganism cannot be in the service of temporal power."[11] Paganism appears more a form of sensibility than a given political credo, and with the exhaustion of Christianity, one should not rule out its renewed flourishing in Europe.

Paganism Against the Monotheist Desert

Two thousand years of Judeo-Christian monotheism has left its mark on Western civilization. In view of this, it should not come as a surprise that glorification of paganism, as well as the criticism of the Bible and Judeo-Christian ethics — especially when they come from the right-wing spectrum of society — are unlikely to gain popularity in the secular city. It suffices to look at American society, where attacks against Judeo-Christian principles are frequently looked at with suspicion, and where the Bible and the Biblical myth of god's "chosen people" still play a significant role in the American constitutional dogma.[12] Although the secular city has by now become indifferent to the Judeo-Christian theology, principles that derive from Judeo-Christian ethics, such as "peace", "love", and "universal brotherhood", are still showing healthy signs of life. In the secular city, many liberal and socialist thinkers, while abandoning their belief in Judeo-Christian theology, have not deemed it wise to abandon the ethics taught by the Bible. Whatever one may think about the seemingly obsolete, dangerous, or even derogatory connotation of the term "European paganism", it is important to note that this connotation is largely due to the historical and political influence of Christianity. Etymologically, paganism is related to the beliefs and rituals that were in usage in European villages and countryside. But paganism, in its modern version, may connote also a certain sensibility and a "way of life" that remains irreconcilable with Judeo-Christian monotheism. To some extent European peoples continue to be "pagans" because their national memory, their geographic roots, and, above all, their ethnic allegiances, which often contain allusions to ancient myths, fairy tales, and forms of folklore bear peculiar marks of pre-Christian themes. Even the modern resurgence of separatism and regionalism in Europe appears as an offshoot of pagan residues. As Markale observes, "the dictatorship of Christian ideology has not silenced those ancient customs; it has only suppressed them into the shadow of the unconscious" (p. 16). The fact that all of Europe is today swept by growing nationalism bears witness to the permanency of the pagan sense of tribal historical memory. In European culture, polytheistic beliefs began to dwindle with the consolidation of Christianity. In the centuries to come, the European system of explanation, whether in theology or, later on, in sociology, politics, or history gradually came under the sway of the Judeo-Christian outlook of the world. David Miller observes that Judeo-Christian monotheism considerably altered the Europeans' approach to the social sciences as well as to the overall perception of the world. In view of these changes, who can reassure us about our own objectivity, especially when we try to understand the pagan world with the goggles of the postmodern Judeo-Christian man? It is no wonder that when paganism was removed from Europe the perceptual and epistemological disruptions in sciences also followed suit. Consequently, with the consolidation of the Judeo-Christian belief, the world and the world phenomena came under the sway of the fixed concepts and categories governed by the logic of "either-or", "true or false", and "good or evil", with seldom any shadings in between. The question, however, arises whether in the secular city — a city replete with intricate choices and complex social differences that stubbornly refuse all categorizations — this approach remains desirable. It is doubtful that Judeo-Christian monotheism can continue to offer a valid solution for the understanding of the increasingly complex social reality that modern man faces in the secular city. Moreover, the subsequent export of Judeo-Christian values to the antipodes of the world caused similar disruptions, yielding results opposite from those originally espoused by the Westerners, and triggering virulent hatred among non-Western populations. Some authors have quite persuasively written that Christian ecumenism, often championed as the "white man's Christian burden", has been one of the main purveyors of imperialism, colonialism, and racism in the Third World.[14] In the modern secular city, the century-long and pervasive influence of Christianity has significantly contributed to the view that each glorification of paganism, or, for that matter, the nostalgia of the Greco-Roman order, is outright strange or at best irreconcilable with contemporary society. Recently, however, Thomas Molnar, a Catholic philosopher who seems to be sympathetic to the cultural revival of paganism, noted that modern adherents of neo-paganism are more ambitious than their predecessors. Molnar writes that the aim of pagan revival does not have to mean the return to the worship of ancient European deities; rather, it expresses a need to forge another civilization or, better yet, a modernized version of the "scientific and cultural Hellenism" that was once a common reference for all European peoples. And with visible sympathy for the polytheistic endeavors of some modern pagan conservatives, Molnar adds:

> The issue is not how to conquer the planet but rather how to promote an oikumena of the peoples and civilizations that have rediscovered their origins. The assumption goes that the domination of stateless ideologies, notably the ideology of American liberalism and Soviet socialism, would come to an end. One believes in rehabilitated paganism in order to restore to peoples their genuine identity that existed before monotheist corruption.[15]

Such a candid view by a Catholic may also shed some light on the extent of disillusionment among Christians in their secular cities. A secularized world full of affluence and richness does not seem to have stifled the spiritual needs of man. How else to explain that throngs of European and American youngsters prefer to trek to pagan Indian ashrams rather than to their own sacred sites obscured by Judeo-Christian monotheism?

Anxious to dispel the myth of pagan "backwardness", and in an effort to redefine European paganism in the spirit of modern times, the contemporary protagonists of paganism have gone to great lengths to present its meaning in a more attractive and scholarly fashion. One of their most outspoken figures, Alain de Benoist, summarizes the modern meaning of paganism in the following words:

> Neo-paganism, if there is such a thing as neo-paganism, is not a phenomenon of a sect, as some of its adversaries, but also some of the groups and chapels,

sometimes well-intentioned, sometimes awkward, frequently funny and completely marginal, imagine ... [W]hat worries us today, at least according to the idea that we have about it, is less the disappearance of paganism but rather its resurgence under primitive and puerile form, affiliated to that "second religiosity", which Spengler justifiably depicted as characteristic of cultures in decline, and of which Julius Evola writes that they correspond generally to a phenomenon of evasion, alienation, confused compensation, without any serious repercussion on reality.[16]

Paganism, as a profusion of bizarre cults and sects, is not something modern pagan thinkers have in mind. A century ago, pagan philosopher Friedrich Nietzsche had already observed in *Der Antichrist* that, when a nation becomes too degenerate or too uprooted, it must place its energy into various forms of Oriental cults, and simultaneously "it must change its own God" (p. 979). Today, Nietzsche's words sound more prophetic than ever. Gripped by decadence and rampant hedonism, the masses from the secular city are looking for the vicarious evasion in the presence of Indian gurus or amidst a host of Oriental prophets. But beyond this Western semblance of transcendence, and behind the Westerners' self-hatred accompanied by puerile infatuation with Oriental mascots, there is more than just a transitory weariness with Christian monotheism. When modern cults indulge in the discovery of perverted paganism, they also may be in search of the sacred that was driven underground by the dominating Judeo-Christian discourse.

From Monotheist Desert to Communist Anthropology

Has monotheism introduced into Europe an alien "anthropology" responsible for the spread of egalitarian mass society and the rise of totalitarianism, as some pagan thinkers seem to suggest? Some authors appear to support this thesis, arguing that the roots of tyranny do not lie in Athens or Sparta, but are traceable, instead, to Jerusalem. In a dialogue with Molnar, de Benoist suggests that monotheism upholds the idea of only one absolute truth; it is a system where the notion of the enemy is associated with the evil, and where the enemy must be physically exterminated (cf. Deut. 13). In short, observes de Benoist, Judeo-Christian universalism, two thousand years ago, set the stage for the rise of modern egalitarian aberrations and their modern secular offshoots, including communism.

> That there are totalitarian regimes "without God", is quite obvious, the Soviet Union for example. These regimes, nonetheless, are the "inheritors" of the Christian thought in the sense as Carl Schmitt demonstrated that the majority of modern political principles are secularized theological principles. They bring down to earth a structure of exclusion; the police of the soul yield its place to the police of the state; the ideological wars follow up to the religious wars.[17]

Similar observations were echoed earlier by the philosopher Louis Rougier as well as by the political scientist Vilfredo Pareto, both of whom represented the "old guard" of pagan thinkers and whose philosophical researches were directed toward the rehabilitation of European political polytheism. Both Rougier and Pareto are in agreement that Judaism and its perverted form, Christianity, introduced into the European conceptual framework an alien type of reasoning that leads to wishful thinking, utopianism, and the ravings about the static future.[18] Similar to latter-day Marxists, early Christian belief in egalitarianism must have had a tremendous impact on the deprived masses of northern Africa and Rome, insofar as it promised equality for the "wretched of the earth", for *odium generis humani*, and all the *proles* of the world. Commenting on Christian proto-communists, Rougier recalls that Christianity came very early under the influence of both the Iranian dualism and the eschatological visions of the Jewish apocalypses. Accordingly, Jews and, later on, Christians adopted the belief that the good who presently suffer would be rewarded in the future. In the secular city, the same theme was later interwoven into modern socialist doctrines that promised secular paradise. "There are two empires juxtaposed in the space", writes Rougier, "one governed by God and his angels, the other by Satan and Belial." The consequences of this largely dualistic vision of the world resulted, over a period of time, in Christian-Marxist projection of their political enemies as always wrong, as opposed to Christian-Marxist attitude considered right. For Rougier, the Greco-Roman intolerance could never assume such total and absolute proportions of religious exclusion; the intolerance towards Christians, Jews, and other sects was sporadic, aiming at certain religious customs deemed contrary to Roman customary law (such as circumcision, human sacrifices, sexual and religious orgies).[19] By cutting themselves from European polytheistic roots, and by accepting Christianity, Europeans gradually began to adhere to the vision of the world that emphasized the equality of souls, and the importance of spreading God's gospel to all peoples, regardless of creed, race, or language (Paul, Galatians 3:28). In the centuries to come, these egalitarian cycles, in secularized forms, entered first the consciousness of Western man and, after that, entire human-kind. Alain de Benoist writes:

> According to the classical process of the development and degradation of cycles, the egalitarian theme has entered our culture from the stage of the myth (equality before God), to the stage of ideology (equality before people); after that, it has passed to the stage of "scientific pretension" (affirmation of the egalitarian fact). In short, from Christianity to democracy, and after that to socialism and Marxism. The most serious reproach that one can formulate against Christianity is that it has inaugurated this egalitarian cycle by introducing into European thought a revolutionary anthropology, with universalist and totalitarian character.[20]

One could probably argue that Judeo-Christian monotheism, as much as it implies universalism and egalitarianism, also suggests religious exclusiveness that directly emanates from the belief in one undisputed truth. The consequence of the Christian belief in theological oneness — e.g., that there is only one God, and therefore only one truth — has naturally led, over the centuries, to Christian temptation to obliterate or downplay all other truths and values. One can argue that when one sect proclaims its religion as the key to the riddle of the universe and if, in addition, this sect claims to have universal aspirations, the belief in equality and the suppression of all human differences will follow suit. Accordingly, Christian intolerance toward "infidels" could always be justified as a legitimate response against those who departed from the belief in Yahveh's truth.

Hence, the concept of Christian "false humility" toward other confessions, a concept that is particularly obvious in regard to Christian attitude toward Jews. Although almost identical in their worship of one god, Christians could never quite reconcile themselves to the fact that they also had to worship the deity of those whom they abhorred in the first place as a deicide people. Moreover, whereas Christianity always has been a universalist religion, accessible to everybody in all corners of the world, Judaism has remained an ethnic religion of only the Jewish people.[21] As de Benoist writes, Judaism sanctions its own nationalism, as opposed to the nationalism of the Christians, which is constantly belied by the Christian universalist principles. In view of this, "Christian anti-Semitism", writes de Benoist, "can justifiably be described as a neurosis." Might it be that the definite disappearance of anti-Semitism, as well as virulent inter-ethnic hatred, presupposes first the recantation of the Christian belief in universalism?

Pagan Notion of the Sacred

To the critics who argue that polytheism is a thing of the prehistoric and primitive mind, incompatible with modern societies, one could respond that paganism is not necessarily a return to "paradise lost" or a nostalgia for the restoration of the Greco-Roman order. For pagan conservatives, to pledge allegiance to "paganism" means to rekindle Europe's historical origins, as well as to revive some sacred aspects of life that existed in Europe prior to the rise of Christianity. One could also add that, as far as the alleged supremacy or modernity of Judeo-Christianity over the backwardness of Indo-European polytheism is concerned, Judeo-Christian religions, in terms of their modernity, are no less backward than pagan religions. To emphasize this point de Benoist writes:

> Just as it was yesterday a grotesque spectacle to see the "pagan idols" denounced by Christian missionaries, who were themselves enamored of their own bric-a-bracs, so it is somewhat ridiculous to see the (European) "past" denounced by those who never tire of praising Judeo-Christian continuity, and who refer us to

the example of "always modern" Abraham, Jacob, Isaac, and other proto-historic Beduins.[22]

According to some pagan thinkers, Judeo-Christian rationalization of historical time has precluded the projection of one's own national past and, in so doing, it has significantly contributed to the "desertification" of the world. In the last century, Ernest Renan observed that Judaism is oblivious of the notion of the sacred, because the "desert itself is monotheistic".[23] In a similar tone, Alain de Benoist in *L'éclipse*, while quoting Harvey Cox's *The Secular City*, writes that the loss of the sacred, which is causing today the "disenchantment" of the modern polity, resulted as the legitimate consequence of the Biblical renunciation of history. First, the disenchantment of nature had started with the Creation; the desacralization of politics with the Exodus; and the deconsecration of values with the Alliance of Sinai, especially after the interdiction of idols (p. 129). Continuing with similar analyses, Mircea Eliade, an author himself influenced by pagan world, adds that Judaic resentment of pagan idolatry stems from the ultra-rational character of Mosaic laws that rationalize all aspects of life by means of a myriad of prescriptions, laws, and interdictions:

> Desacralization of the Nature, devaluation of cultural activity, in short, the violent and total rejection of cosmic religion, and above all the decisive importance conferred upon spiritual regeneration by the definite return of Yahveh, was the prophets' response to historical crises menacing the two Jewish kingdoms.[24]

Some might object that Catholicism has its own form of the sacred and that, unlike some other forms of Judeo-Christian beliefs, it displays its own spiritual transcendence. But there are reasons to believe that the Catholic concept of the sacred does not emerge *sui generis*, but rather as a substratum of the Christian amalgam with paganism. As de Benoist notes, Christianity owes its manifestation of the sacred (holy sites, pilgrimages, Christmas festivities, and the pantheon of saints) to the indomitable undercurrent of pagan and polytheistic sensibility. Therefore, it seems that the pagan revival today represents less a normative religion, in the Christian sense of the word, than a certain spiritual equipment that stands in contrast to the religion of Jews and Christians. Consequently, as some pagan thinkers suggest, the possible replacement of the monotheistic vision of the world by the polytheistic vision of the world could mean not just the "return of gods" but the return of the plurality of social values as well. Courage, personal honor, and spiritual and physical self-surpassment are often cited as the most important virtues of paganism. In contrast to Christian and Marxian utopian optimism, paganism emphasizes the profound sense of the tragic — the tragic as seen in Greek tragedies — that sustains man in his Promethean plight and that makes his life worth living.[25] It is the pagan sense of the tragic that can explain man's destiny — destiny, which for old Indo-Europeans "triggered action, endeavor, and selfsurpassment".[26] Hans Günther summarizes this point in the following words:

> [I]ndo-European religiosity is not rooted in any kind of fear, neither in fear of deity nor in fear of death. The words of the Latterday Roman poet, that fear first created the Gods (Statius, Thebais, 3:661: *primus in orbe fecit deos timor*), cannot be applied to the true forms of Indo-European religiosity, for wherever it has unfolded freely, the "fear of the Lord" (Proverbs, Solomon 9, 10; Psalm 11, 30) has proved neither the beginning of belief nor of wisdom.[27]

Some have suggested that the greatest civilizations are those that have shown a strong sense of the tragic and that have had no fear of death.[28] In the pagan concept of the tragic, man is encouraged to take responsibility before history because man is the only one who gives history a meaning. Commenting on Nietzsche, Giorgio Locchi writes that, in pagan cosmogony, man alone is considered a forger of his own destiny (*faber suae fortunea*), exempt from biblical or historical determinism, "divine grace", or economic and material constraints.[29] Paganism stresses a heroic attitude toward life as opposed to the Christian attitude of culpability and fear toward life. Sigrid Hunke writes of the essentialization of life, since both life and death have the same essence and are always contained in both. The life, which at any moment is face-to-death and with-death, renders the future permanent in each instant, and life becomes eternal by acquiring an inscrutable profundity, and by assuming the value of eternity. For Hunke, along with other authors of pagan sensibility, in order to restore these pagan virtues in the secular city, man must first abandon the dualistic logic of religious and social exclusion, "a logic which has been responsible for extremism not only among individuals, but also among parties and peoples, and which, starting out from Europe, has disseminated into the world this dualistic split that has acquired planetary proportions."[30] To achieve this ambitious goal, Western man must first rethink the meaning of history.

The Terror of History

Modern pagans remind us that Judeo-Christian monotheism has substantially altered man's attitude toward history. By assigning history a specific goal, Judeo-Christianity has devalued all past events, except those that display the sign of Yahveh's theophany. Undoubtedly, Yahveh does admit that man may have a history, but only insofar as history is bestowed with an assigned goal, a certain goal, and a specific goal. Should man, however, continue to cling to the concept of history that evokes collective memory of his tribe or people, he runs the risk of provoking Yahveh's anger. For Jews, Christians, as well as Marxists, historicity is not the real essence of man; the real essence of man is beyond history. One could observe that the Judeo-Christian concept of the end of history correlates well with modern egalitarian and pacifist doctrines that inspire themselves, often unknowingly, with the Biblical proverb: "the wolf also shall dwell with the lamb, and the leopard shall lie down with the kid" (Isa. 11:6). De Benoist notes in *L'éclipse* that, unlike the pagan concept of history that involves organic solidarity and communal ties, the monotheistic concept of history creates divisions. Accordingly, Yahveh must forbid "mixtures" between the present and the past, between people and the divine, between Israel and the goyim (p. 132). Christians, of course, will reject Jewish exclusiveness — as their century-long religious proselytism amply demonstrates — but they will, nonetheless, retain their own brand of exclusiveness against "infidel" Moslems, pagans, and other "false believers". Contrary to the Judeo-Christian dogma that asserts that historical time starts from one unique father, in European paganism there are no traces of the beginning of the time; instead, historical time is seen as a perpetual recommencement, the "eternal return" emanating from multiple and different fathers. In pagan cosmogony, as de Benoist writes, time is the reflection of the non-linear or spheric conception of history, a conception in which the past, the present, and the future are not perceived as stretches of cosmic time irrevocably cut off from each other, or following each other on the single line. Instead, present, past, and future are perceived as dimensions of actuality (*L'éclipse*, p. 131). In pagan cosmogony, it is incumbent to each people to assign itself a role in history, which in practice means that there cannot be self-appointed peoples occupying the central stage in history. Similarly, just as it is erroneous to speak about one truth, it is equally wrong to maintain that entire humanity must pursue the same and unique historical direction, as proposed by Judeo-Christian universalism and its secular fallout "global democracy". The Judeo-Christian concept of history suggests that the flow of' historical time is monolinear and, therefore, limited by its significance and meaning. Henceforth, for Jews and Christians, history can be apprehended only as a totality governed by a sense of ultimate end and historical fulfillment. History for both Jews and Christians appears at best parenthetical, at worst an ugly episode or a "valley of tears", which one of these days must be erased from earth and transcended by paradise. Furthermore, Judeo-Christian monotheism excludes the possibility of historical return or "recommencement"; history has to unfold in a predetermined way by making its way toward a final goal. In the modern secular city, the idea of Christian finality will be transposed into a myth of a finite "classless" society, or the apolitical and ahistorical liberal consumer society. Here is how de Benoist sees it in *L'éclipse*:

> Legitimization by the future that replaces legitimization of the immemorial times authorizes all uprootedness, all "emancipations" regarding the adherence in its original form. This utopian future that replaces a mythic past is incidentally always the generator of deceptions, because the best that it announces must constantly be put off to a later date. Temporality is no longer a founding element of the deployment of the being who tries to grasp the game of the world.

> Temporality is pursued from one goal, reached from one end; expectation and no longer communion.
>
> To submit globally the historical becoming to an obligatory meaning means in fact to shut history in the reign of objectivity, which reduces choices, orientations, and projects. (155–56)

Only the future can enable Jews and Christians to "rectify" the past. Only the future assumes the value of redemption. Henceforth, historical time for Jews and Christians is no longer reversible; from now on each historical occurrence acquires the meaning of divine providence, of "God's" finger, or theophany. In the secular city, this line of monolinear thinking will give birth to the "religion" of progress and the belief in boundless economic growth. Did not Moses receive the Laws at a certain place and during a certain time, and did not Jesus later preach, perform miracles, and was he not crucified at a specifically recorded time and place? Did not the end of history begin for Communists with the Bolshevik Revolution, and for liberals with the American century? These "divine" interventions in human history are never again to be repeated. Eliade summarizes this point in the following words:

> Under the "pressure of history" and supported by the prophetic and Messianic experience, a new interpretation of historical events dawns among the children of Israel. Without finally renouncing the traditional concept of archetypes and repetitions, Israel attempts to "save" historical events by regarding them as active presences of Yahweh.... Messianism gives them a new value, especially by abolishing their [historical events] possibility of repetition ad infinitum. When the Messiah comes, the world will be saved once and for all and history will cease to exist.[31]

Directly commanded by the will of Yahweh, history henceforth functions as a series of events, with each event becoming irrevocable and irreversible. History is not only discarded, but also fought against. Pierre Chaunu, a contemporary French historian, observes that "the rejection of history is a temptation of those civilizations that have emerged out of Judeo-Christianity."[32] In a similar tone, Michel Maffesoli writes that totalitarianism occurs in those countries that are hostile to history, and he adds: "We enter now into the reign of finality propitious to political eschatology whose outcome is Christianity and its profane forms, liberalism and Marxism..."[33]

The foregoing observations might need some comments. If one accepts the idea of the end of history, as proposed by monotheists, Marxists, and liberals, to what extent, then, can the entire historical suffering be explained? How is it possible, from liberal and Marxist points of view, to "redeem" past oppressions, collective sufferings, deportations, and humiliations that have filled up history? Suffice it to say that this enigma only underscores the difficulty regarding the concept of distributive justice in the egalitarian secular city. If a truly egalitarian society miraculously emerges, it will be, inevitably, a society of the elect — of those who, as Eliade noted, managed to escape the pressure of history by simply being born at a right time, at a right place, and in a right country. Paul Tillich noted, some time ago, that such equality would result in immense historical inequality, since it would exclude those who, during their lifetime, lived in unequal society, or — if one can borrow Arthur Koestler's words — who perished with a "shrug of eternity".[34] These quotes from Koestler and Eliade illustrate the difficulties of modern salutary ideologies that try to "arrest" time and create a secular paradise. Would it not be better in times of great crisis to borrow the pagan notion of cyclical history? This seems to be the case with some East European peoples who, in times of crisis or catastrophes, frequently resort to popular folklore and myths that help them, in an almost cathartic manner, better to cope with their predicament. Locchi writes:

> The new beginning of history is feasible. There is no such thing as historical truth. If historical truth truly existed then there would be no history. Historical truth must time and again be obtained; it must always be translated into action. And this is exactly — for us — the meaning of history.[35]

We might conclude that for Christians it is Christ who defines the value of a human being, for a Jew it is Judaism that gauges someone's "choseness", and for Marx it is not the quality of man that defines the class, but rather the quality of the class that defines man. One thus becomes "elected" by virtue of his affiliation to his class or his religious belief.

Pagans or Monotheists: Who is More Tolerant?

As observed, Yahveh, similar to his future secular successors, in the capacity of the single truth-maker, is opposed to the presence of other gods and other values. As a reductionist, whatever exists beyond his fold must be either punished or destroyed. One can observe that, throughout history, the monotheistic true believers have been encouraged, in the name of "higher" historic truths, to punish those who strayed away from Yahveh's assigned direction. Walter Scott writes:

> In many instances the Mosaic law of retaliation, an "eye for eye, tooth for tooth", was invoked by the Israelites to justify the atrocities which they visited upon their fallen enemies … The history of the Israelite campaigns shows that the Hebrews were most often the aggressors.[36]

Thus, in the name of historical truth, the ancient Hebrews could justify the slaughtering of Canaanite pagans, and in the name of Christian revelation, Christian states legitimized wars against infidel heretics, Jews, and pagans. It would be imprecise, however, in this context to downplay the pagan violence. The Greek destruction of the city of Troy, the Roman destruction of Carthage, clearly point to the frequently total and bloody nature of wars conducted by the ancient Greeks and Romans. Yet, it is also important to stress that seldom do we find among the ancients the self-righteous attitude toward their victories that accompanied Christian and Jewish military victories. Seldom, if ever, did the Romans or the Greeks attempt, after the military destruction of their opponents, to convert them to their own deities. By contrast, both the Gospel and the Old Testament are interspersed with acts of self-congratulatory justice that will, in turn, justify "redeeming" violence against opponents. Similarly, in the modern secular city, to wage war for democracy has become a particularly nefarious means for erasing all different polities that refuse the "theology" of global progress and that shun the credo of "global democracy". To underscore this point, Pierre Gripari writes that Judaism, Christianity, and their secular offshoots Nazism, socialism, and liberalism, are barbarian doctrines that cannot have their place in the modern world (p. 60). By contrast, notes de Benoist, a system that recognizes an unlimited number of gods acknowledges also the plurality of cults offered in their honor, and above all, the plurality of customs, political and social systems, and conceptions of the world of which these gods are sublime expressions.[37] It follows from this that pagans, or believers in polytheism, are considerably less inclined to intolerance. Their relative tolerance is primarily attributed to the acceptance of the notion of the "excluded third" (*der ausgeschlossene Dritte*), as well as the rejection of Judeo-Christian dualism. To underscore pagan relative tolerance, it is worth mentioning the attitude of Indo-European pagans toward their opponents during military confrontation. Jean Haudry remarks that war for pagans was conducted according to strict regulations; war was declared according to the rituals that beseeched first the help of gods and asked for their anger against the adversary. The conduct of war was subject to well-defined rules and consequently, "the victory consisted of breaking the resistance, and not necessarily of destroying the adversary" (p. 161). In view of the fact that Judeo-Christianity does not permit relative truths, or different and contradictory truths, it will frequently adopt the policy of total war toward its opponents. Eliade writes that the "intolerance and fanaticism characteristic of the prophets and missionaries of the three monotheistic religions, have their model and justification in the example of Yahveh."[38] How does the monotheist intolerance transpire in the purportedly tolerant secular city? What are the secular consequences of Judeo-Christian monotheism in our epoch? In contemporary systems, it is the opposite, the undecided, i.e., those who have not taken sides, and those who refuse modern political eschatologies — that become the targets of ostracism or persecution: those who today question the utility of the ideology of "human rights", globalism, or equality. Those, in short, who reject the liberal and communist credo. In conclusion, one could say that, in the very beginning of its development,

Judeo-Christian monotheism set out to demystify and desacralize the pagan world by slowly supplanting ancient pagan beliefs with the reign of the Judaic Law. During this century-long process, Christianity gradually removed all pagan vestiges that coexisted with it. The ongoing process of desacralization and the *Entzauberung* of life and politics appear to have resulted not from Europeans' chance departure from Christianity, but rather from the gradual disappearance of the pagan notion of the sacred that coexisted for a long time with Christianity. The paradox of our century is that the Western world is saturated with Judeo-Christian mentality at the moment when churches and synagogues are virtually empty.

MONOTHEISM VS. POLYTHEISM

by Alain de Benoist

Introduction and translation by Tomislav Sunic

Can we still conceive of the revival of pagan sensibility in an age so profoundly saturated by Judeo-Christian monotheism and so ardently adhering to the tenets of liberal democracy? In popular parlance, the very word "paganism" may incite some to derision and laughter. Who, after all, wants to be associated with witches and witchcraft, with sorcery and black magic? Worshiping animals or plants, or chanting hymns to Wotan or Zeus, in an epoch of cable television and "smart weapons", does not augur well for serious intellectual and academic inquiry. Yet, before we begin to heap scorn on paganism, we should pause for a moment. Paganism is not just witches and witches' brew; paganism also means a mix of highly speculative theories and philosophies. Paganism is Seneca and Tacitus; it is an artistic and cultural movement that swept over Italy under the banner of the Renaissance. Paganism also means Friedrich Nietzsche, Martin Heidegger, Charles Darwin, and a host of other thinkers associated with the Western cultural heritage. Two thousand years of Judeo-Christianity have not obscured the fact that pagan thought has not yet disappeared, even though it has often been blurred, stifled, or persecuted by monotheistic religions and their secular offshoots. Undoubtedly, many would admit that in the realm of ethics all men and women of the world are the children of Abraham. Indeed, even the bolder ones who somewhat self-righteously claim to have rejected the Christian or Jewish theologies, and who claim to have replaced them with "secular humanism", frequently ignore that their self-styled secular beliefs are firmly grounded in Judeo-Christian ethics. Abraham and Moses may be dethroned today, but their moral edicts and spiritual ordinances are much alive. The global and disenchanted world, accompanied by the litany of human rights, ecumenical society, and the rule of law, are these not principles that can be traced directly to the Judeo-Christian messianism that resurfaces today in its secular version under the elegant garb of modern "progressive" ideologies? And yet, we should not forget that the Western world did not begin with the birth of Christ. Neither did the religions of ancient Europeans see the first light of the day with Moses in the desert. Nor did our much-vaunted democracy begin with the period of Enlightenment or with the proclamation of American independence. Democracy and independence, all of this existed in ancient Greece, albeit in its own unique social and religious context. Our Greco-Roman ancestors, our predecessors who roamed the woods of central and northern Europe, also believed in honor, justice, and virtue, although they attached to these notions a radically different meaning. Attempting to judge, therefore, ancient European political and religious manifestations through the lens of our ethnocentric and reductionist glasses could mean losing sight of how much we have departed from our ancient heritage, as well as forgetting that modern intellectual epistemology and methodology have been greatly influenced by the Bible. Just because we profess historical optimism — or believe in the progress of the modem "therapeutic state" — does not necessarily mean that our society is indeed the "best of all worlds." Who knows, with the death of Communism, with the exhaustion of liberalism, with the visible depletion of the congregations in churches and synagogues, we may be witnessing the dawn of neopaganism, a new blossoming of old cultures, a return to the roots that are directly tied to our ancient European precursors. Who can dispute the fact that Athens was the homeland of Europeans before Jerusalem became their frequently painful edifice? Great lamenting is heard from all quarters of our disenchanted and barren world today. Gods seem to have departed, as Nietzsche predicted a century ago, ideologies are dead, and liberalism hardly seems capable of providing man with enduring spiritual support. Maybe the time has come to search for other paradigms? Perhaps the moment is ripe, as Alain dc Benoist would argue, to envision another cultural and spiritual revolution — a revolution that might well embody our pre-Christian European pagan heritage?

Tomislav Sunic

* * *

Nietzsche well understood the meaning of "Athens against Jerusalem". Referring to ancient paganism, which he called "the greatest utility of polytheism", he wrote in *The Joyful Wisdom*:

> There was then only one norm, the man and even people believed that it had this one and ultimate norm. But, above himself, and outside of himself, in a distant over-world a person could see a multitude of norms: the one God was not the denial or blasphemy of the other Gods! It was here that the right of individuals was first respected. The inventing of Gods, heroes, and supermen of all kinds, as well as co-ordinate men and undermen — dwarfs, fairies, centaurs, satyrs, demons, devils was the inestimable preliminary to the justification of the selfishness and sovereignty of the individual: the freedom that was granted to one God in respect to other Gods, was at last given to the individual himself in respect to laws, customs, and neighbors. Monotheism, on the contrary, the rigid consequence of one normal human being — consequently, the belief in a normal God, beside whom there are only false spurious Gods — has perhaps been the greatest danger of mankind in the past.

Jehovah is not only a "jealous" god, but he can also show hatred: "Yet, I loved Jacob, and I hated Esau" (Malachi 1:3). He recommends hatred to all those who call out his name: "Do not I hate them, O Lord that hate thee? And am not I grieved with those that rise up against thee? I hate them with perfect hatred: I count them mine enemies" (Psalm 139: 21–22). "Surely thou wilt slay the wicked, o God" (Psalm 139:19). Jeremiah cries out: "Render unto them a recompense, O Lord, according to the work of their hands. . . . Persecute and destroy them in anger from under the heavens of the Lord" (Lamentations 3:64–66). The book of Jeremiah is a long series of maledictions and curses hurled against peoples and nations. His contemplation of future punishments fills him with gloomy delight. "Let them be confounded that persecute me, but let not me be confounded: ... bring upon them the day of evil, and destroy them with double destruction" (Lam. 17:18). "Therefore deliver up their children to the famine, and pour out their blood by the force of the sword; and let their wives be bereaved of their children, and be widows; and let their men be put to death" (Lam. 18:21). Further on, Jehovah promises the Hebrews that he will support them in their war efforts: "When the Lord thy God shall cut off the nations from before thee, whither thou goest to possess them, and thou succeedest them, and dwellest in their land" (Deuteronomy 12:29). "But of the cities of these people, which the Lord thy God doth give thee for an inheritance, thou shalt save alive nothing that breatheth" (Deut. 20:16). Jehovah himself gave an example of genocide by provoking the Deluge against the humanity that sinned against him. While he resided with the Philistine King Achish, David also practiced genocide (1 Samuel 27:9). Moses organized the extermination of the Midian people (Numbers 31:7). Joshua massacred the inhabitants of Hazor and Anakim. "And Joshua at that time turned back, and took Hazor, and smote the king thereof with the sword: for Hazor beforetime was the head of all those kingdoms. And they smote all the souls that were therein with the edge of the sword, utterly destroying them: there was not any left to breathe: and he burnt Hazor with fire" (Joshua 11:10–11, 20–21). The messianic king extolled by Solomon was also known for his reign of terror: "May he purify Jerusalem for all gentiles who trample on it miserably, may he exterminate by his wisdom, justice the sinners of this country... May he destroy the impious nations with the words from his mouth." Hatred against pagans is also visible in the books of Esther, Judith, etc. "No ancient religion, except that of the Hebrew people has known such a degree of intolerance", says Emile Gillabert in *Moïse et le phénomène judéo-chrétien* (1976). Renan had written in similar terms:

> The intolerance of the Semitic peoples is the inevitable consequence of their monotheism. The Indo-European peoples, before they converted to Semitic ideas, had never considered their religion an absolute truth. Rather, they conceived of it as a heritage of the family, or the caste, and in this way they remained foreign to intolerance and proselytism. This is why we find among these peoples the liberty of thought, the spirit of inquiry and individual research.

Of course, one should not look at this problem in a black and white manner, or for instance compare and contrast one platitude to another platitude. There have always been, at all times, and everywhere, massacres and exterminations. But it would be difficult to find in the pagan texts, be they of sacred or profane nature, the equivalent of what one so frequently encounters in the Bible: the idea that these massacres could be morally justified, that they could be deliberately authorized and ordained by one god, "as Moses the servant of the Lord commanded" (Joshua 11:12). Thus, for the perpetrators of these crimes, good consciousness continues to rule, not despite these massacres, but entirely for the sake of the massacres. A lot of ink has been spilled over this tradition of intolerance. Particularly contentious are the words of Jesus as recorded by Luke: "If any man come to me, and hate not his father, and mother, and wife, and children, and brethren, and sisters, yea, and his own life also, he cannot be my disciple" (Luke 14:26). Some claim to perceive in the word "hate" a certain form of Hebraism; apparently, these words suggest that Jesus had to be absolutely preferred to all other human beings. Some claim to see in it traces of Gnostic contamination that suggest renouncement, despoliation of goods, and the refusal of procreation. In this context, the obligation to "hate" one's parents is to be viewed as a corollary of not wishing to have children. These interpretations remain pure conjecture. What is certain is that Christian intolerance began to manifest itself very early. In the course of history this intolerance was directed against "infidels" as well as against pagans, Jews, and heretics. It accompanied the extermination of all aspects of ancient culture — the murder of Julius of Hypati, the interdiction of pagan cults, the destruction of temples and statues, the suppression of the Olympic Games, and the arson, at the instigation of the town's Bishop Theophilus of Sarapeum, of Alexandria in A.D. 389, whose immense library of 700,000 volumes had been collected by the Ptolemeys. Then came the forced conversions, the extinction of positive science, persecution, and pyres. Ammianus Marcellinus said: "The wild beasts are less hostile to people than Christians are among themselves." Sulpicius Severus wrote: "Now everything has gone astray as the result of discords among bishops. Everywhere, one can see hatred, favours, fear, jealousy, ambition, debauchery, avarice, arrogance, sloth: there is general corruption everywhere." The Jewish people were the first to suffer from Christian monotheism. The causes of Christian anti-Semitism, which found its first "justification" in the Gospel of John (probably written under the influence of Gnosticism, and to which many studies have been devoted) lie in the proximity of the Jewish and Christian faiths. As Jacques Solé notes: "One persecutes only his neighbors." Only a "small gap" separates Jews from Christians, but as Nietzsche says, "the smallest gap is also the least bridgeable." During the first centuries of the Christian era anti-Semitism grew out of the Christian claim to be the successor of Judaism, and bestowing on it its "truthful" meaning. For Christians, "salvation is of the Jews" (John 4:22), but it is only Christianity that can be *verus Israel*. Hence the expression *perfidi*, applied to the Jews until recently by the Church in prayers during Holy Friday — an expression meaning "without faith", and whose meaning is different from the modem word "perfidious". The origins of modern totalitarianism are not difficult to trace. In a secular form, they are tied to the same radical strains of intolerance whose religious causes we have just examined. Saint Paul was the first to formulate this distinction. With his replacement of the Law by Grace, Paul distinguished between the "Israel of God" and the "Israel after the flesh" (1 Corinthians 10:18), which also led him to oppose circumcision: "For he is not a Jew, which is one outwardly; neither is that circumcision, which is outward in the flesh: But he is a Jew, which is one inwardly; and circumcision is that of the heart, in the spirit, and not in the letter; whose praise is not of men, but of God" (Romans 2:28–29). Conclusion: "For we are the circumcision" (Philippians 3:3). This argument has, from the Christian point of view, certain coherence. As Claude Tresmontant says, if the last of the nabis from Israel, the rabbi Yohushua of Nazareth, that is to say Jesus, is really a Messiah, then the vocation of Israel to become the "beacon of nations" must be fully accomplished, and the universalism implied in this vocation must be put entirely into practice. Just as the Law that has come to an end with Christ (in a double sense of the word) is no longer necessary, so has the distinction between Israel and other nations become futile as well: "There is neither Jew nor Greek" (Galatians 3:28). Consequently, universal Christianity must become verus Israel. This process, which originated in the Pauline reform, has had a double consequence. On the one hand, it has resulted in the persecution of Jews who, by virtue of their "genealogical" proximity, are represented as the worst enemies of Christianity. They are the adversaries who refuse to "convert", who refuse to recognize Christianity as the "true Israel". As Shmuel Trigano notes, "by projecting itself as the new Israel, the West has given to Judaism a de facto jurisdiction, albeit not the right to be itself." This means that the West can become "Israelite" to the extent that it denies Jews the right to be Israelites. Henceforth, the very notion of "Judeo-Christianity" can be defined as a double incarceration. It imprisons "the Christian West", which by its own deliberate act has subordinated itself to an alien "jurisdiction", and which by doing so denies this very same jurisdiction to its legitimate (Jewish) owners. Furthermore, it imprisons the Jews who, by virtue of a religion different from their own, are now undeservedly caught in the would-be place of their "accomplishment" by means of a religion that is not their own. Trigano further adds: "If Judeo-Christianity laid the foundations of the West, then the very place of Israel is also the West." Subsequently, the requisites of "Westernization" must also become the requisites of assimilation and "normalization", and the denial of identity. "The crisis of Jewish normality is the crisis of the westernization of Judaism. Therefore, to exit from the West means for the Jews to turn their back to their 'normality', that is, to open themselves up to their otherness." This seems to be why

Jewish communities today criticize the "Western model", only after they first adopt their own specific history of a semi-amnesiac and semi-critical attitude. In view of this, Christian anti-Semitism can be rightly described as neurosis. As Jean Blot writes, it is because of its "predisposition toward alienation" that the West is incapable of "fulfilling itself or rediscovering itself." And from this source arises anti-Semitic neurosis. "Anti-semitism allows the anti-Semite to project onto the Jew his own neuroses. He calls him a stranger, because he himself is a stranger, a crook, a powerful man, a parvenu; he calls him a Jew, because he himself is this Jew in the deepest depth of his soul, always on the move, permanently alienated, a stranger to his own religion and to God who incarnates him." By replacing his original myth with the myth of biblical monotheism, the West has turned Hebraism into its own superego. As an inevitable consequence, the West had to turn itself against the Jewish people by accusing them of not pursuing the "conversion" in terms of the "logical" evolution proceeding from Sinai to Christianity. In addition, the West also accused the Jewish people of attempting, in an apparent "deicide", to obstruct this evolution. Many, even today, assume that if Jews were to renounce their distinct identity, "the Jewish problem" would disappear. At best, this is a naive proposition, and at worst, it masks a conscious or unconscious form of anti-Semitism. Furthermore, this proposition, which is inherent in the racism of assimilation and the denial of identity, represents the reverse side of the racism of exclusion and persecution. In the West, notes Shmuel Trigano, when the Jews were not persecuted, they "were recognized as Jews only on the condition that they first ceased to be Jews." Put another way, in order to be accepted, they had to reject themselves; they had to renounce their own Other in order to be reduced to the Same. In another type of racism, Jews are accepted but denied; in the first, they are accepted but are not recognized. The Church ordered Jews to choose between exclusion (or physical death) or self-denial (spiritual and historical death). Only through conversion could they become "Christians, as others". The French Revolution emancipated Jews as individuals, but it condemned them to disappear as a "nation"; in this sense, they were forced to become "citizens, as others". Marxism, too, attempted to ensure the "liberation" of the Jewish people by imposing on them a class division, from which their dispersion inevitably resulted. The origins of modern totalitarianism are not difficult to trace. In a secular form, they are tied to the same radical strains of intolerance whose religious causes we have just examined. The organization of totalitarianism is patterned after the organization of the Christian Church, and in a similar manner totalitarianisms exploit the themes of the "masses" — the themes inherent in contemporary mass democracy. This secularization of the system has, in fact, rendered totalitarianism more dangerous — independently of the fact that religious intolerance often triggers, in return, an equally destructive revolutionary intolerance. "Totalitarianism", writes Gilbert Durand, "is further strengthened, in so far as the powers of monotheist theology (which at least left the game of transcendence intact) have been transferred to a human institution, to the Grand Inquisitor." It is a serious error to assume that totalitarianism manifests its real character only when it employs crushing coercion. Historical experience has demonstrated — and continues to demonstrate — that there can exist a "clean" totalitarianism, which, in a "soft" manner, yields the same consequences as the classic kinds of totalitarianism. "Happy robots" of *1984* or of *Brave New World* have no more enviable conditions than prisoners of the camps. In essence, totalitarianism did not originate with Saint-Just, Stalin, Hegel, or Fichte. Rather, as Michel Maffesoli says, totalitarianism emerges "when a subtle form of plural, polytheistic, and contradictory totality, that is inherent in organic interdependency" is superseded by a monotheistic one. Totalitarianism grows out of a desire to establish social and human unity by reducing the diversity of individuals and peoples to a single model. In this sense, he argues, it is legitimate to speak of a "polytheist social arena, referring to multiple and complementary gods" versus a "monotheistic political arena founded on the illusion of unity." Once the polytheism of values "disappears, we face totalitarianism." Pagan thought, on the other hand, which fundamentally remains attached to rootedness and to the place, and which is a preferential center of the crystallization of human identity, rejects all religious and philosophical forms of universalism.

PART II
CULTURAL PESSIMISM

HISTORY AND DECADENCE: SPENGLER'S CULTURAL PESSIMISM TODAY

Oswald Spengler (1880–1936) exerted considerable influence on European conservatism before the Second World War. Although his popularity waned somewhat after the war, his analyses, in the light of the disturbing conditions in the modern polity, again seem to be gaining in popularity. Recent literature dealing with gloomy postmodernist themes suggests that Spengler's prophecies of decadence may now be finding supporters on both sides of the political spectrum. The alienating nature of modern technology and the social and moral decay of large cities today lend new credence to Spengler's vision of the impending collapse of the West. In America and Europe an increasing number of authors perceive in the liberal permissive state a harbinger of "soft" totalitarianism that may lead decisively to social entropy and conclude in the advent of "hard" totalitarianism.[1]

Spengler wrote his major work *The Decline of the West* (*Der Untergang des Abendlandes*) against the background of the anticipated German victory in World War I. When the war ended disastrously for the Germans, his predictions that Germany, together with the rest of Europe, was bent for irreversible decline gained a renewed sense of urgency for scores of cultural pessimists. World War I must have deeply shaken the quasi-religious optimism of those who had earlier prophesied that technological inventions and international economic linkages would pave the way for peace and prosperity. Moreover, the war proved that technological inventions could turn out to be a perfect tool for man's alienation and, eventually, his physical annihilation. Inadvertently, while attempting to interpret the cycles of world history, Spengler probably best succeeded in spreading the spirit of cultural despair to his own as well as future generations.

Like Gianbattista Vico, who two centuries earlier developed his thesis about the rise and decline of cultures, Spengler tried to project a pattern of cultural growth and cultural decay in a certain scientific form: "the morphology of history" — as he himself and others dub his work — although the term "biology" seems more appropriate considering Spengler's inclination to view cultures as living organic entities, alternately afflicted with disease and plague or showing signs of vigorous life.[2] Undoubtedly, the organic conception of history was, to a great extent, inspired by the popularity of scientific and pseudoscientific literature, which, in the early twentieth century, began to focus attention on racial and genetic paradigms in order to explain the patterns of social decay. Spengler, however, prudently avoids racial determinism in his description of decadence, although his exaltation of historical determinism often brings him close to Marx — albeit in a reversed and hopelessly pessimistic direction. In contrast to many egalitarian thinkers, Spengler's elitism and organicism conceived of human species as of different and opposing peoples, each experiencing its own growth and death, and each struggling for survival. "Mankind," writes Spengler, should be viewed as either a "zoological concept or an empty word." If ever this phantom of "mankind" vanishes from the circulation of historical forms, "we shall then notice an astounding affluence of genuine forms." Apparently, by form (*Gestalt*) Spengler means the resurrection of the classical notion of the nation-state, which, in the early twentieth century, came under fire from the advocates of the globalist and universalist polity. Spengler must be credited, however, with pointing out that the frequently used concept "world history", in reality encompasses an impressive array of diverse and opposing cultures without common denominator; each culture displays its own forms, pursues its own passions, and grapples with its own life or death. "There are blossoming and aging cultures," writes Spengler, "peoples, languages, truths, gods, and landscapes, just as there are young and old oak trees, pines, flowers, boughs and petals — but there is no aging 'mankind.'"[3] For Spengler, cultures seem to be growing in sublime futility, with some approaching terminal illness, and others still displaying vigorous signs of life. Before culture emerged, man was an ahistorical creature; but he becomes again ahistorical and, one might add, even hostile to history: "as soon as some civilization has developed its full and final form, thus putting a stop to the living development of culture" (2:58; 2:48).

Spengler was convinced, however, that the dynamics of decadence could be fairly well predicted, provided that exact historical data were available. Just as the biology of human beings generates a well-defined life span, resulting ultimately in biological death, so does each culture possess its own aging "data", normally lasting no longer than a thousand years — a period, separating its spring from its eventual historical antithesis, the winter, of civilization. The estimate of a thousand years before the decline of culture sets in corresponds to Spengler's certitude that, after that period, each society has to face self-destruction. For example, after the fall of Rome, the rebirth of European culture started anew in the ninth century with the Carolingian dynasty. After the painful process of growth, self-assertiveness, and maturation, one thousand years later, in the twentieth century, cultural life in Europe is coming to its definite historical close.

As Spengler and his contemporary successors see it, Western culture now has transformed itself into a decadent civilization fraught with an advanced form of social, moral, and political decay. The first signs of this decay appeared shortly after the Industrial Revolution, when the machine began to replace man, when feelings gave way to ratio. Ever since that ominous event, new forms of social and political conduct have been surfacing in the West — marked by a widespread obsession with endless economic growth and irreversible human betterment — fueled by the belief that the burden of history can finally be removed. The new plutocratic elites, that have now replaced organic aristocracy, have imposed material gain as the only principle worth pursuing, reducing the entire human interaction to an immense economic transaction. And since the masses can never be fully satisfied, argues Spengler, it is understandable that they will seek change in their existing polities even if change may spell the loss of liberty. One might add that this craving for economic affluence will be translated into an incessant decline of the sense of public responsibility and an emerging sense of uprootedness and social anomie, which will ultimately and inevitably lead to the advent of totalitarianism. It would appear, therefore, that the process of decadence can be forestalled, ironically, only by resorting to salutary hard-line regimes.

Using Spengler's apocalyptic predictions, one is tempted to draw a parallel with the modern Western polity, which likewise seems to be undergoing the period of decay and decadence. John Lukacs, who bears the unmistakable imprint of Spenglerian pessimism, views the permissive nature of modern liberal society, as embodied in America, as the first step toward social disintegration. Like Spengler, Lukacs asserts that excessive individualism and rampant materialism increasingly paralyze and render obsolete the sense of civic responsibility. One should probably agree with Lukacs that neither the lifting of censorship, nor the increasing unpopularity of traditional values, nor the curtailing of state authority in contemporary liberal states, seems to have led to a more peaceful environment; instead, a growing sense of despair seems to have triggered a form of neo-barbarism and social vulgarity. "Already richness and poverty, elegance and sleaziness, sophistication and savagery live together more and more," writes Lukacs.[5] Indeed, who could have predicted that a society capable of launching rockets to the moon or curing diseases that once ravaged the world could also become a civilization plagued by social atomization, crime, and an addiction to escapism? With his apocalyptic predictions, Lukacs, similar to Spengler, writes: "This most crowded of streets of the greatest civilization: this is now the hellhole of the world."

Interestingly, neither Spengler nor Lukacs nor other cultural pessimists seems to pay much attention to the obsessive appetite for equality, which seems to play, as several contemporary authors point out, an important role in decadence and the resulting sense of cultural despair. One is inclined to think that the process of decadence in the contemporary West is the result of egalitarian doctrines that promise much but deliver little, creating thus an endless feeling of emptiness and frustration among the masses of economic-minded and rootless citizens. Moreover, elevated to the status of modern secular religions, egalitarianism and economism inevitably follow their own dynamics of growth, which is likely to conclude, as Claude Polin notes, in the "terror of all against all" and the ugly resurgence of democratic totalitarianism. Polin writes: "Undifferentiated man is par excellence a quantitative man; a man who accidentally differs from his neighbors by the quantity of economic goods in his possession; a man subject to statistics; a man who spontaneously reacts in accordance to statistics".[6] Conceivably, liberal society, if it ever gets gripped by economic duress and hit by vanishing opportunities, will have no option but to tame and harness the restless masses in a Spenglerian "muscled regime."

Spengler and other cultural pessimists seem to be right in pointing out that democratic forms of polity, in their final stage, will be marred by moral and social convulsions, political scandals, and corruption on all social levels. On top of it, as Spengler predicts, the cult of money will reign supreme, because "through money democracy destroys itself, after money has destroyed the spirit" (2: p. 582; 2: p. 464). Judging by the modern development of capitalism, Spengler cannot be accused of far-fetched assumptions. This economic civilization founders on a major contradiction: on the one hand its religion of human rights extends its beneficiary legal tenets to everyone, reassuring every individual of the legitimacy of his earthly appetites; on the other, this same egalitarian civilization fosters a model of economic Darwinism, ruthlessly trampling under its feet those whose interests do not lie in the economic arena.

The next step, as Spengler suggests, will be the transition from democracy to salutary Caesarism; substitution of the tyranny of the few for the tyranny of many. The neo-Hobbesian, neo-barbaric state is in the making:

> Instead of the pyres emerges big silence. The dictatorship of party bosses is backed up by the dictatorship of the press. With money, an attempt is made to lure swarms of readers and entire peoples away from the enemy's attention and bring them under one's own thought control. There, they learn only what they must learn, and a higher will shapes their picture of the world. It is no longer needed — as the baroque princes did — to oblige their subordinates into the armed service. Their minds are whipped up through articles, telegrams, pictures, until they demand weapons and force their leaders to a battle to which these wanted to be forced. (2: p. 463).

The fundamental issue, however, which Spengler and many other cultural pessimists do not seem to address, is whether Caesarism or totalitarianism represents the antithetical remedy to decadence or, rather, the most extreme form of decadence? Current literature on totalitarianism seems to focus on the unpleasant side effects of the bloated state, the absence of human rights, and the pervasive control of the police. By contrast, if liberal democracy is indeed a highly desirable and the least repressive system of all hitherto known in the West — and if, in addition, this liberal democracy claims to be the best custodian of human dignity — one wonders why it relentlessly causes social uprootedness and cultural despair among an increasing number of people? As Claude Polin notes, chances are that, in the short run, democratic totalitarianism will gain the upper hand since the security it provides is more appealing to the masses than is the vague notion of liberty.[7] One might add that the tempo of democratic process in the West leads eventually to chaotic impasse, which necessitates the imposition of a hard-line regime.

Although Spengler does not provide a satisfying answer to the question of Caesarism vs. decadence, he admits that the decadence of the West needs not signify the collapse of all cultures. Rather, it appears that the terminal illness of the West may be a new lease on life for other cultures; the death of Europe may result in a stronger Africa or Asia. Like many other cultural pessimists, Spengler acknowledges that the West has grown old, unwilling to fight, with its political and cultural inventory depleted; consequently, it is obliged to cede the reigns of history to those nations that are less exposed to debilitating pacifism and the self-flagellating feelings of guilt that, so to speak, have become the new trademarks of the modern Western citizen. One could imagine a situation where these new virile and victorious nations will barely heed the democratic niceties of their guilt-ridden former masters, and may likely, at some time in the future, impose their own brand of terror that could eclipse the legacy of the European Auschwitz and the Gulag. In view of the ruthless civil and tribal wars all over the decolonized African and Asian continent, it seems unlikely that power politics and bellicosity will disappear with the "decline of the West". So far, no proof has been offered that non-European nations can govern more peacefully and generously than their former European masters. "Pacifism will remain an ideal," Spengler reminds us, "war a fact. If the white races are resolved never to wage a war again, the colored will act differently and be rulers of the world."[8]

In this statement, Spengler clearly indicts the self-hating *Homo europeanus* who, having become a victim of his bad conscience, naively thinks that his truths and verities must remain irrefutably valid forever, forgetting that his eternal verities may one day be turned against him. Spengler strongly attacks this Western false sympathy with the deprived ones — a sympathy that Nietzsche once depicted as a twisted form of egoism and slave moral. "This is the reason," writes Spengler, why this "compassion moral", in the day-to-day sense, "evoked among us with respect, and sometimes strived for by the thinkers, sometimes longed for, has never been realized" (1: p. 449; 1: p. 350).

This form of political masochism could be well studied particularly among those contemporary Western egalitarians who, with the decline of socialist temptations, substituted for the archetype of the European exploited worker, the iconography of the starving African. Nowhere does this change in political symbolics seem more apparent than in the current Western drive to export Western forms of civilization to the antipodes of the world. These Westerners, in the last spasm of a guilt-ridden shame, are probably convinced that their historical repentance might also secure their cultural and political longevity. Spengler was aware of these paralyzing attitudes among Europeans, and he remarks that, if a modern European recognizes his historical vulnerability, he must start thinking beyond his narrow perspective and develop different attitudes toward different political convictions and verities. What do Parsifal or Prometheus have to do with the average Japanese citizen, asks Spengler? "This is exactly what is lacking in the Western thinker," continues Spengler, "and which precisely should have never lacked in him; insight into historical relativity of his achievements, which are themselves the manifestation of one and unique, and of only one existence" (1: p. 31; 1: p. 23). On a somewhat different level, one wonders to what extent the much-vaunted dissemination of universal human rights can become a valuable principle for non-Western peoples if Western universalism often signifies blatant disrespect for all cultural particularities.

Even with their eulogy of universalism, as Serge Latouche has recently noted, Westerners have, nonetheless, secured the most comfortable positions for themselves. Although they have now retreated to the back stage of history, vicariously, through their humanism, they still play the role of the undisputable masters of the non-white-man show. "The death of the West for itself has not been the end of the West in itself", adds Latouche.[9] One wonders whether such Western attitudes to universalism represent another form of racism, considering the havoc these attitudes have created in traditional Third World communities. Latouche appears correct in remarking that European decadence best manifests itself in its masochistic drive to deny and discard everything that it once stood for, while simultaneously sucking into its orbit of decadence other cultures as well. Yet, although suicidal in its character, the Western message contains mandatory admonishments for all non-European nations. He writes:

> The mission of the West is not to exploit the Third World, nor to christianize the pagans, nor to dominate by white presence; it is to liberate men (and even more so women) from oppression and misery. In order to counter this self-hatred of the anti-imperialist vision, which concludes in red totalitarianism, one is now compelled to dry the tears of white man, and thereby ensure the success of this westernization of the world. (p. 41)

The decadent West exhibits, as Spengler hints, a travestied culture living on its own past in a society of different nations that, having lost their historical consciousness, feel an urge to become blended into a promiscuous "global polity". One wonders what would he say today about the massive immigration of non-Europeans to Europe? This immigration has not improved understanding among races, but has caused more racial and ethnic strife that, very likely, signals a series of new conflicts in the future.

But Spengler does not deplore the "devaluation of all values" nor the passing of cultures. In fact, to him decadence is a natural process of senility that concludes in civilization, because civilization is decadence. Spengler makes a typically German distinction between culture and civilization, two terms that are, unfortunately, used synonymously in English. For Spengler civilization is a product of intellect, of completely rationalized intellect; civilization means uprootedness and, as such, it develops its ultimate form in the modern megapolis that, at the end of its journey, "doomed, moves to its final self-destruction" (2: p. 127; 2: p. 107). The force of the people has been overshadowed by massification; creativity has given way to "kitsch" art; genius has been subordinated to the terror of reason. He writes:

> Culture and civilization. On the one hand the living corpse of a soul and, on the other, its mummy. This is how the West European existence differs from 1800 and after. The life in its richness and normalcy, whose form has grown up and matured from inside out in one mighty course stretching from the adolescent days of Gothics to Goethe and Napoleon — into that old artificial, deracinated life of our large cities, whose forms are created by intellect. Culture and civilization. The organism born in countryside, that ends up in petrified mechanism. (1: p. 453; 1: p. 353)

In yet another display of determinism, Spengler contends that one cannot escape historical destiny: "the first inescapable thing that confronts man as an unavoidable destiny, which no thought can grasp, and no will can change, is a place and time of one's birth: everybody is born into one people, one religion, one social status, one stretch of time and one culture."[10] Man is so much constrained by his historical environment that all attempts at changing one's destiny are hopeless. And, therefore, all flowery postulates about the improvement of mankind, all liberal and socialist philosophizing about a glorious future regarding the duties of humanity and the essence of ethics, are of no avail. Spengler sees no other avenue of redemption except by declaring himself a fundamental and resolute pessimist:

> Mankind appears to me as a zoological quantity. I see no progress, no goal, no avenue for humanity, except in the heads of the Western progress-Philistines ... I cannot see a single mind and even less a unity of endeavors, feelings, and understandings in these barren masses of people. (*Selected Essays*, p. 73-74; 147).

The determinist nature of Spengler's pessimism has been criticized recently by Konrad Lorenz who, while sharing Spengler's culture of despair, refuses the predetermined linearity of decadence. In his capacity of ethologist and as one of the most articulate neo-Darwinists, Lorenz admits the possibility of an interruption of human phylogenesis — yet also contends that new vistas for cultural development always remain open. "Nothing is more foreign to the evolutionary epistemologist, as well, to the physician," writes Lorenz, "than the doctrine of fatalism".[11] Still, Lorenz does not hesitate to criticize vehemently decadence in modern mass societies that, in his view, have already given birth to pacified and domesticated specimens unable to pursue cultural endeavors. Lorenz would certainly find positive resonance with Spengler himself in writing:

> This explains why the pseudodemocratic doctrine that all men are equal, by which is believed that all humans are initially alike and pliable, could be made into a state religion by both the lobbyists for large industry and by the ideologues of communism (p. 179–80).

Despite the criticism of historical determinism that has been leveled against him, Spengler often confuses his reader with Faustian exclamations reminiscent of someone prepared for battle rather than reconciled to a sublime demise. "No, I am not a pessimist," writes Spengler in "Pessimism", for "pessimism means seeing no more duties. I see so many unresolved duties that I fear that time and men will run out to solve them" (p. 75). These words hardly cohere with the cultural despair that earlier he so passionately elaborated. Moreover, he often advocates force and the toughness of the warrior in order to stave off Europe's disaster.

One is led to the conclusion that Spengler extols historical pessimism or "purposeful pessimism" (*Zweckpessimismus*), as long as it translates his conviction of the irreversible decadence of the European polity; however, once he perceives that cultural and political loopholes are available for moral and social regeneration, he quickly reverts to the eulogy of power politics. Similar characteristics are often to be found among many poets, novelists, and social thinkers whose legacy in spreading cultural pessimism played a significant part in shaping political behavior among European conservatives prior to World War II.[12] One wonders why they all, like Spengler, bemoan the decadence of the West if this decadence has already been sealed, if the cosmic die has already been cast, and if all efforts of political and cultural rejuvenation appear hopeless? Moreover, in an effort to mend the unmendable, by advocating a Faustian mentality and will to power, these pessimists often seem to emulate the optimism of socialists rather than the ideas of those reconciled to impending social catastrophe.

For Spengler and other cultural pessimists, the sense of decadence is inherently combined with a revulsion against modernity and an abhorrence of rampant economic greed. As recent history has shown, the political manifestation of such revulsion may lead to less savory results: the glorification of the will-to-power and the nostalgia of death. At that moment, literary finesse and artistic beauty may take on a very ominous turn. The recent history of Europe bears witness to how easily cultural pessimism can become a handy tool for modern political titans. Nonetheless, the upcoming disasters have something uplifting for the generations of cultural pessimists whose hypersensitive nature — and disdain for the materialist society — often lapses into political nihilism. This nihilistic streak was boldly stated by Spengler's contemporary Friedrich Sieburg, who reminds us that "the daily life of democracy with its sad problems is boring, but the impending catastrophes are highly interesting."[13]

One cannot help thinking that, for Spengler and his likes, in a wider historical context, war and power politics offer a regenerative hope against the pervasive feeling of cultural despair. Yet, regardless of the validity of Spengler's visions or nightmares, it does not take much imagination to observe in the decadence of the West the last twilight-dream of a democracy already grown weary of itself.

"GEMEINSCHAFT AND GESELLSCHAFT": A SOCIOLOGICAL VIEW OF THE DECAY OF MODERN SOCIETY

by Alain de Benoist and Tomislav Sunic

Peaceful modern societies that respect the individual evolved from age-old family ties. The transition from band-type societies, through clan and tribal organizations, into nation-states was peaceful only when accomplished without disruption of the basic ties that link the individual to the larger society by a sense of a common history, culture and kinship. The sense of "belonging" to a nation by virtue of such shared ties promotes cooperation, altruism and respect for other members. In modern times, traditional ties have been weakened by the rise of mass societies and rapid global communication, factors that bring with them rapid social change and new philosophies that deny the significance of the sense of nationhood, and emphasize individualism and individualistic goals. The cohesion of societies has consequently been threatened, and replaced by multicultural and multi-ethnic societies and the overwhelming sense of lost identity in the mass global society in which Western man, at least, has come to conceive himself as belonging.

Sociologically, the first theorist to identify this change was the Arab scholar Ibn Khaldun (1332–1406), who emphasized the tendency for mass urban societies to break down when the social solidarity characteristic of tribal and national societies disappeared. Ibn Khaldun saw dramatically the contrast between the morality of the nationalistic and ethnically unified Berbers of North Africa and the motley collation of peoples who called themselves Arabs under Arabic leadership, but did not possess the unity and sense of identity that had made the relatively small population of true Arabs who had built a widespread and Arabic-speaking Empire. Later it was Ferdinand Tönnies (1855–1936) who introduced this thought to modern sociology. He did so in his theory of *gemeinschaft* and *gesellschaft* (*Gemeinschaft und Gesellschaft*, 1887). This theory revealed how early tribal or national (*gemeinschaft*) societies achieved harmonious collaboration and cooperation, more or less automatically, due to the common culture and sense of common genetic and cultural identity in which all members were raised. This avoided major conflicts concerning basic values since all shared a common set of mores and a common sense of destiny. However, as history progressed, larger multi-ethnic and multicultural societies began to develop, and these Tönnies described as being united by *gesellschaft* ties. These were not united by any common set of values or historical identity, and collaboration was only maintained due to the need to exchange goods and services. In short, their existence came to depend on economic relations, and as a result of the diversity of cultural values, the lack of any "family feeling", and the emphasis on economic exchange and economic wealth, conflict over wealth and basic values was likely to disrupt the harmony of such societies at any time. In political terms, liberalism developed to eulogize the freedom of individuals from claims to national loyalty and support for national destiny, while Marxism grew out of the dissatisfaction felt by those who were less successful in achieving wealth and power, which now came to represent the primary goals of the individuals who were left at the mercy of the modern mass *gesellschaft* society. Nationalism and any sense of loyalty to the nation as a distinct ethnic kinship unit came to be anathematized by both liberals and Marxists.

* * *

"A specter is haunting Europe — a specter of communism," wrote Marx in the preface of *The Manifesto*. A century later this specter became a mere phantom, with liberalism the dominant force. Over the last several decades, liberalism used communism as a scarecrow to legitimize itself. Today, however, with the bankruptcy of communism, this mode of "negative legitimization" is no longer convincing. At last, liberalism, in the sense of the emphasis on the individual above and even against that of the nation, actually endangers the individual by undermining the stability of the society that gives him identity, values, purpose and meaning, the social, cultural and biological nexus to which he owes his very being.

Fundamentally, classical liberalism was a doctrine that, out of an abstract individual, created the pivot of its survival. In its mildest form, it merely emphasized individual freedom of action, and condemned excessive bureaucratic involvement by government. But praiseworthy though its defense of individual freedom was, its claim that the ideal system is that in which there is the least possible emphasis on nationhood, leads to situations that in fact endanger the freedom of the individual. In its extreme form, classical liberalism has developed into universal libertarianism, and at this point it comes close to advocating anarchy.

From the sociological standpoint, in its extreme form, modern internationalist liberalism defines itself totally in terms of the *gesellschaft* society of Tönnies. It denies the historical concept of the nation state by rejecting the notion of any common interest between individuals who traditionally shared a common heritage. In the place of nationhood, it proposes to generate a new international social pattern centered on the individual's quest for optimal personal and economic interest. Within the context of extreme liberalism, only the interplay of individual interests creates a functional society — a society in which the whole is viewed only as a chance aggregate of anonymous particles. The essence of modern liberal thought is that order is believed to be able to consolidate itself by means of all-out economic competition, that is, through the battle of all against all, requiring governments to do no more than set certain essential ground rules and provide certain services that the individual alone cannot adequately provide. Indeed, modern liberalism has gone so far along this path that it is today directly opposed to the goals of classical liberalism and libertarianism in that it denies the individual any inalienable right to property, but still shares with modern liberalism and with libertarianism an antagonism toward the idea of nationhood. Shorn of the protection of a society that identifies with its members because of a shared national history and destiny, the individual is left to struggle for his own survival, without the protective sense of community that his forebears enjoyed since the earliest of human history.

Decadence in modern mass multicultural societies begins at a moment when there is no longer any discernable meaning within society. Meaning is destroyed by raising individualism above all other values, because rampant individualism encourages the anarchical proliferation of egotism at the expense of the values that were once part of the national heritage, values that give form to the concept of nationhood and the nation state, to a state that is more than just a political entity, and that corresponds to a particular people who are conscious of sharing a common heritage for the survival of which they are prepared to make personal sacrifices.

Man evolved in cooperating groups united by common cultural and genetic ties, and it is only in such a setting that the individual can feel truly free, and truly protected. Men cannot live happily alone and without values or any sense of identity: such a situation leads to nihilism, drug abuse, criminality and worse. With the spread of purely egotistic goals at the expense of the altruistic regard for family and nation, the individual begins to talk of his rights rather than his duties, for he no longer feels any sense of destiny, of belonging to and being a part of a greater and more enduring entity. He no longer rejoices in the secure belief that he shares in a heritage that it is part of his common duty to protect — he no longer feels that he has anything in common with those around him. In short, he feels lonely and oppressed. Since all values have become strictly personal, everything is now equal to everything; e.g., nothing equals nothing.

"A society without strong beliefs," declared Régis Debray in his interview with J. P. Enthoven in *Le Nouvel Observateur*, (October 10, 1981), "is a society about to die." Modern liberalism is particularly critical of nationalism. Hence, the question needs to be raised: Can modern liberal society provide strong unifying communal beliefs in view of the fact that on the one hand it views communal life as nonessential, while on the other, it remains impotent to envision any belief — unless this belief is reducible to economic conduct?

Moreover, there seems to be an obvious relationship between the negation and the eclipse of the meaning and the destruction of the historical dimension of the social corpus. Modern liberals encourage "narcissism"; they live in the perpetual now. In liberal society, the individual is unable to put himself in perspective, because putting himself in perspective requires a clear and a collectively perceived consciousness of common heritage and common adherence. As Régis Debray remarks, "In the capacity of isolated subjects men can never become the subjects of action and acquire the capability of making history" (*Critique de la raison politique*, op. cit. p. 207). In liberal societies, the suppression of the sense of meaning and identity embedded in national values, leads to the dissolution of social cohesion as well as to the dissolution of group consciousness. This dissolution, in turn, culminates in the end of history.

Being the most typical representative of the ideology of egalitarianism, modern liberalism, in both its libertarian and socialist variants, appears to be the main factor in this dissolution of the ideal of nationhood. When the concept of society, from the sociological standpoint, suggests a system of simple 'horizontal interactions,' then this notion inevitably excludes social form. As a manifestation of solidarity, society can only be conceived in terms of shared identity — that is, in terms of historical values and cultural traditions (cf. Edgar Morin: "The communal myth gives society its national cohesion"). By contrast, liberalism undoes nations and systematically destroys their sense of history, tradition, loyalty, and value. Instead of helping man to elevate himself to the sphere of the superhuman, it divorces him from all 'grand projects' by declaring these projects 'dangerous' from the point of view of equality. No wonder, therefore, that the management of man's individual well-being becomes his sole preoccupation. In the attempt to free man from all constraints, liberalism brings man under the yoke of other constraints that now downgrade him to the lowest level. Liberalism does not defend liberty; it destroys the independence of the individual. By eroding historical memories, liberalism extricates man from history. It proposes to ensure his means of existence, but robs him of his reason to live and deprives him of the possibility of having a destiny.

There are two ways of conceiving of man and society. The fundamental value may be placed on the individual, and when this is done the whole of mankind is conceived as the sum total of all individuals — a vast faceless proletariat — instead of as a rich fabric of diverse nations, cultures, and races. It is this conception that is inherent in liberal and socialist thought. The other view, which appears to be more compatible with man's evolutionary and socio-biological character, is when the individual is seen as enjoying a specific biological and cultural legacy — a notion that recognizes the importance of kinship and nationhood. In the first instance, mankind, as a sum total of individuals, appears to be "contained" in each individual human being; that is, one becomes first a "human being", and only then, as by accident, a member of a specific culture or a people. In the second instance, mankind comprises a complex phylogenetic and historic network, whereby the freedom of the individual is guaranteed by the protection of his family, by his nation, which both provide him with a sense of identity and with a meaningful orientation to the entire world population. It is by virtue of their organic adherence to the society of which they are a part that men build their humanity.

As exponents of the first concept we encounter Descartes, the Encyclopaedists, and the emphasis on "rights"; nationality and society emanate from the individual, by elective choice, and are revokable at any time. As proponents of the second concept we find J. G. Herder and G. W. Leibniz, who stress the reality of cultures and ethnicity. Nationality and society are rooted in biological, cultural and historical heritage. The difference between these two concepts becomes particularly obvious when one compares how they visualize history and the structure of the real. Nationalists are proponents of holism. Nationalists see the individual as a kinsman, sustained by the people and community, which nurtures and protects him, and with which he is proud to identify. The individual's actions represent an act of participation in the life of his people, and freedom of action is very real because, sharing in the values of his associates, the individual will seldom seek to threaten the basic values of the community with which he identifies. Societies that lack this basic sense of national unity are inherently prone to suffer from repeated situations wherein the opposing values of its egotistical members conflict with each other.

Furthermore, proponents of nationhood contend that a society or a people can survive only when: a) they remain aware of their cultural and historical origins; b) when they can assemble around a mediator, be it individual or symbolic, who is capable of reassembling their energies and catalyzing their will to have a destiny; c) when they can retain the courage to designate their enemy. None of these conditions have been realized in societies that put economic gain above all other values and that consequently:

a) dissolve historical memories;

b) extinguish the sublime and eliminate subliminal ideals;

c) assume that it is possible not to have enemies.

The results of the rapid change from national or tribal-oriented societies to the modern, anti-national individualism prevalent in contemporary "advanced" societies have been very well described by Cornelius Castoriadis: "Western societies are in absolute decomposition. There is no longer a vision of the whole that could permit them to determine and apply any political action ... Western societies have practically ceased to be [nation] states ... Simply put, they have become agglomerations of lobbies that, in a myopic manner, tear the society apart; where nobody can propose a coherent policy, and where everybody is capable of blocking an action deemed hostile to his own interests." (*Libération*, December, 16 and 21, 1981)

Modern liberalism has suppressed patriotic nationhood into a situation in which politics has been reduced to a "delivery service" decision-making process resembling the economic "command post", statesmen have been reduced to serving as tools for special interest groups, and nations have become little more than markets. The heads of modern liberal states have no options but to watch their citizenry being somatized by civilizational ills such as violence, delinquency, and drugs.

Ernst Jünger once remarked that the act of veiled violence is more terrible than open violence (*Journal IV*, September 6, 1945). And he also noted: "Slavery can be substantially aggravated when it assumes the appearance of liberty." The tyranny of modern liberalism creates the illusion inherent in its own principles. It proclaims itself for liberty and cries out to defend "human rights" at the moment when it oppresses the most. The dictatorship of the media and the "spiral of silence" appear to be almost as effective in depriving the citizenry of its freedom as imprisonment. In the West, there is no need to kill: suffice it to cut someone's microphone. To kill somebody by silence is a very elegant kind of murder, which in practice yields the same dividends as a real assassination — an assassination that, in addition, leaves the assassin with good conscience. Moreover, one should not forget the importance of such a type of assassination. Rare are those who silence their opponents for fun.

Patriotic nationhood does not target the notion of "formal liberties", as some rigorous Marxists do. Rather, its purpose is to demonstrate that "collective liberty", i.e., the liberty of peoples to be themselves and to continue to enjoy the privilege of having a destiny, does not result from the simple addition of individual liberties. Proponents of nationhood instead contend that the "liberties" granted to individuals by liberal societies are frequently nonexistent; they represent simulacra of what real liberties should be. It does not suffice to be free to do something. Rather, what is needed is one's ability to participate in determining the course of historical events. Societies dominated by modern liberal traditions are "permissive" only insofar as their general macrostability strips the populace of any real participation in the actual decision-making process. As the sphere in which the citizenry is permitted to "do everything" becomes larger, the sense of nationhood becomes paralyzed and loses its direction.

Liberty cannot be reduced to the sentiment that one has about it. For that matter, both the slave and the robot could equally well perceive themselves as free. The meaning of liberty is inseparable from the founding anthropology of man, an individual sharing a common history and common culture in a common community. Decadence vaporizes peoples, frequently in the gentlest of manners. This is the reason why individuals acting as individuals can only hope to flee tyranny, but cooperating actively as a nation they can often defeat tyranny.

The above text is based on an original essay by Alain de Benoist. Translated and interpreted by Tomislav Sunic.

EMILE CIORAN AND THE CULTURE OF DEATH

Historical pessimism and the sense of the tragic are recurrent motives in European literature. From Heraclitus to Heidegger, from Sophocles to Schopenhauer, the exponents of the tragic view of life point out that the shortness of human existence can only be overcome by the heroic intensity of living. The philosophy of the tragic is incompatible with the Christian dogma of salvation or the optimism of some modern ideologies. Many modern political theologies and ideologies set out from the assumption that "the radiant future" is always somewhere around the corner, and that existential fear can best be subdued by the acceptance of a linear and progressive concept of history. It is interesting to observe that individuals and masses in our post-modernity increasingly avoid allusions to death and dying. Processions and wakes, which not long ago honored the postmortem communion between the dead and the living, are rapidly falling into oblivion. In a cold and super-rational society of today, someone's death causes embarrassment, as if death should have never occurred, and as if death could be postponed by a deliberate "pursuit of happiness". The belief that death can be outwitted through the search for the elixir of eternal youth and the "ideology of good looks", is widespread in modern TV-oriented society. This belief has become a formula for social and political conduct.

The French-Romanian essayist, Emile Cioran, suggests that the awareness of existential futility represents the sole weapon against theological and ideological deliriums that have been rocking Europe for centuries. Born in Romania in 1911, Cioran very early came to terms with the old European proverb that geography means destiny. From his native region, which was once roamed by Scythian and Sarmatian hordes, and in which more recently, secular vampires and political Draculas are taking turns, he inherited a typically "balkanesque" talent for survival. Scores of ancient Greeks shunned this area of Europe, and when political circumstances forced them to flee, they preferred to search for a new homeland in Sicily or Italy — or today, like Cioran, in France. "Our epoch," writes Cioran, "will be marked by the romanticism of stateless persons. Already the picture of the universe is in the making in which nobody will have civic rights."[1] Similar to his exiled compatriots Eugene Ionesco, Stephen Lupasco, Mircea Eliade, and many others, Cioran came to realize very early that the sense of existential futility can best by cured by the belief in a cyclical concept of history, which excludes any notion of the arrival of a new messiah or the continuation of techno-economic progress.

Cioran's political, aesthetic and existential attitude towards being and time is an effort to restore the pre-Socratic thought, which Christianity, and then the heritage of rationalism and positivism, pushed into the periphery of philosophical speculation. In his essays and aphorisms, Cioran attempts to cast the foundation of a philosophy of life that, paradoxically, consists of a total refutation of all living. In an age of accelerated history it appears to him senseless to speculate about human betterment or the "end of history." "Future," writes Cioran, "go and see it for yourselves if you really wish to. I prefer to cling to the unbelievable present and the unbelievable past. I leave to you the opportunity to face the very Unbelievable."[2] Before man ventures into daydreams about his futuristic society, he should first immerse himself in the nothingness of his being, and finally restore life to what it is all about: a working hypothesis. On one of his lithographs, the 16th century French painter, J. Valverde, sketched a man who had skinned himself. This awesome man, holding a knife in one hand and his freshly peeled off skin in the other, resembles Cioran, who now teaches his readers how best to shed their hide of political illusions. Man feels fear only on his skin, not on his skeleton. How would it be for a change, asks Cioran, if man could have thought of something unrelated to being? Has not everything that transpires caused stubborn headaches? "And I think about all those whom I have known," writes Cioran, "all those who are no longer alive, long since wallowing in their coffins, for ever exempt of their flesh — and fear."[3]

The interesting feature about Cioran is his attempt to fight existential nihilism by means of nihilism. Unlike many of his contemporaries, Cioran is averse to the voguish pessimism of modern intellectuals who bemoan lost paradises, and who continue pontificating about endless economic progress. Unquestionably, the literary discourse of modernity has contributed to this mood of false pessimism, although such pessimism seems to be more induced by frustrated economic appetites, and less by what Cioran calls, "metaphysical alienation". Contrary to J. P. Sartre's existentialism that focuses on the rupture between being and non-being, Cioran regrets the split between the language and reality, and therefore the difficulty to fully convey the vision of existential nothingness. In a kind of alienation popularized by modern writers, Cioran detects the fashionable offshoot of "Parisianism" that elegantly masks a warmed-up version of a thwarted belief in progress. Such a critical attitude towards his contemporaries may be the reason why Cioran has never had eulogies heaped upon him, and why his enemies like to dub him "reactionary". To label Cioran a philosopher of nihilism may be more appropriate in view of the fact that Cioran is a stubborn blasphemer who never tires from calling Christ, St. Paul, and all Christian clergymen, as well as their secular Freudo-Marxian successors, outright liars and masters of illusion. To reduce Cioran to some preconceived intellectual and ideological category cannot do justice to his complex temperament, nor can it objectively reflect his complicated political philosophy. Each society, be it democratic or despotic, as a rule, tries to silence those who incarnate the denial of its sacrosanct political theology. For Cioran all systems must be rejected for the simple reason that they all glorify man as an ultimate creature. Only in the praise of non-being, and in the thorough denial of life, argues Cioran, man's existence becomes bearable. The great advantage of Cioran is, as he says, is that "I live only because it is in my power to die whenever I want; without the idea of suicide I would have killed myself long time ago."[4] These words testify to Cioran's alienation from the philosophy of Sisyphus, as well as his disapproval of the moral pathos of the dung-infested Job. Hardly any biblical or modern democratic character would be willing to contemplate in a similar manner the possibility of breaking away from the cycle of time. As Cioran says, the paramount sense of beatitude is achievable only when man realizes that he can at any time terminate his life; only at that moment will this mean a new "temptation to exist". In other words, it could be said that Cioran draws his life force from the constant flow of the images of salutary death, thereby rendering irrelevant all attempts of any ethical or political commitment. Man should, for a change, argues Cioran, attempt to function as some form of saprophytic bacteria; or better yet as some amoebae from the Paleozoic era. Such primeval forms of existence can endure the terror of being and time more easily. In a protoplasm, or lower species, there is more beauty then in all philosophies of life. And to reiterate this point, Cioran adds: "Oh, how I would like to be a plant, even if I would have to attend to someone's excrement!"[5]

Perhaps Cioran could be depicted as a trouble maker, or as the French call it a *trouble-fête*, whose suicidal aphorisms offend bourgeois society, but whose words also shock modern socialist day-dreamers. In view of his acceptance of the idea of death, as well as his rejection of all political doctrines, it is no wonder that Cioran no longer feels bound to egoistical love of life. Hence, there is no reason for him to ponder over the strategy of living; one should rather start thinking about the methodology of dying, or better yet how never to be born. "Mankind has regressed so much," writes Cioran, and "nothing proves it better than the impossibility to encounter a single nation or a tribe in which a birth of a child causes mourning and lamentation."⁶ Where are those sacred times, inquires Cioran, when Balkan Bogumils and France's Cathars saw in child's birth a divine punishment? Today's generations, instead of rejoicing when their loved ones are about to die, are stunned with horror and disbelief at the vision of death. Instead of wailing and grieving when their offsprings are about to be born, they organize mass festivities:

> If attachment is an evil, the cause of this evil must be sought in the scandal of birth — because to be born means to be attached. The purpose of someone's detachment should be the effacement of all traces of this scandal — the ominous and the least tolerable of all scandals.⁷

Cioran's philosophy bears a strong imprint of Friedrich Nietzsche and Indian Upanishads. Although his inveterate pessimism often recalls Nietzsche's *Weltschmerz*, his classical language and rigid syntax rarely tolerates romantic or lyrical narrative, nor the sentimental outbursts that one often finds in Nietzsche's prose. Instead of resorting to thundering gloom, Cioran's paradoxical humor expresses something that in the first place should have never been verbally construed. The weakness of Cioran prose lies probably in his lack of thematic organization. At times his aphorisms read as broken-off scores of a well-designed musical masterpiece, and sometimes his language is so hermetic that the reader is left to grope for meaning.

When one reads Cioran's prose the reader is confronted by an author who imposes a climate of cold apocalypse that thoroughly contradicts the heritage of progress. Real joy lies in non-being, says Cioran, that is, in the conviction that each willful act of creation perpetuates cosmic chaos. There is no purpose in endless deliberations about higher meaning of life. The entire history, be it the recorded history or mythical history, is replete with the cacophony of theological and ideological tautologies. Everything is *éternel retour*, a historical carousel, with those who are today on top, ending tomorrow at the bottom.

> I cannot excuse myself for being born. It is as if, when insinuating myself in this world, I profaned some mystery, betrayed some very important engagement, made a mistake of indescribable gravity.⁸

This does not mean that Cioran is completely insulated from physical and mental torments. Aware of the possible cosmic disaster and neurotically persuaded that some other predator may at any time deprive him of his well-planned privilege to die, he relentlessly evokes the set of death bed pictures. Is this not a truly aristocratic method to alleviate the impossibility of being?

> In order to vanquish dread or tenacious anxiety, there is nothing better than to imagine one's own funeral: efficient method, accessible to all. In order to avoid resorting to it during the day, the best is to indulge in its virtues right after getting up. Or perhaps make use of it on special occasions, similar to Pope Innocent IX who ordered the picture of himself painted on his death-bed. He would cast a glance at his picture every time he had to reach an important decision…[9]

At first, one may be tempted to say that Cioran is fond of wallowing in his neuroses and morbid ideas, as if they could be used to inspire his literary creativity. So exhilarating does he find his distaste for life that he suggests that, "he who succeeds in acquiring them has a future that makes everything prosper; success as well as defeat."[10] Such frank description of his emotional spasms makes him confess that success for him is as difficult to bear as much as a failure. One and the other cause him headache.

The feeling of sublime futility with regard to everything that life entails goes hand in hand with Cioran's pessimistic attitude towards the rise and fall of states and empires. His vision of the circulation of historical time recalls Vico's *corsi e ricorsi*, and his cynicism about human nature draws on Spengler's "biology" of history. Everything is a merry-go-round, and each system is doomed to perish the moment it makes its entrance onto the historical scene. One can detect in Cioran's gloomy prophecies the forebodings of the Roman stoic and emperor Marcus Aurelius, who heard in the distance of the Noricum the gallop of the barbarian horses, and who discerned through the haze of Panonia the pending ruin of the Roman Empire. Although today the actors are different, the setting remains similar; millions of new barbarians have begun to pound at the gates of Europe, and will soon take possession of what lies inside:

> Regardless of what the world will look like in the future, Westerners will assume the role of the Graeculi of the Roman Empire. Needed and despised by new conquerors, they will not have anything to offer except the jugglery of their intelligence, or the glitter of their past.[11]

Now is the time for the opulent Europe to pack up and leave, and cede the historical scene to other more virile peoples. Civilization becomes decadent when it takes freedom for granted; its disaster is imminent when it becomes too tolerant of every uncouth outsider. Yet, despite the fact that political tornados are lurking on the horizon, Cioran, like Marcus Aurelius, is determined to die with style. His sense of the tragic has taught him the strategy of *ars moriendi*, making him well prepared for all surprises, irrespective of their magnitude. Victors and victims, heroes and henchmen, do they not all take turns in this carnival of history, bemoaning and bewailing their fate while at the bottom, while taking revenge when on top? Two thousand years of Greco-Christian history is a mere trifle in comparison to eternity. One caricatural civilization is now taking shape, writes Cioran, in which those who are creating it are helping those wishing to destroy it. History has no meaning, and therefore, attempting to render it meaningful, or expecting from it a final burst of theophany, is a self-defeating chimera. For Cioran, there is more truth in occult sciences than in all philosophies that attempt to give meaning to life. Man will finally become free when he takes off the straitjacket of finalism and determinism, and when he realizes that life is an accidental mistake that sprang up from one bewildering astral circumstance. Proof? A little twist of the head clearly shows that "history, in fact, boils down to the classification of the police: After all, does not the historian deal with the image which people have about the policeman throughout epochs?"[12] To succeed in mobilizing masses in the name of some obscure ideas, to enable them to sniff blood, is a certain avenue to political success. Had not the same masses that carried on their shoulders the French Revolution in the name of equality and fraternity several years later, also brought on their shoulders an emperor with new clothes — an emperor on whose behalf they ran barefoot from Paris to Moscow, from Jena to Dubrovnik? For

Cioran, when a society runs out of political utopia there is no more hope, and consequently there cannot be any more life. Without utopia, writes Cioran, people would be forced to commit suicide; thanks to utopia they commit homicides.

Today there are no more utopias in stock. Mass democracy has taken their place. Without democracy life makes little sense; yet democracy has no life of its own. After all, argues Cioran, had it not been for a young lunatic from the Galilee, the world would be today a very boring place. Alas, how many such lunatics are hatching today their self-styled theological and ideological derivatives! "Society is badly organized," writes Cioran, "it does nothing against lunatics who die so young."[13] Probably all prophets and political soothsayers should immediately be put to death, "because when the mob accepts a myth — get ready for massacres or better yet for a new religion."[14]

Unmistakable as Cioran's resentments against utopia may appear, he is far from deriding its creative importance. Nothing could be more loathsome to him than the vague cliché of modernity that associates the quest for happiness with a peaceful pleasure-seeking society. Demystified, disenchanted, castrated, and unable to weather the upcoming storm, modern society is doomed to spiritual exhaustion and slow death. It is incapable of believing in anything except in the purported humanity of its future bloodsuckers. If a society truly wishes to preserve its biological well-being, argues Cioran, its paramount task is to harness and nurture its "substantial calamity"; it must keep a tally of its own capacity for destruction. After all, have not his native Balkans, in which secular vampires are today again dancing to the tune of butchery, also generated a pool of sturdy specimens ready for tomorrow's cataclysms? In this area of Europe, which is endlessly marred by political tremors and real earthquakes, a new history is today in the making — a history that will probably reward its populace for the past suffering.

Whatever their past was, and irrespective of their civilization, these countries possess a biological stock that one cannot find in the West. Maltreated, disinherited, precipitated in the anonymous martyrdom, torn apart between wretchedness and sedition, they will perhaps know in the future a reward for so many ordeals, so much humiliation and for so much cowardice.[15]

Is this not the best portrayal of that anonymous "eastern" Europe that according to Cioran is ready today to speed up the world history? The death of communism in Eastern Europe might probably inaugurate the return of history for all of Europe. Conversely, the "better half" of Europe, the one that wallows in air-conditioned and aseptic salons, that Europe is depleted of robust ideas. It is incapable of hating and suffering, and therefore of leading. For Cioran, society becomes consolidated in danger and it atrophies in peace: "In those places where peace, hygiene and leisure ravage, psychoses also multiply... I come from a country that, while never learning to know the meaning of happiness, has also never produced a single psychoanalyst."[16] The raw manners of new East European cannibals, not "peace and love" will determine the course of tomorrow's history. Those who have passed through hell are more likely to outlive those who have only known the cozy climate of a secular paradise.

These words of Cioran are aimed at the decadent *France la Doulce* in which afternoon chats about someone's obesity or sexual impotence have become major preoccupations on the hit parade of daily concerns. Unable to put up resistance against tomorrow's conquerors, this Western Europe, according to Cioran, deserves to be punished in the same manner as the noblesse of the *ancien régime*, which, on the eve of the French Revolution, laughed at its own image, while praising the image of the *bon sauvage*. How many among those good-natured French aristocrats were aware that the same *bon sauvage* was about to roll their heads down the streets of Paris? "In the future," writes Cioran, "if mankind is to start all over again, it will be with the outcasts, with the mongols from all parts, with the dregs of the continents."[17] Europe is hiding in its own imbecility in front of an approaching catastrophe. Europe? "The rots that smell nice, a perfumed corpse."[18]

Despite gathering storms Cioran is comforted by the notion that he at least is the last heir to the vanishing "end of history". Tomorrow, when the real apocalypse begins, and as the dangers of titanic proportions take final shape on the horizon, then, even the word "regret" will disappear from our vocabulary. "My vision of the future," continues Cioran is so clear, "that if I had children I would strangle them immediately."[19]

After a good reading of Cioran's opus one must conclude that Cioran is essentially a satirist who ridicules the stupid existential shiver of modern masses. One may be tempted to argue that Cioran offers an elegant *vade mecum* for suicide designed for those, who like him, have thoroughly delegitimized the value of life. But as Cioran says, suicide is committed by those who are no longer capable of acting out optimism, e.g. those whose thread of joy and happiness breaks into pieces. Those like him, the cautious pessimists, "given that they have no reason to live, why would they have a reason to die?"[20] The striking ambivalence of Cioran's literary work consists of the apocalyptic forebodings on the one hand, and enthusiastic evocations of horrors on the other. He believes that violence and destruction are the main ingredients of history, because the world without violence is bound to collapse. Yet, one wonders why is Cioran so opposed to the world of peace if, according to his logic, this peaceful world could help accelerate his own much-craved demise, and thus facilitate his immersion into nothingness? Of course, Cioran never moralizes about the necessity of violence; rather, in accordance with the canons of his beloved reactionary predecessors Josephe de Maistre and Nicolo Machiavelli, he asserts that "authority, not verity, makes the law", and that consequently, the credibility of a political lie will also determine the magnitude of political justice. Granted that this is correct, how does he explain the fact that authority, at least the way he sees it, only perpetuates this odious being from which he so dearly wishes to absolve himself? This mystery will never be known other than to him. Cioran admits however, that despite his abhorrence of violence, every man, including himself is an integral part of it, and that every man has at least once in his life contemplated how to roast somebody alive, or how to chop off someone's head:

> Convinced that troubles in our society come from old people, I conceived the plan of liquidating all citizens past their forties — the beginning of sclerosis and

mummification. I came to believe that this was the turning point when each human becomes an insult to his nation and a burden to his community... Those who listened to this did not appreciate this discourse and they considered me a cannibal... Must this intent of mine be condemned? It only expresses something that each man, who is attached to his country, desires in the bottom of his heart: liquidation of one half of his compatriots.[21]

Cioran's literary elitism is unparalleled in modern literature, and for that reason he often appears as a nuisance for modern and sentimental ears poised for the lullaby words of eternal earthly or spiritual bliss. Cioran's hatred of the present and the future, his disrespect for life, will certainly continue to antagonize the apostles of modernity who never tire of chanting vague promises about the "better here-and-now."

His paradoxical humor is so devastating that one cannot take it at face value, especially when Cioran describes his own self. His formalism in language, his impeccable choice of words, despite some similarities with modern authors of the same elitist caliber, make him sometimes difficult to follow. One wonders whether Cioran's arsenal of words such as "abulia", "schizophrenia", "apathy", etc., truly depict a *nevrosé*, which he claims to be.

If one could reduce the portrayal of Cioran to one short paragraph, then one must depict him as an author who sees in the modern veneration of the intellect a blueprint for spiritual gulags and the uglification of the world. Indeed, for Cioran, man's task is to wash himself in the school of existential futility, for futility is not hopelessness; futility is a reward for those wishing to rid themselves of the epidemic of life and the virus of hope. Probably, this picture best befits the man who describes himself as a fanatic without any convictions — a stranded accident in the cosmos who casts nostalgic looks towards his quick disappearance.

"To be free is to rid oneself forever from the notion of reward; to expect nothing from people or gods; to renounce not only this world and all worlds, but salvation itself; to break up even the idea of this chain among chains." (*Le mauvais démiurge*)

THE RIGHT STUFF (DRUGS AND DEMOCRACY)

Morphine is said to be good for people subject to severe depressions, or even pessimism. Although the drug first surfaced in a laboratory at the end of the last century, its basis, opium, had been used earlier by many aristocratic and reactionary thinkers. A young and secretive German romantic, Novalis, enjoyed eating and smoking opium juice, probably because he had always yearned to alleviate his nostalgia for death. Probably in order to write his poem *Sehnsucht nach dem Tode*. Early poets of Romanticism rejected the philosophy of rationalism and historical optimism. They turned inward to their irrational feelings, shrouding themselves in the pensive loneliness that opiates endlessly offer.

Once upon a distant time we met Homer's Odysseus, who was frequently nagged by the childish behavior of his pesky sailors. Somewhere along the shores of northern Africa, Odysseus and his sailors had strayed away into the mythical land of the lotus flower. As soon as his sailors began to eat the lotus plant, they sank into forgetfulness, and immediately forgot their history and their homeland. It was with great pain that Odysseus succeeded in extracting them from artificial paradises. What can be worse for a nation than to erase its past and lose its collective memory?

Unlike many modern wannabe conservatives and televangelists, Greeks and Romans were not hypocrites. They frankly acknowledged the pleasures of wine and women. *Sine Cerere et Bacco friget Venus* — without food and wine sexual life withers away, too.

The escape from industrial reality and the maddening crowd was one of the main motives for drug use among some reactionary poets and thinkers, who could not face the onset of mass society. The advent of early liberalism and socialism was accompanied not only by factory chimneys, but also by loneliness, decay, and decadence. If one could, therefore, not escape to the sunny Mediterranean, then one had to craft one's own artificial paradise in rainy and foggy London. The young English Tory Thomas

De Quincey, in his essay *Confessions of an English Opium Eater*, relates his Soho escapades with a poor prostitute Anna, as well as his spiritual journeys in the aftertaste of opium. De Quincey has a feeling that one life-minute lasts a century, finally putting an end to the reckless flow of time.

The mystique of opium was also grasped by the mid-19th century French symbolist and poet Charles Baudelaire. He continued the aristo-nihilistic-revolutionary-conservative tradition of dope indulgence via the water pipe, i.e., the Pakistani *hookah*. Similar to the lonely albatross, Baudelaire observes the decaying France in which the steamroller of coming liberalism and democratism mercilessly crushes all aesthetics and all poetics.

When studying the escapism of postmodernity, it is impossible to circumvent the leftist subculture and its pseudo-intellectual sycophants of 1968. The so-called sixty-eighters hollered out not only for liberty from all political authority, but also for free sex and drugs. Are these leftist claims not part of the modern religion of human rights? At the beginning of the 60's, the musical alter egos of the Western left, the Rolling Stones and Bob Dylan, called out to millions of young people throughout America and Europe, telling intruders to "get off of my cloud" and concluding that "everybody must get stoned."

Predictably, the right-wing answer to the decadence of liberal democracy was nihilistic counter-decadence. The main difference, however, between these two is that reactionary and rightist addicts do drugs for elitist and esoteric purposes. By their temperament and literary style they reject all democracy — whether it is of a socialist or liberal brand. When in the 20th century the flow of history switched from first gear into fifth gear, many rightist poets and thinkers posed a question: What to do after the orgy? The French right-leaning author Jean Cocteau answered the question this way: "Everything that we do in our life, even when we love, we perform in a rapid train running to its death. Smoking opium means getting off the train."

Hashish and marijuana change the body language and enhance social philanthropy. Smoking joints triggers abnormal laughter. Therefore, hashish may be described as a collectivistic drug custom-designed for individuals who by their lifestyle loathe solitude and who, like Dickens' proverbial Ms. Jellyby, indulge in vicarious humanism and unrepentant globalism. In today's age of promiscuous democracy, small wonder that marijuana is inhaled by countless young people all over liberalized Europe and America. In the permissive society of today, one is allowed to do everything — provided one does not rock the boat, i.e., "bogart" political correctness. Just as wine, over the last 2,000 years, has completely changed the political profile of the West, so has marijuana, over the last 30 years, completely ruined the future of Western youth. If Stalin had been a bit more intelligent he would have solemnly opened marijuana fields in his native Transcaucasia. Instead, communist tyrants resorted to the killing fields of the Gulag. The advantage of liberalism and social democracy is that via sex, drugs, and rock 'n' roll, by means of consumerism and hedonism, they function perfectly well; what Communism was not able to achieve by means of the solid truncheon, liberalism has achieved by means of the solid joint. Indisputably, Western youth can be politically and correctly controlled when herded in techno-rap concerts and when welcomed in cafés in Holland, where one can freely buy marijuana as well as under-the-table "crack", "speedball", and "horse". Are these items not logical ingredients of the liberal theology of human rights?

Cocaine reportedly induces eroticism and enhances the sex act. The late French fascist dandy and novelist Pierre Drieu La Rochelle liked coke, desiring all possible drugs and all impossible women. The problem, however, is that the coke intaker often feels invisible bugs creeping from his ankles up to his knees, so that he may imagine himself sleeping not with a beautiful woman but with scary reptiles. In his autobiographical novels *Le feu follet* and *L'homme couvert de femmes*, La Rochelle's hero is constantly covered by women and veiled by opium and heroin sit-ins. In his long intellectual monologues, La Rochelle's hero says: "A French-woman, be she a whore or not, likes to be held and taken care of; an American woman, unless she hunts for a husband, prefers a passing relationship… Drug users are mystics in a materialistic age. Given that they can no longer animate and embellish this world, they do it in a reverse manner on themselves." Indeed, La Rochelle's hero ends up in suicide — with heroin and revolver. In 1945, with the approaching victory of the Allies, and in the capacity of the intellectual leader of the defunct Eurofascist international, Pierre Drieu La Rochelle also opted for suicide.

The English conservative and aristocrat Aldous Huxley is unavoidable in studying communist pathology (*Brave New World Revisited*) and Marxist subintellectual schizophrenia (*Grey Eminence*). As a novelist and essayist his lifelong wish had been to break loose from the flow of time. Mexican mescaline and the artificial drug L.S.D. enabled him new intellectual horizons for observing the end of his world and the beginning of a new, decadent one. Apparently, mescaline is ideal for sensing the colors of late impressionist and pointillist painters. Every drop on Seurat's silent water, every touch on Dufy's leaf, or every stone on the still nature of old Vermeer, pours away into thousands of billions of new colors. In the essay *The Doors of Perception*, Huxley notes that "mescaline raises all colors to a higher power and makes the percipient aware of innumerable fine shades of difference, to which, at ordinary times, he is completely blind." His intellectual experiments with hallucinogenic drugs continued for years, and even on his deathbed in California in 1963, he asked for and was given L.S.D. Probably to depart more picturesquely into timeless infinity.

And what to say about the German centenarian, enigmatic essayist and novelist Ernst Jünger, whom the young Adolf Hitler in Weimar Germany also liked to read, and whom Dr. Joseph Goebbels wanted to lure into pro-Nazi collaboration? Yet Jünger, the aristocratic loner, refused all deals with the Nazis, preferring instead his martial travelogues. In his essay *Annäherungen: Drogen and Rausch*, Jünger describes his close encounters with drugs. He was also able to cut through the merciless wall of time and sneak into floating eternity. "Time slows down ... The river of life flows more gently... The banks are disappearing." While both the French president François Mitterrand and the German chancellor Helmut Kohl, in the interest of Franco-German reconciliation, liked meeting and reading the old Jünger, they shied away from his contacts with drugs.

Ernst Jünger's compatriot, the essayist, early expressionist, and medical doctor Gottfried Benn, also took drugs. His medical observations, which found their transfigurations in his poems *Kokain* and *Das Verlorene Ich*, were collected by Benn as a doctor and mortician in Berlin of the liberal-Weimarian Germany in decay. He records in his poetry nameless human destinies stretched out dead on the tables of his mortuary. He describes the dead meat of prostitutes out of whose bellies crawl squeaking mice. A connoisseur of French culture and genetics, Benn was subsequently offered awards and political baits by the Nazis, which he refused to swallow. After the end of the war, like thousands of European artists, Benn sank into oblivion. Probably, also because he once remarked that "mighty brains are strengthened not on milk but on alkaloids."

Modern psychiatrists, doctors, and sociologists are wrong in their diagnosis of drug addiction among large segments of Western youth. They fail to realize that to combat drug abuse one must prevent its social and political causes before attempting to cure its deadly consequences. Given that the crux of the modern liberal system is the dictatorship of well-being and the dogma of boundless economic growth, many disabused young people are led to believe that everybody is entitled to eternal fun. In a make-believe world of media signals, many take for granted instant gratification by projecting their faces on the characters of the prime-time soaps. Before they turn into drug addicts, they become dependent on the videospheric surreality of television, which in a refined manner tells them that everybody must be handsome, rich, and popular. In an age of TV-mimicry, headless young masses become, so to speak, the impresarios of their own narcissism. Such delusions can lead to severe depressions, which in turn can lead to drugs and suicide. Small wonder that in the most liberal countries of the West, notably California, Holland, and Denmark, there is also the highest correlation between drug addiction and suicide.

If drug abuse among some reactionary and conservative thinkers has always been an isolated and Promethean death wish to escape time, the same joint in leftist hands does more than burn the fingers of the individual: it poisons the entire society.

PART III

RACE / THE THIRD REICH

THE BEAUTY AND THE BEAST: RACE AND RACISM IN EUROPE

No word in the modern Western parlance is as scary as the word "race". It is avoided like the plague by contemporary opinion makers, except when they gleefully use its verbal derivative "racist" against right-wingers, White nationalists, forever looming "neo-Nazis", and their proverbial bed fellows "anti-Semites". In modern science, let alone in the social sciences, the word and the concept of race is denounced as a social construct, not being admitted as biological reality, despite overwhelming evidence that race is not just skin deep and that different races worldwide show marked differences in behavior, cultural achievements, and in IQ. As professor Daniel A. Beach recently noted: "Race pervades a great deal of social and interpersonal issues with which we must contend, yet we have no effective way of talking about it."

Unlike their colleagues in the social sciences, many Western biologists and geneticists are well aware of differences among races, yet they prefer to resort to esoteric verbiage and expressions, such as "mapping the genome", or "different gene pools" or "different haplotypes", when doing research on the tricky subject of race.

Prior to the early 20th century the words "race" and "racist" were rarely used in the English, French, or German languages in Europe. Everybody knew which race he belonged to. The etymology of the word "race" is still unclear, although most likely it derives from the old Latin word *radix*, meaning roots, or the German *reiza*, meaning family lineage. Its significance became ideologically loaded only in the late 1920s. Over the last 50 years, it has undergone a total semantic distortion. Indeed, if one were to follow the logic and discourse of professional antiracists, peoples of European ancestry must be all certified racists. Why? Because it is still an unwritten rule that White males and females all over the West mate and date solely within their own race.

European *Gestalt*: In Quest of Order and Form

The concept of eugenics is now associated with National Socialism and has come to be understood among the educated classes as the epitome of evil. In fact, however, eugenic measures were a standard family practice from time immemorial among European tribes. Undoubtedly, each family had to be prolific with a multitude of children able to work on the land or to guard the household. This meant allowing and frequently facilitating the death of children who were sickly or had disabilities.

Until recently in the European countryside when a young girl and boy were about to start dating, parents first inquired about whether their respective fathers or mothers were alcoholics, whether somebody in their family tree had some serious illness, such as diabetes, tuberculosis, or some nervous disorder — or even inborn proclivity to criminal behavior. A semi-literate, yet intelligent European peasant or farmer did not have to be versed in sociobiology or have a degree in molecular biology in order to realize that hereditary diseases of the unfortunate partner could easily be transmitted to the newborns, with deadly social consequences for the entire family.

In France it is still common to hear the expression "elle est de bonne race" ("she is of good breed or character") for a good looking and healthy woman. In the Croatian or the Serbian language one can hear among young adults the colloquial adjective *rasna* ("raceful") when depicting a good and healthy looking woman. In such particular instances "race" is more a synonym of good health and good looks and less a scientific term for a distinctive European appearance.

After 1945 everything changed. The whole hell of moralizing and do-good pontificating broke loose. The more degenerate, the more maladaptive and the uglier — the better. The role of the environment became a sacrosanct dogma of liberal and communist world improvers, while blind faith in progress became a shining path for a promiscuous end of history. Especially the German word *Rasse*, which was commonly used in the 1920s, 30s and the early 40s, came to be highly uncomfortable for postwar German politicians who were themselves to be groomed by the Allies in self-hate and guilt feelings about their race. *Rasse* is a sharp monosyllabic word whose consonant "s" requires the speaker to emit a hissing sound.

Hence the reason that the legacy of National Socialism and thousands of German titles dealing with race, racial hygiene, racial studies, racial mixing, etc., had to disappear from library shelves, only to reappear as a subject of criminal proceedings in modern Germany. The German ruling class today is quick to raise the red flag against scholars who dare to use this word in a normative and value free manner. Shortly after WWII, thousands of books dealing with race and racial differences were burned and destroyed by the Allies. Institutes specializing in racial hygiene, such as *Deutsche Gesellschaft für Rassenhygiene* or the prestigious *Kaiser Wilhelm Institut für Anthropologie*, were closed down. Hundreds of European doctors and specialists in genetics and biology — if not spirited out furtively to the U.S.A. or the U.S.S.R. — were hunted down as war criminals, or denounced as proverbial Nazi quacks. (See Manfred Heinemann, *Hochschuloffiziere und Wiederaufbau des Hochschulwesens in Westdeutschland, 1944-1952*. See also Reinhard Grohnert, *Die Entnazifizierung in Baden 1945-1949*).

In Gods We Trust: Ancient "Ethnic Profiling"

The word "race" did not exist but the sense of racial beauty and racial awareness was firmly grounded in the minds of ancient Europeans. In Homer's *Iliad* most gods and goddesses are fair skinned and light eyed. Athena is described by Pindar as as the "blond and blue eyed goddess", whereas tricksters or fickle persons, personified by satyrs and centaurs had repulsive Levantine features with wooly hair, thick lips and hooked noses. (R. Peterson, *The Classical World*, 1985, pp. 30-31).

In the Middle Ages one encounters those grotesque images of ugliness on basilicas and cathedrals where gargoyles were used as ornamented water spouts projecting from roofs or water fountains. Those negative images displaying non-European racial traits would be banned today, as our modern multiracial pontiffs do not tolerate racial stereotyping, or what they euphemistically call "ethnic profiling". Likely, many out-group individuals in modern American or European cities would detect in those figures strange resemblance to their own non-European facial traits.

In a well researched, yet forgotten book, Professor Allen G. Roper (*Ancient Eugenics*, 1913) provides a great many citations from ancient Greek and Latin texts describing eugenic practices by the old Greeks and Romans. Infanticide was not considered a barbaric act, but a paramount political necessity for a city-state in perennial crisis and warfare. They did not have a luxury of feeding genetic misfits, potential crooks, or the dregs of racial outgroups. The Spartan leader Solon drafted the first eugenic laws, and the Stoic Roman philosopher Seneca encouraged infanticide for misfits. "We drown the weaklings and the monstrosity. It is not passion but reason to separate the useless from the fit."

In ancient Rome of the Republic, racial purity and close-knit bonds among kin were extremely valued. The whole concept of the city-state was premised on a small family unit, with the typical *pater familias* at the helm. Even today in popular unwritten culture in Europe, a saying goes that a "person's character can best be recognized in his facial features." Conversely, "a person's distorted character follows his distorted countenance," a saying that was common in ancient Rome ("*Distortum vultum sequitur distortio morum.*").

It is a dangerous mistake, very widespread among White European American nationalists, to assert that the ancient Greeks were all of Nordic ancestry. As I have written elsewhere, the blond dolichocephalic faces that one finds painted on old Greek murals or pottery, or even bronze busts of Roman and Greek leaders, had primarily normative value; they were meant as the enhanced ideal type for what White Europeans should be — not the reflection of what they looked like in real life.

This is particularly relevant because of childish quarrels among European and American White nationalists and self-proclaimed Aryans. Such people often imagine ancient Spartan warriors as blond giants — or even picture the Waffen S.S. as superhuman extraterrestrial beings.

It should come as no surprise that the concept of beauty and race in pre-war Europe, and particular in pre-war Germany, witnessed a return to romanticized classicism. Models from antiquity and the Renaissance were adapted to the prevailing spirit of the times. Numerous German sculptors worked on their projects while benefiting from the logistic and financial support of the National Socialist political elite. Their sculptures resembled, either by form, or by composition, the works of Praxiteles or of Phidias of ancient Greece, or those executed by Michelangelo during the Renaissance. The most prominent German sculptors in the Third Reich were Arno Breker, Josef Thorak and Fritz Klimsch, who although enjoying the significant logistical support of the National Socialist regime, were never members of the N.S.D.A.P.

After the Second World War, as the result of pressure from the Allies, Europe — and to a large extent America itself — were forced to open its doors to abstract art (Jackson Pollock, Piet Mondrian, etc.) and, consequently Euro Americans and in particularly the Germans had to stifle the production of their traditional figurative art. A large number of paintings and other works of art executed during the Third Reich were either removed or destroyed. Several hundred sculptures were demolished or trashed during the Allied air bombardments. After the war, a considerable number of works of art were confiscated by the Americans, because of "their pornographic character." In the spring of 1947, 8,722 paintings and sculptures of German artists were transported to the United States. Of these, only a small number have been returned to the Federal Republic of Germany.

The concept of racial beauty in ancient Greece or during the Renaissance in the 15th century Italy was often used as a pedagogical and graphic tool to provide the sense of order and form (*Gestalt*). In traditional Europe and

America, the vast majority of citizens were never ever the replicas of these hyperreal beauties represented on busts or sculptures.

Paintings of women by the late Italians Botticelli or Titian, or sculptures by the modern Germans Breker or Thorak, did not suggest that that all Italian and German women have elongated Gothic limbs, thin noses and Nordic cranial index.

The whole purpose of classicism and neoclassicism, particularly in plastic art, but also in philosophy and literature suggested that Europeans had to abide by the cosmic rules of racial form and order. Whatever and whoever departs from order — brings in decadence and death.

The word and epithet "racist" and "racism" are usually hurled against White nationalists, never ever scathing other racial non-European outgroups. Over the last fifty years, no effort has been spared by the Western system and its mediacracy to pathologize White Western peoples into endless atonement and perpetual guilt feelings about their White race. The intended goal was to create a perception that all non-European races and outgroups are immune to sentiments of xenophobia or racial exclusion. The incessant anti-White propaganda and the idealization of non-Whites have attained grotesque dimensions, resulting in clinical self-hate and neurotic behavior among the majority of Whites.

Were such sickening attitudes of White Europeans and White Americans not suicidal, they would appear laughable at best. The sense of territorial imperative, the seething interracial hate is far more salient and violent among and amidst non-Whites than among Whites.

Beauty of the Beast

Mexican Americans do not like African Americans. Neither do American Asians like African Americans and Mexican Americans combined (see AmRen's list of racial conflict in the U.S.). In a likely scenario of Whites becoming a displaced minority in the U.S.A. and Europe, other races would soon be at each other's throat with violence surpassing the imagination of White peoples.

Similarly, in South Africa, the influential Xhosa tribesmen, who hold important political positions, resent Zulus, but so are they themselves the target of hate by Ndebele and Kwazulus. In Rwanda, Tutsis, who consider themselves more "European" and more civilized, hate Hutus, but so do Hutus hate Tutsis. Generally, Arab-speaking populations in northern Africa and the Middle East resent dark, Black neighbors below the Sahara belt.

The Sikhs in Punjab consider themselves the best-looking people on the Indian subcontinent, ridiculing as less human the populace in neighboring Rajasthan. It is a common practice among Indian women, but also among women in the Middle East, not to expose themselves to sun, as White skin has more charm and provides huge social prestige. The ex-president of Pakistan, Benazir Bhutto, with her quasi-Euro-Mediterranean facial traits and complexion, gave her country an enormous sense of pride.

A Mexican cabbage picker from Salinas in California's Central Valley is often encouraged by do-good U.S. liberal White attorneys to yammer about being discriminated by Whites, and, of course, this is standard procedure for organizations like the anti-White A.D.L. Yet it would never cross the cabbage picker's mind to voice similar grievances or ask the A.D.L. to remedy his lot in his native Mexico. It is considered an unwritten rule that the bulk of the Mexican diplomatic corps should be made up of Whites, *hidalgos* of sorts, so that a California *cholo* never dares to envisage his niche amidst them. He knows very well his socio-racial place, and if not tempted by robbing or stealing he can only dream in his barrio about having his sister or daughter married to a light skinned Anglo. Former Mexican president Vicente Fox (who did his best to make the U.S. a non-White country by ridding Mexico of its dark-skinned citizens) looked more like a picture perfect antebellum *gringo* than like an LA "beaner."

In Turkey high social positions and political perks, as well as diplomatic postings are the protected turf of individuals whose ancestry goes back to White slaves from 16th century Southeastern Europe and the 18th century Transcaucasia — not to the steppes of Turkmenistan. There is no worse insult for a Turk or an Iranian to dub them "Arabs" — which they are not. In the Red Light District of Istanbul, Aksaray, a stupendous 6-foot White Russian hooker is very, very pricy indeed, whereas a ride with a tiny Filipino woman costs almost nothing. The father of modern Turkey, Kemal Pasha Ataturk, was a tall man with blue eyes of either Illyrian or Slavic ancestry, who spent more time brooding over modern Turks as hypothetical descendants of the Indo-European Hittites than recounting the exploits of pillaging Asiatic horsemen. It would never, ever cross the mind of a stocky half-Mongoloid, unibrow blue collar worker in Ankara to ask for his share of Turkish social glitz — except when he arrives to Germany or Belgium with already good premonition of Germany's self-hate and its tax payers' largesse.

"We" vs. "They" — the "Other" is the basic conceptual pillar in the studies of racial psychology, whereby every racial group or sub-group dreams to be a bit more of the Other, provided that the Other is genetically better equipped. Thus, an attractive White European or American woman with recessive Mediterranean genes may nervously pluck the stubborn hair on her upper lip or depilate her widow's peak. Or a short Alpine-headed man from southern France may purchase high-heeled boots. These are often issues of social acceptance or social rejection. Sometimes they can be matters of life or death.

One can only imagine the dramatic self-perception of non-Whites landing in America or in Europe, however modest or low their IQ may be. After all, which non-European mother, be it in Berlin, Stockholm, or San Antonio, does not strive to see, or at least project her son or daughter into a better gene pool, however much she may envy or hate her White host? And if her son is already doomed to be a victim of poor heredity, then some hyper-real surgical trick might do the job — as witnessed by the facial escapades of the Western hero, the late pop star Michael Jackson.

The Painful Otherness

The normative concept of beauty and the general code of social and political conduct and civility are exclusively of European origin. This includes the famous "body language" practiced by White liberal politicians and avidly mimicked by non-white politicians. Hence the norm for all peoples, of all races worldwide is to accept White Otherness either by emulating or mimicking its phenotype. The Western heritage, regardless of whether it is despised or loved by non-Europeans, is viewed either consciously or subconsciously as the ideal type and role model for all.

The major crime of the liberal system and its human rights pontiffs is that on the one hand it preaches diversity and uniqueness of each culture and each ethnic group, while on the other hand, because of its egalitarian, levelling and procrustean tactics, it fosters discriminatory policies against all races and all peoples wordwide.

The liberal ideology of global "panmixia" destroys individual cultures of different peoples, while imposing feelings of cultural and racial inferiority on all. Thus, many non-Europeans, especially if cultivated, are implicitly forced to be ashamed of their roots, while accepting something that is alien to their psychophysical and cultural heritage.

While Europeans of different ethnic origins and with different facial traits (Dinaric, Alpine, Mediterranean, Nordic) do not have trouble in blending in, non-European races have considerable difficulties. This often results in feelings of racial exclusion, and consequently in criminal activities, especially among younger newcomers to the U.S.A. or to Europe.

In a little known, yet highly significant preface to the second edition of his once famous book (*Rasse und Seele* [Race and Soul], 2nd edition, 1943), and following the attacks by the Vatican clergy against the racial laws of Nationalist Socialist Germany, the once-famous German psychologist and anthropologist Ludwig Ferdinand Clauss, wrote:

> We have been accused of considering only the Nordic race as worthy and all other races as inferior. Wherever such "evidence" was believed, it has affected us negatively.
>
> This is especially true because the word "Nordic" is easily misunderstood and misinterpreted by laymen, which has created all kinds of mischief. This was entirely mistaken and unnecessary.
>
> It is true that in Germany and elsewhere, a number of books and booklets have been published that assert this sort of thing. From the beginning, the

psychology of race clearly teaches us that each race finds ultimate value in itself ... In the final analysis it is the only factor that determines racial-spiritual values.

Every race bears within itself its own value system and standard of excellence; and no race can be evaluated by the standards of any other race ... Only a person who could stand above all races and transcend race would be able to make "objective" statements about a given human race ... Such a person does not exist, however, because to be human means to be conditioned and determined by race. Perhaps God knows the true hierarchy of races, but we humans do not. The German Volk or Nation is a mixture of various races, in which the Nordic race clearly predominates. However, there is an admixture of "Blood" in the German Volk (for example Mediterranean). Today it is no longer possible to sow mistrust between friendly peoples ... Each step in international and colonial politics confirms the tenets of racial psychology and increases its usefulness (practical utility) in dealing with different peoples. Its goal is not to divide and separate nations, but rather to connect them by objectively establishing enlightened understanding between them.

Clauss is labelled a "Nazi scholar" by his Jewish and liberal detractors, although some of his remarks run counter to Hollywood custom-designed "Nazi Nordicists" and self-proclaimed Aryans, all the more because Clauss, like many German anthropologists, wrote much about Bedouins, and is still considered an authority on Arabic culture.

The Jew vs. the Same

It would be interesting to find out what was crossing the mind of the Jewish American author Susan Sontag, who famously said that "the White race is the cancer of human history." If one grants that the White race is a cancer, Sontag is putting herself in an awkward position. Does she reject being White? Implicitly she suggested that Jews are not Whites, which only confirms the thesis of hundreds if not millions of White racialists that Jews constitute a unique racial/ethnic group — and not just a different culture or a different religion.

Consequently, can Sontag's Jewish compatriots be Whites — in the sense their White Euro-American liberal friends want them to be? Her defamatory comments on Whites imply that Jews do not fall into the category of Whites. But as practice has shown in Jew-Gentile relationships all over the West, neither do they like being called "Jews" by non-Jews — except when they need to capitalize on their Jewishness, both figuratively and financially. Yet implicitly, many Jews, while rejecting Whiteness in its "anti-Semitic" "right-wing", or "Nazi" connotation — are not at all opposed to displaying their Whiteness. The late Israeli Prime Minister Yitzhak Rabin, with his feigned self-assertiveness, must have been well aware that his quasi-Nordic facial traits would be popular with his fellow Jews.

Many Jews quite rightly resent the German word and the concept of *Mischlinge* (crossbreeds) or *Mauscheljude* (trickster Jew or hidden Jew). At the same time, many Jews like to conceal as much as they can their original Turko-Kazharic-Semitic features. As I wrote earlier, the more things look hyper-real, the more real they get eventually. By the same logic, if Jews get upset by anti-Semites, why not call Jews Semites? Most likely this would be an offensive word for them too.

Tons of books on this subject are very difficult to obtain, especially if written in German. As a result, this most incendiary topic of our times is debated only in private or avoided completely. One thing is when Jewish authors like Salcia Landmann (*Die Juden als Rasse*, 1981) and Jon Entine (*Abraham's Children: Race, Identity, and the DNA of the Chosen People*) write objectively — albeit from a Jewish perspective — about the "Jews as a race." Yet it is quite a different story when a famous German anthropologist and eugenicist, also dubbed a "Nazi", Otmar von Verschuer, writes about "the Jewish race." It appears that the expression and the concept "the Jewish race" can only have safe passage and scholarly legitimacy when used and discussed by Jews.

In April 1988, several weeks before I was awarded a PhD degree in political science at the University of California — Santa Barbara, I had a private and casual dinner with a famous author of human ecology, professor emeritus Garrett Hardin. After a beer or two, he told me, if I recall his words well: "Look, Tom, I have been lecturing in biology; I can get away with saying things to my students about race that you will never, ever be able to in humanities."

Being young and living in the allegedly freest country in the world, I did not exactly understand what he meant. Years later I grasped the meaning of his words. I realized that there are academic fields in humanities that are subject to strict inquisitorial control and to undisputed canons of political rectitude. This sacred triangle consists of three subjects: a) modern historiography; b) Jewish power and influence; and c) the race question. Lecturing in an open an honest way on these topics means receiving a kiss of academic death.

Intellectual terror in American colleges is well hidden behind the garb of feigned academic conviviality and the "have-a-wonderful-day" rhetoric of superficially friendly peers. Yet it has far more insidious effects than the naked terror I experienced in a drab ex-communist Europe.

Apart from being a derogatory, value-laden word that immediately lends itself to an array of catastrophic fantasies and judgment-day scenarios, the word "Nazi" also gives birth to a schizoid behavior among a number of White nationalists, particularly in America. Many of them seriously project in their minds National Socialist Germany as a country populated by Albino-like Nordic-*Übermenschen* possessing a hidden force that could be resuscitated any day either in Patagonia or on astral UFOs. As noted previously in *The Occidental Observer*, the false re-enactment of political events leads to their farcical repetition — with dangerous political consequences. In our postmodernity, the overkill of false images leads to the real kill. The often rowdy and infantile behavior of such "proud Aryan internet warriors" scares off serious White people who could otherwise be of some help in these decisive days of struggle for Western civilization. We must ask ourselves: *Cui bono*? Who benefits?

Indeed, the surreal image of National Socialism as exclusively Nordic has been promoted by the left — antifascist scholars, environmentalists, Freudo-Boasians, various Jewish and pro-Jewish academic think tanks, the caviar-left, the gated community White liberals, etc. How? For decades, they have been cranking out an overkill of one-sided books and movies on National Socialism and racism, and this for two simple reasons. First, it pays well and provides lush media and academic sinecures. Secondly, there has been a well-conceived pedagogical project ever since 1945 to prevent a critical re-examination of race and racism.

The Many Faces of National Socialism

For starters, the second most powerful National Socialist man in the Third Reich was a dark-haired "shrunken German" (*nachgedunkelter Schrumpfgermane*), the proverbial Joseph Goebbels, a thin man, little over 5 feet tall, whose stature and face resembled more an ancient Roman quaestor than a blond fighting machine. His thin lips, a round protruding occiput, sad, yet very sharp eyes, testified to a man who under different historical circumstances would have made an excellent professor in comparative literature. Goebbels was born in the German province of Westphalia, close to France. In the 1st century A.D., this area was an important Roman military outpost and a region in which many Germans today still show distinct Mediterranean facial traits.

The much discussed German anti-Slavic policies, which were based on the alleged racial inferiority of Slavs, are nonsense — all the more so since at least one out of three Germans carries the name of Slavic origin. Prior to 1945, well over 15 million Germans were born and lived in the Slavic speaking areas of East Europe, including the third-ranking man in the National Socialist command, the Russian-Baltic born German Alfred Rosenberg. Rosenberg's face shows Nordic features with a slight Alpine Slavic streak.

The linguistic approach to the study of races should not be neglected because it was common for many Slavs all over Europe to change their names to German names ("Weber", "Bauer", "Schmitt"), just as it was common for many Germans to change their names to Slavic ones. One needs to open up the white pages in Vienna, or in the once heavily Polish-populated Rhine basin, or in Berlin, to realize that one in every three German names ends with the Slavic syllable, such as "ski", "tschc", or "c".

In former Prussia — which is today under Russian and Polish jurisdiction — lived a significant number of Germans of French ancestry with names like "Fontane", "de Maizière", or "Lafontaine", bearing witness to a significant group of expelled 16th century French Protestant Huguenots, many of whom became prominent German leaders and scholars. Unlike all other European kingdoms, 18th-century Prussia under Frederick the Great was the first country to endorse the American Declaration of Independence. Prussia was then the most tolerant place on earth, attracting Enlightenment philosophers from France and from other parts of Europe.

Some of the highest-ranking German generals in the Wehrmacht were of Slavic-German origin. Their family names are clearly Slavic and their skull morphology points to a large variety of all European subracial types, from the Alpine (*ostisch*), the Mediterranean (*westisch*) to the Nordic: Hans Hellmich, Curt Badinski, Bruno Chrobeck, Emil Dedek, Heinrich Domansky, Walter Dybilasz, Erich Glodkowski, Kurt Mierzinsky, Adalbert Mikulicz, Bronislaw Pawel, Georg Radziej, Hans Radisch, Franz Zednicek, Walter von Brauchitsch. So were the other High German officers such as the master of panzer warfare, the round-headed Heinz Guderian, who was of distant Armenian origin, or the tall and big-nosed Wilhelm Canaris, who was of Italian/Greek origin. (See the important book by Christopher Dolbeau — practically unknown in France — *Face au Bolchevisme: Petit dictionnaire des résistances nationales à l'Est de l'Europe: 1917–1989*. (Against Bolshevism: A Little Dictionary of National Resistances in East Europe: 1917–1989).

The Beautiful Beast?

To assume, therefore, that the Institute for Racial Hygiene in Germany or the Gestapo were checking the names or the cranial index of High German officials, before admitting them to high military positions is academic lunacy. Yet a type of deliberate lunacy is still alive in some influential anti-German conspiratorial circles in the West and in America. The alleged racism of Germans against Slavs was part and parcel of the Allied propaganda and later of the Frankfurt School, whose goal was to whip up Slavs during and after WWII into anti-German frenzy. By accepting more than one million volunteers from Russia, Ukraine, Croatia, Slovakia, etc. in the Wehrmacht and by allowing half a million non-German European volunteers in the Waffen S.S., the German high military command thought it could create its own version of united Europe and successfully fight the war on two fronts.

Even the very bad guys — the men most feared by communists and Jews all over Europe and only trusted by Adolf Hitler in the last year of the war — were not quite the paradigms of the "Nazi Nordic" supermen. Or were they? Those haunting five were: the S.S. Gestapo and Interpol chief, the Austrian-born Ernst Kaltenbrunner; the Czech-Moravian-born S.S. Reichskommissar and Foreign Minister hopeful, Arthur Seyss Inquart (real name Arthur Zajtich); the Austrian-born S.S. Chief of Special Forces, whose name appears to be of Hungarian origin, Otto Skorzeny; the Italian, Trieste-born S.S. police chief of Slovenian origin, Odilo Globocnik, who put down the Warsaw Jewish ghetto uprising in late April 1943; and finally the Croatian-born Wehrmacht general, Lothar von Rendulic, who, even long after the war, was considered an expert on terrorist communist guerila warfare. Many of their fellow travelers — the ones who escaped suicide or the Allied gallows — played a crucial role in the development of the U.S. strategy for Cold War Communist containment.

Physically, all these men could be described as of the Dinaro-Nordic mixture, with prominent long heads and, to top it off, they are well over 6 foot tall, with Kaltenbrunner measuring 6' 7" (201 cm) and Skorzeny 6' 4" (194 cm). It is striking that all five were born in the former Austro-Hungarian Empire, an area of Europe where Hitler himself was born and that he knew best.

Traditionally, tall stature has been a matter of pride and a trademark of ethnic groups in this part of southeast *Mitteleuropa*. From Bavaria to Austria, along the German-speaking northern Italian province of South Tyrol and stretching further along the Croatian coast down to Montenegro, this part of Europe had been literally the military highway of different European and non-European armies since time immemorial. It is a convergence point of all European ethnicities: Goths, Celts, Latins, Illyrians and Slavs, with some inescapable Asiatic, Turkic recessive genes still to be detected, particularly further inland in the eastern Balkans. The Roman Emperor Marcus Aurelius in the 3rd century brought hundreds of thousands Roman legionaries to defend the *limes* on the Danube against Barbarians. The same can be said of the Goths who settled there in the 4th century and of Napoleon's *Grande Armée*, which went on foot all the way from Paris to Vienna, then further north to Moscow and then further south to the Croatian coastal and medieval town of Dubrovnik. There was a brief Mongol incursion in the 13th century, followed later, from the late 15th to the early 18th century, by lengthy and painful Turkish invasions, which the populace in this region holds in very bitter memory. The German derivative of the noun *Türke*, the past participle verb *getürkt* ("faked", "screwed up") has a very derogatory meaning today. So does the noun *Turčin* among Croats, or *Turco* in Italian — words still used to depict gross and violent behavior.

It is a common sight in the capital city of Bolzano, in South Tyrol and in the Croat coastal town of Split, to see lank long-limbed women who are 6 feet tall. Incidentally, the tallest man in Europe was a Croat, Grgo Kusić (1892–1918), who was 7'9" tall (2.37m) and who served in the Royal Guard of the late Austrian emperor Franz Joseph II. His contemporary, the Montenegrin Princess Helena measured 6' and was married to the late Italian King Victor Emmanuel III, who measured a modest 5'.

California governor Arnold Schwarzenegger also comes from this region. Born in the small village of Thal, right on the Slovenian-Styrian Austrian border, his physique and facial traits are not quite common for this region. He is a typical Nordic specimen — highly intelligent, although his square jaw is reminiscent of old Cro-Magnon chromosomes. Although born as a provincial "hillbilly" (*Bergtrottel* in colloquial German), after being successfully coached by his wife Maria (a member of the Kennedy dynasty), he learned the ropes of political survival in America. A few Californian pep talks about multiracial conviviality, coupled with his generous donations to Jewish organizations, made him a success story that his lookalikes in Austria could only dream of. Otherwise, under different historical circumstances, he would have ended up like his father, singing a different political tune — albeit with another heavy accent.

The term "racism" has a generic meaning today, denoting social ostracism of outgroups, or in the worst case scenario, depicting an act of savagery meted out by some race or some warring party to another race or ethnic group. In the standard usage today the word "racism" is not necessarily a referent for a different skin color, or a depiction of someone's high or low cognitive ability. As a result of constant semantic shifts the word "racism" is used to describe a form of barbarism, generally viewed as despicable and contrary to the most basic norms of human conduct.

German Endtimes

If one accepts this very general and generic definition of racism, then the German people, shortly after WWII, became a prime victim of the most massive form of racism and racial discrimination — unseen and unheard of at any time in the history of mankind. The scope of terror inflicted to the German people during the Allied firebombing of German cities, the degree of suffering experienced by millions of German civilians in Eastern Europe in the aftermath of the war, goes beyond human imagination. By its scope and its sophistication this peculiar type of cruelty against Germans is hardly comparable to any earlier tragedy of any other race or ethnicity in Africa or Asia during colonial times. It had clear racial, linguistic and judicial overtones still awaiting an objective scholarly examination.

Numerous books have been published by prominent authors, including the well-known American legal scholar Alfred de Zayas, the German historian Franz W. Seidler, and the Canadian historian James Bacque on the expulsion of Germans, the policy of starving of hundreds of thousands of surrendered German soldiers along the Rhine river that was carried out by the Allied commander Dwight Eisenhower, the grand theft of German property, mass rapes of over 2 million German women by Soviet soldiers, slave labor of captured young German children, etc.. Yet most of these books, although based on solid forensic research and physical evidence, are barely accessible, and they are never mentioned in higher education in the U.S.A. or in Europe.

Expulsion of Germans from Czechoslovakia

Germany's European allies, such as Hungary, or the wartime France, dearly paid for their collaboration with Germany too. Few French students, let alone American students, know that over 70,000 French civilians perished under American bombs from 1942 to 1944. They cannot be blamed, as there are no sites of commemoration for the bombs' victims in France. Tiny Croatia, which remained the loyal ally of Germany to the last day of WWII, paid a heavy price too, losing the best part of its gene pool, after its middle class had been wiped out by Yugoslav Communists. Although considered today the most beautiful country in Europe and a prime tourist destination, Croatia is essentially a huge graveyard. In 1945, it became the largest communist killing field of ethnic Germans and Croats in Europe.

It is still common in the Karst area in the mountains of southern Croatia to stumble upon small ravines and pits with rusted German helmets, rosary beads, and scattered bones. Beyond the carnage of WWII and its immediate aftermath, the root causes of the recent interethnic war in the Balkans are the direct outcome of forcible Allied creation at Yalta and Potsdam of the artificial multicultural entity known as Yugoslavia.

The question that comes to mind is: Why is this unique form of racism against Germans not debated in public as is for instance the plight of Jews during WWII? While acknowledging that others suffered greatly during WWII and that Germany also committed large-scale atrocities against others, one still wonders: Why are the enormous crimes against the Germans simply not discussed?

The answer may not be hard to find. We are still living in the period where history has been written by the victors. The topic of the war and post-war German losses cannot be debated in academe or in public life because the gigantic scale of German suffering would automatically and immediately eclipse all other competing victimologies combined.

What is striking is that there is still no official tally as to the number of German civilians and soldiers who perished in the period from 1938 to 1950. Why has the German government never released the exact casualty figure? One can only read in some marginal revisionist journals or hear occasional rumours that 6 to 12 million Germans perished during that time span — but there is no official document endorsing this allegation. And this silence is very, very telling indeed.

Crying Wolf

Racism against Germans had been well thought out and was brought to its academic perfection before the war's end. An influential American Jewish businessman, Theodore Kaufman, published in 1940 a small pamphlet titled *Germany Must Perish!* In the 1942 pamphlet *Kill*, his counterpart, the high Soviet-Jewish official Ilya Ehrenburg, unabashedly urged Soviets solders to spare no mercy against the Germans: "The Germans are not human beings. Henceforth the word German means to us the most terrible curse. From now on the word 'German' will trigger your rifle."

The Morgenthau Plan, devised by two ethnic Jews — Secretary of the Treasury Henry Morgenthau, Jr. and Assistant Treasury Secretary Harry Dexter White — would have killed 10 million Germans by starvation and disease in the first two years after the war. (White has been named as a Soviet spy on the basis of the Venona documents.) This would have been in addition to the 1 million that had been killed in saturation bombing and 3 million in forced expulsions. As Secretary of War Henry L. Stimson wrote in his diary, "I found around me, particularly Morgenthau, a very bitter atmosphere of personal resentment against the entire German people without regard to individual guilt of the Nazis."

As recounted by Joseph Bendersky, American military officers commonly believed that there were many anti-German Jews in the U.S. military government after World War II who were bent on de-nazification and revenge. "Feeling inhibited from speaking publicly by alleged Jewish power, a number of officers, as well as some government officials, complained incessantly in private that Jewish 'refugees in American uniforms,' together with Jews in the U.S. government, unduly affected American policy toward Germany in a variety of detrimental ways" (p. 364). Refugee officers (i.e., German Jews returning as members of the U.S. military government) treated Germans brutally, including sadistic beatings and starvation (p. 365). In general, these Jews advocated harsh treatment, the concept of collective guilt, and trials for general staff officers. The reputation of these refugee officers was so bad that the Army ended up firing personnel who had entered the U.S. after 1933.

Although modern mainstream historiography and the media downplay Kaufmann's little booklet and Ehrenburg's hectoring of Soviet soldiers, their words had a significant psychological impact on the behavior of Allied soldiers.

Anti-German hatred did not stop when the war was over. It is still well alive and thriving, albeit by resorting to far more sophisticated methods. Over the last 70 years anti-German racism, under the guise of the fluid word 'antifascism' has been the pivot of the "negative legitimacy" of Western civilization in the eyes of intellectual elites. Anti-German hatred still represents the unavoidable pillar of the world order, including international law. Any dent in it would seriously harm the modern system and would possibly bring it down.

There is also a psychological dimension to a racist act. Usually the bigger the magnitude of a racist crime the more intellectual effort is needed by its perpetrator to hide it, or explain it away, either by propagandistic or by pedagogical tools. Perpetrators of huge racist crimes, such as those committed by the Allies against the German people, were subsequently obliged to project their own crimes on their German victims. By reversing the semantics of the word 'racism', they were able to carry out their own racist policies, while at the same time naming the German victim as an exemplary role model of racism. Consequently, the victors of WWII had no other option but to trivialize or hush up their crimes, while simultaneously doctoring up the image of their own victimhoods while ascribing their own evildoing as a racially inborn trait of the defeated German side. The postmodern liberal "antifascist" and "antiracist" discourse of "crying wolf" — blaming the Other for one's own dark and criminal secrets, can be traced to good old fable teller Aesop and his allegories about human duplicity.

Freda Utley, a former communist intellectual, who very early learned the meta-language of the Allied propaganda and who later turned into an anticommunist writer, observed the psychology of the victors and their usage of semantic pyrotechnics. As early as 1948 she knew what would become of Germany:

> A thoughtful American professor, whom I met in Heidelberg, expressed the opinion that the United States military authorities on entering Germany and seeing the ghastly destruction wrought by our obliteration bombing were fearful that knowledge of it would cause a revulsion of opinion in America and might prevent the carrying out of Washington's policy for Germany by awakening sympathy for the defeated and realization of our war crimes. This, he believes, is the reason why a whole fleet of aircraft was used by General Eisenhower to bring journalists, Congressmen, and churchmen to see the concentration camps; the idea being that the sight of Hitler's starved victims would obliterate consciousness of our own guilt. Certainly it worked out that way. (Freda Utley, *The High Cost of Vengeance* (Chicago: Henry Regnery Co. 1949)

Judicial Review or Racial Review?

There is also a judicial aspect of modern anti-German racism, well observed by the German legal scholar Carl Schmitt, who witnessed himself this unparalleled German drama. Wars declared "good" and specifically wars fought in the name of "democracy and human rights," are the most barbaric ones. A democratic warrior is obliged to place his enemy below democratic standards, or simply set him outside the category of human beings. This was likely the image of Germans crossing the mind of American commanders when given orders to firebomb German cities. There were no longer "bad Krauts" residing in the crosshairs of the bombers, but monstrous beasts — a unique type of bacteria, a special form of disease that needed to be chemically removed in order to make the word safe for democracy.

Psychologically speaking American aircraft pilots or naive GIs had perfect consciousness, being firmly convinced that some ugly telluric creatures from the Bible, some stray Gogs or Magogs, lived down under in the medieval cities of Cologne, Dresden, Bremen, and Munich. It is no accident that the largest Allied firebombing — of Hamburg in July 1943 — had a code name from the Old Testament: 'Gomorrah.'

This pattern of demonization of the adversary was first used by the North against the South in legitimizing the Union aggression in 1863 and later on in brainwashing the Southerners. More recently it was used by George W. Bush and his neocon advisors in legitimizing military intervention in Iraq, notably by parroting the expression "Axis of Evil", put together by his Canadian-American Jewish advisor David Frum in subliminal reference to Axis countries of WWII. In both historical instances, *Deuteronomy*, Chapter VII, with its prescriptions for genocide, was used as a handbook against unchosen ones. As Schmitt writes:

> Hostility becomes so absolute that even the most ancient sacral differentiation between the enemy and the criminal disappears in the paroxysm of self-righteousness. To doubt one's own justice appears as treason; to show interest in the opponent's arguments is viewed as treacherousness, and the attempt to start discussion is considered as agreement with the enemy. (*Ex Captivitate Salus, Erfahrungen der Zeit 1945/47* (Köln: Greven Verlag, 1950, p. 58).

After 1945, with the hindsight of the Allied terror bombing and fresh memories of immense suffering, the mimicry of political rectitude amidst the new German ruling class was comprehensive. Hundreds of thousands of German intellectuals had to be purged from schools and universities and newspapers and also obliged to fill out the demeaning Questionnaires (*Fragebogen*), while renouncing over and over again their "authoritarian personality." The high priests of the Frankfurt School, specialists in "laundering the German character", accomplished their work meticulously. (See Caspar Schrenck von Notzing; also my *Homo Americanus*.) In the decades to come German politicians had to prove that they could perform their liberal democratic tasks better than their American tutors. Given that all signs of nationalism, let alone racialism, had to be erased, the only form of patriotism allowed to Germans was "constitutional patriotism": "*The German people had to adapt itself to the constitution, instead of adapting the constitution to the German people,*" writes the German legal scholar, Günther Maschke (*Das bewaffnete Wort* ("Die Verschwörung der Flakhelfer") (Wien und Lepzig: Karolinger Verlag, 1997) p. 74; my emphasis).

The word 'German' has become synonymous with evil. German studies in the U.S. academe have been thoroughly neglected; any mentioning of "German culture" is still reminiscent of the time span stretching from 1933 to 1945. Today, the Germans are a thoroughly neurotic people, a case of the victor's successful cultural (and genetic?) engineering — probably the most unique case in the history of mankind.

The peculiar hatred of German tormentors must be put into wider psychological perspective and possibly also described by an evolutionary psychologist. It was largely the subconscious knowledge of their low character in comparison to the Germans that tormentors of the German people acted in such a barbaric fashion.

The German people, as the synthesis of all European races and residing in the place where North and West meet South and East in Europe, are in many ways the most accomplished of all Indo-European peoples. Rising from the ashes of WWII, they have built the strongest, most productive economy in Europe. Germans have a special sense of space and order (*Ordnung* and *Ortung*), which other European peoples do not have to the same degree. There is a joke that even a German drug addict knows how to neatly dispose of his used needles.

In addition, the German language is the richest Indo-European language. It enables hundreds of thousands of neologisms and compound nouns; it is timeless and endless and ideal for philosophical speculation. Unlike the English language and even more so the highly contextual French language (which is full of antonyms and homonyms), the German language is a straightforward and a very "earthbound" language, having in addition a solid normative grammar. Alas, unlike French, its major fault is that it does not give speakers latitude for diplomatic weaseling.

The paradox of our postmodernity is that despite being the most demonized people on earth, Germans are the most welcome people anywhere. Unlike the French, the English, and let alone the Americans, who are resented, if not despised in foreign countries, German businessmen, tourists and even their politically correct elites, are welcome everywhere. From the Arabic casbahs to India's bazaars, barefooted-street kids yell in great respect when they spot Germans: "Alemani! Alemani!" Officially, even Germany's former arch-enemies in Russia and Israel reserve to German diplomats a far more lavish treatment than they do to other foreign diplomats.

Subconsciously everybody knows that something terrible and unspeakable happened to Germans. But it is not deserving loud and open discourse — at least not for now.

In late June 1944, the Anglo-American troops were well entrenched in Normandy after successfully cutting off German supply lines from the north-eastern part of France. On their way to the borders of the Reich, the Americans GIs would occasionally capture small military units wearing German uniforms that they first took for Japanese soldiers. It turned out that these were Turkmen and Azeri soldiers fighting on the Western front under German patronage.

Bizarre interracial encounters not only occurred in the Pacific between the Japanese and Americans, but also in north-western Italy, in the province of Friuli, where it was common in April 1945 to spot retreating pockets of Asian civilians and slanted-eyed soldiers in German uniforms fleeing the incoming Soviet advance along with their German allies (Christopher Dolbeau, *Face au Bolchevisme: 1917–1989*, 2002, pp. 302–303; see also, Patrik von zur Mühlen, *Zwischen Hakenkreuz und Sowjetstern*, 1971).

In the last year of the war, National Socialist Germany, which over the last 60 years has been maligned for its real and surreal racist prejudices and practices, had hundreds of thousands of non-European volunteers fighting the global war against Communism and colonialism. Many of those non-European troops had firmly believed that that N.S. Germany would provide them with independence from the rule of colonial France and England. The German Wehrmacht had thousands of Arab fighters, Indian fighters, and even two black fighters from Guadeloupe fighting alongside with the Germans, such as the famous Louis Joachim-Eugène and Norbert Désirée!

Space does not allow recounting each individual event that took place after the end of hostilities. But although meagre, the literature on non-European fighters in the German Wehrmacht sheds a different light on the already highly complex picture of German racial policies in the Third Reich. However, what is clear today is that 70 years after the war, neither the winning side nor to the losing side benefited from the conflict. In fact as a prominent German historian Ernst Nolte writes (*Der europäische Bürgerkrieg 1917–1945: Nationalsozialismus und Bolschewismus*, 1987), this was the largest European civil war in history, substantially draining the White gene pool.

All subsequent events in the world up to the present, be they on the theoretical or institutional level, be they in the field of social sciences or world politics, are directly linked to this largest intra-White bloodshedding in history.

Race or Religion?

In the late 1940's hundreds of prominent National Socialist dignitaries managed to escape to Egypt, Turkey and Syria. Most converted to Islam, married there and adopted Muslim names. A substantial number of them played a crucial role in early Egyptian politics under president Gamal Abdel Nasser, providing valuable intelligence to Egyptians and Syrians on the newly born state of Israel. Numerous ex-S.S. intelligence officers, academics and physicians, such as Hans Appler — alias Sakah Chaffar, Joachim Daemling — alias Ibrahim Mustafa, Ludwig Heiden — alias El Hadj, Aribert Heim — alias Tarek Hussein Farid, and many, many others are still warmly remembered in the Syrian and Egyptian intelligence community.

It is quite common among White nationalists in Europe and America to single out Muslim immigrants as the major threat to White Euro-American societies because their demographic growth is likely to turn Europe into an Islamic state. The United Kingdom, France, or for that matter the European Union as a whole, have a large number of South Asian and Arab Muslims. One study found that there were at least 15 million Muslims in the E.U., and possibly as many as 23 million. This number does not include over 10 million White autochthonous European Muslims, particularly in the Balkans.

Yet a sharp difference must be made between race and religion. For example, only one third of Catholics in the world today are White, with two thirds being of mixed race living mostly in Latin America and the Philippines. One need only take a walk in St. Peter's Square in Rome to spot swarms of non-European Catholic seminarians. Unlike Judaism, which is a highly ethnocentric monotheistic religion, the other two monotheistic religions, also born in the Middle East — Islam and Christianity — ignore, at least in theory, the distinction between race and religion.

There are also double standards in depicting the deluge of Muslim non-European outgroups into Europe and America. These groups are unquestionably changing the racial profile of their White host countries. But while it is relatively safe to criticize the alleged violent nature of Islam in academic circles, one rarely hears that the violence against non-Jews in the Old Testament shows that Judaism is inherently violent.

And in the contemporary world, why criticize the violent nature of Islam while avoiding criticism of the violent nature of Zionism?

Many White nationalists are justly concerned about the inflow of non-European races. But many of these non-Europeans, such as Hindus residing in the UK, are extremely resentful of Islam. Ethnic and religious conflict in the future may well be a complex affair, as it already is in the United States, where Latinos have ethnically cleansed Blacks from some areas of Southern California.

The whole liberal hypocrisy on race was well described by Alain Brossat, who notes that in France making fun of Arabs or describing them as terrorists, obscurantists, or enemies of democracy and republicanism is considered protected free speech. On the other hand, making fun of rabbis or vehemently criticizing the politics of the state of Israel will result in draconian penalties.

To make the subject of race even more complicated, during different historical eras the Catholic Church endorsed highly promiscuous policies of miscegenation, particularly in Latin America during Spanish rule. From the 16th to the 19th century, a few Spanish White settlers and hordes of ordinary criminals from all parts of Europe found a safe haven in fertile Paraguay, only to be forced by the powerful Jesuit clergy to marry Guarani Indian women — simply because there were no White women around.

The Christian Gospel of "love thy neighbour" certainly played an additional role in the process of miscegenation all over Latin America. There has been a gradual depletion of the White gene pool caused by racial mongrelisation. This has often resulted in frequent coup d'états and poor economic growth, despite the fact that Latin America is rich in natural resources.

Moreover, the interplay of race and religion is further complicated by the fact that there are well over 10 million indigenous Muslims in Europe, mostly Bosnians and Albanians whose gene pool is relatively well preserved and who are often more European than White European Christians. Bosnian Muslims present a very peculiar case, being all of European stock with a high number of strikingly blond people. In the Middle Ages their ancestors were renowned as heretics, known as "Bogumils", with strong ties to French Cathars and Albingensians.

In the late 15th century with the onslaught of Turks against Europe, Bosnian Bogumils converted in droves to Islam — partly because of their hostility to the Vatican, and partly because their White race propelled them quickly into lucrative positions in the Ottoman hierarchy. The Ottomans offered them prestigious titles — "beys", "pashas", or "grand viziers." Valued and praised because of their physical stature and race, Slavic

Muslims, including the Albanians, who are of old Indo-European Illyrian stock, played for centuries an important role as elite soldiers known as janissaries who were posted as provincial rulers throughout the Ottoman empire, which in some periods stretched from today's Algeria in the west to Yemen in the East, and all the way to Hungary in central Europe.

During WWII, many Bosnian and Albanian Muslims were highly regarded by N.S. Germany. The Catholic pro-fascist Croat leader, Ante Pavelić built a large mosque in the heart of the Croatian baroque city of Zagreb, while frequently referring to Bosnian Muslims as the "purest Croats." In 1943, under the supervision of Heinrich Himmler, a Bosnian Waffen S.S. *Handschar* was established under German command.

The story of race and racism in the Third Reich is complex and endless in its scope. It still needs to be objectively written. Surprisingly perhaps, some "half-Jews" or "quarter-Jews" played a significant political and military role in N.S. Germany; many took part in the anti-communist campaign in the East. Among the famous "Mischlings", or crossbreeds, was the famous German admiral Bernhard Rogge, Field Marshal Erhard Milch, Field Marshal von Manstein (born Lewinski), the panzer general Fritz Bayerlein, etc. In his book, *Hitler's Jewish Soldiers*, the Jewish American historian Bryan Mark Rigg estimates that between 120,000 to 160,000 Germans of Jewish extraction served in the Wehrmacht.

Heredity and race are crucial elements in someone's political and social behavior. But a person possessing the highest qualities of his race — but without a culture that preserves and enhances his race — turns into a biological unit with a meaningless life. Culture must always come as the final veneer on a person's racial make-up. Even among Third Reich scholars the most frequent word was not *Rasse* (race), but, rather, the word *Ausbildung*, which denotes character building (often wrongly translated into English as 'education'). High IQ and other positive racial characteristics can in no way substitute for strong will and moral integrity. These traits are influenced genetically and they differ between the races. But there are strong cultural influences on these traits as well. The phenomenon whereby so many Whites have accepted the death of their culture and the surrender of lands they have held for centuries is the product of a pathological culture, not pathological genes.

It still remains a great mystery why the great White race, once capable of great deeds and daring adventure from Cape Verde to Patagonia and from the Arctic Circle to New Zealand, is now more and more inclined to a domesticated life with no risks, always ready to meekly accept its own cultural and political eclipse as a moral imperative. Must it wait for the real interracial warfare in order to retrieve its ingroup identity?

ART IN THE THIRD REICH: 1933–1945

When writing about or discussing the plastic and figurative arts in Germany during the period stretching from 1933 to 1945, one must inevitably mention the cultural or pseudo-cultural works of art that highlighted the epoch of National Socialism. During that short and troubled period of time, art was also a reflection of modern European history, and, therefore, it must be examined, or, for that matter, conceptualized, within the larger geopolitical framework of Europe as a whole.

National Socialist culture, or the Nazi "(anti)culture", has always been a sensitive subject, whose controversial nature is more apparent today than ever before in the ongoing media warfare between so-called anti-communists and antifascists.

If one accepts the conventional wisdom, widely accepted in all corners of the world, that National Socialism was a form of totalitarianism, one must then also raise the question as to whether there were any authentic cultural successes achieved during the Third Reich at all. Certain parallels can and should be drawn between artistic efforts in the U.S.S.R. and National Socialist Germany, in view of the fact that culture in both systems was dominated by a specific ideology. Does this therefore mean that there were no valuable works of art created in the U.S.S.R., or for that matter in National Socialist Germany? What both National Socialism and Communism had in common was the rejection of "art for art's sake", (*l'art pour l'art*) and the repudiation of middleclass aestheticism. Instead, both political systems favored a committed and normative approach to art, which was supposed to be a tool for the creation of the "new man". On the other hand, from the thematic, aesthetic and stylistic point of view, the differences between art in Communism and art in National Socialism were immense.

After the Second World War, as the result of pressure from the Allies, Germany was forced to open its doors to abstract art (Jackson Pollock, Piet Mondrian, et al.), and, consequently Germany had to stifle the production of its traditional figurative art. Even German artists who were not implicated in the National Socialist regime, including those whom the National Socialist propaganda had labeled "degenerate artists" (*entartete Künstler*) came under the ban. A large number of paintings and other works of art executed during the Third Reich were either removed or destroyed. Several hundred sculptures were demolished or trashed during the Allied air bombardments. After the war, a considerable number of works of art were confiscated by the Americans, because of "their pornographic character." In the spring of 1947, eight thousand, seven hundred and twenty-two (8,722) paintings and sculptures of German artists were transported to the United States. Of these, only a small number has hitherto been returned to the Federal Republic of Germany.

A short outline of art under National Socialism requires knowledge of the historical and political framework of that epoch. Who were those German artists? Were they sympathetic to the National Socialist regime? What did they do before the National Socialist seizure of power in 1933? What became of them after the fall of the Third Reich?

It is important to emphasize the fact that to be an artist in National Socialist Germany did not always imply self-enslavement to the ruling class or blind obedience to political decrees, nor did it necessarily entail membership in the National Socialist Party (N.S.D.A.P.). Yet to be able to have one's artistic works accepted for public exhibition during the period between 1933 and 1945, presupposed at least tacit respect for the concept of beauty as defined by the National Socialist regime. A large number of German artists, who were by no means followers of the National Socialist regime, nevertheless well understood which type of works they could exhibit or display if they wished to remain within the public eye. As was the case with countless artists in every historical epoch and in all political systems from the dawn of time, many German artists were the simple, timorous types, the "flag wavers", as it were, who understood that it was necessary to yield to the whims of the new regime if they did not wish to be left out of the spotlight completely.

Such a servile attitude is not a novel phenomenon in European cultural history. Being a good artist or a good writer does not always entail the artist's possession of moral integrity, guaranteeing that the artist will always be found siding with the oppressed, or shouting at full breath for universal justice. Throughout European history, there were (and still are) excellent artists and thinkers who served (and still serve) criminal governments. A well-known Croatian sculptor, Antun Augustinčić, who was influenced in his youth by the French sculptor Auguste Rodin, made busts of the Croatian pro-fascist Ustashi leader, Ante Pavelić. After World War II, in the new communist Yugoslavia, Augustinčić did the same thing for the communist ruler Marshall Josip Broz Tito. To ponder the question as to the moral and political integrity of the sculptor Augustinčić is one thing; to try to define the subtlety of his artistic achievements is quite another.

Moreover, any appreciation of an artistic work created during the National Socialist epoch requires a precise knowledge of the mentality of the German people, a good knowledge of the *Zeitgeist*, as it influenced a specific work of art at the very moment when it was created. Ignoring the dominant ideas of the first half of the twentieth century cannot help us more accurately to comprehend the artistic range of a particular work of art. The famous French painter, Jacques-Louis David (1748–1825) served with devotion three widely different regimes: the French revolutionary Jacobins; Napoleonic imperialism; and, later, the reactionary monarchists of the French Restoration. David knew well how to adapt his skills to each new system (as a metaphorical and proverbial French *demisolde*!).

However, David's lack of political or moral integrity does not belittle his gift for the static or mobile composition, nor its key element such as strong and realistic brushwork. One might be tempted to mention hundreds of similar cases today, notably when gifted artists and writers adapt to "political correctness" without any scruples and always with the full approval of their "good conscience."

The Political Apparatus in the Service of Culture

It is often forgotten that the major goal of National Socialist propaganda was not the rearrangement of the political field, but rather the promotion of culture. This was especially true in the area of figurative and plastic art. The four most influential people in the Third Reich, i.e., Joseph Goebbels, Albert Speer, Arthur Rosenberg, and the Führer, Adolf Hitler, were focused, over the 12 years of the National Socialist regime, on the concept of the new art, the new architecture, and the new painting. In his youth, at the beginning of the twentieth century, Hitler had painted hundreds of watercolors, some of which have, without doubt, a certain artistic value and seem to be held in high esteem among WWII artifacts dealers, especially in the United States.

Toward the end of his reign, in 1945, Hitler dreamed of opening the largest art gallery in the world, which he had long determined to house in the Austrian city of Linz.

Immense architectural and scientific efforts, such as the launching of the first model of the popular automobile named the *Volkswagen*, and the construction of vast and well-designed motorways, were to a large extent Hitler's own ideas. In his answer to the editor in chief of the cultural newspaper *Kunst dem Volke*, on June 2, 1937, Hitler remarked: "The fact that I made paintings in order to survive, does not now mean that they now deserve to be exposed in the *Haus der Deutschen Kunst* (The House of the German Art)."

As a teenager, imbued by the art and culture of the period of Romanticism, Hitler was influenced by the watercolors of Rudolf von Alt and the oil paintings of Carl von Spitzweg. During the National Socialist regime many journals dealing with art were launched: *Kunst der Nation, Kunst dem Volke, Die Kunst im Dritten Reich,* etc. In 1937, the propaganda minister Goebbels inaugurated the "Chamber of Arts" (*Kunstkammer*), a cultural institution that, from 1935 to 1937, enrolled more than one hundred thousand members. During the period stretching from 1933 to 1945, thirty large art exhibitions, on average, were held each month. This was the case even during the period from 1940 to 1945, when Germany was subject to the regular air bombardments carried out by the Allies.

In 1937, the opening of the "Haus der Deutschen Kunst" took place in Munich. At that time, this was the most significant establishment of its kind in Europe. The first stone of this building — which was 175 meters long — was laid by Hitler himself. Approximately one thousand German artists exposed their works in it from 1937 to 1939.

The Archaic Post-Modernity

National Socialist dignitaries devoted much energy to the promotion of German sculptors and their works, and helped them, considerably, in the execution of massive basreliefs and in the erection of monumental stone and bronze sculptures. The political goal was obvious: to bring the German art as close as possible to the German people, so that any German citizen, regardless of his or her social standing could identify himself or herself with a specific artistic achievement.

It should, therefore, come as no surprise that the German art of that time witnessed a return to classicism. Models from Antiquity and the Renaissance were to some extent adapted to the needs of National Socialist Germany. Numerous German sculptors worked arduously on their projects while benefiting from the logistic and financial support of the political elite. Their sculptures resembled, either by form, or by composition, the works of Praxiteles or of Pheidias of ancient Greece, or those executed by Michelangelo during the Renaissance. The most prominent German sculptors of that time were Arno Breker, Josef Thorak, and Fritz

Klimsch, who although enjoying the significant logistical resources of the National Socialist regime, were never members of the N.S.D.A.P.

Sculptures of naked women, such as "Flora" by Breker, "Girl" by Fehrle, or "Glance" by Klimsch, show excessively beautiful and geometrically pruned women who, sometimes, with their perfect bodies, with their narrow and lengthened ankles, with their well-rounded and well-proportioned breasts, tire the eye of the observer. In addition, the fact that many sculptures show naked males embracing naked females indicates that National Socialism was by no means a "conservative" or "reactionary" movement, and that Puritan and Anglo-Saxon prudishness was completely alien to it. It is difficult to deny the great talents of Breker or Klimsch, even if some critics justly estimate that their sculptures often show traits of solid manufacturing copies of classic artists.

As a young man, Breker lived in France where he was influenced by his future friend and sculptor, Aristide Maillol. After the war, many of Breker's sculptures were destroyed by the American soldiers. In spite of his political troubles, Breker continued to work after the war making busts of his friends and protectors, (Salvador Dali, Hassan II, Louis-Ferdinand Céline, etc). It should be noted that Breker, in the wake of the Allied occupation of Germany, was requested by the Soviets to continue his artistic career in the Soviet Union — an offer that he refused. It goes without saying that it is possible to draw certain parallels between the gigantism of the plastic art in National Socialist Germany and that of the Soviet Union (the naked Prometheus *vis-à-vis* the muscular and shirtless hammer-holding proletarian!). Yet the differences are again glaring: in communist countries one can never find sculptures representing nude women and men — which confirms our thesis that Communism, although politically frightening, was primarily a prudish and conservative system.

Indeed, even today, one can hardly encounter pictorial or plastic representations of embracing couples in China, Cuba, or in North Korea. The sculptures of Venus or nymphs made by Breker or Thorak display nothing provocative or pornographic; they never trigger sexual fantasies or erotic dreams, as is perhaps the case with the stupendous naked beauties painted by the Italian artist Amadeo Modigliani. Upon the faces of the sculptures representing nude women made by German artists, one comes across an enigmatic and aristocratic smile and a deep sense of the tragic, which reflect, symbolically, the pessimism of a whole nation in search of its geopolitical identity. No trace can be found of female coquetry or flirtatiousness, such as one encounters among the nudes painted by the French realist, Gustave Courbet, by the impressionist Edouard Manet, or by Paul Cézanne, the post-impressionist.

The German painting of that time represents a chapter apart. Contrary to widespread ideas, "kitsch" was never part of art in National Socialist Germany, and against "kitsch" in the arts the German National Socialist authorities adopted repressive measures resembling those invoked against the alleged degenerate art. As far as the painting of that time is concerned, Germany suffered a considerable regression in the quality of its pictorial production. The early school of expressionism was abandoned and even severely repressed by the authorities. Expressionism, compared to impressionism of the French source, is paradoxically the typical feature of the German character and temperament, just as it is of other Germanic peoples (Flemmings, Scandinavians).

Yet German artists of the expressionist school did not obtain the regime's green light to exhibit their works. Schools of thought that had emerged from such cultural circles as *Die Brücke* or *Neue Sachligkeit*, and that, at the beginning of the twentieth century had produced some of Europe's great masters, were assailed by the National Socialist censorship. German painters, who, between 1933 and 1945, gained considerable reputation were neo-classicist self-portraitists and landscape painters who avoided pathetic and exaggerated compositions, and attempted to rid artistic work of every trace of the influence of Cubism and abstract art. Overall, one can sense in their paintings the revival of the taste for primitive art and a return to the Flemish masters of the fifteenth century.

Certain parallels can again be drawn with the paintings known as "socialist-realist" in the Soviet Union and other communist countries. However, even here the difference is obvious. Whereas one can see on the paintings of Soviet artists the peasants and workmen adorned with their perpetual grins, and in the background a factory under construction, on the German paintings of that time seldom can one see signs of industrialization. Traces of the asphalt, chimneys spewing fumes, or factories in full gear — such as one can observe among "socialists-realist" painters (and in their titanic and apocalyptic form among the futuristic artists in fascistic Italy!), very rarely appear in the German paintings of that period.

Just as one can draw a comparison between German sculptors and Soviet sculptors, one can also notice a difference between figurative art under Communism and figurative art under National Socialism. In the art galleries of the Third Reich the scenes of handsome rural nymphs abound (Amadeus Dier, Johannes Beutner, Sepp Hilz, etc). These pastoral beauties, which can be observed on oil paintings, exhale family harmony, and seem to anticipate a well-deserved rest after a hard day's work in the cornfields. Also worth mentioning is the artist and wood engraver, Ernst von Dombrowski, whose scenes of country life and young children playing, still win great praise from critics.

In conclusion, one can state that the German sculpture of that time, proclaims, at least as a rule, a message of racial and promethean hygiene, while the paintings of that time reveal a distinct and populist (*völkisch*) tendency that can hardly be misconstrued for any ideological or political speculation.

THE DESTRUCTION OF ETHNIC GERMANS AND GERMAN PRISONERS OF WAR IN YUGOSLAVIA, 1945–1953

From the European and American media, one can often get the impression that World War II needs to be periodically resurrected to give credibility to financial demands of one specific ethnic group, at the expense of others. The civilian deaths of the war's losing side are, for the most part, glossed over. Standard historiography of World War II is routinely based on a sharp and polemical distinction between the "ugly" fascists who lost, and the "good" anti-fascists who won, and few scholars are willing to inquire into the gray ambiguity in between. Even as the events of that war become more distant in time, they seemingly become more politically useful and timely as myths.

German military and civilian losses during and especially after World War II are still shrouded by a veil of silence, at least in the mass media, even though an impressive body of scholarly literature exists on that topic. The reasons for this silence, due in large part to academic negligence, are deep rooted and deserve further scholarly inquiry. Why, for instance, are German civilian losses, and particularly the staggering number of postwar losses among ethnic Germans, dealt with so sketchily, if at all, in school history courses? The mass media — television, newspapers, film and magazines — rarely, if ever, look at the fate of the millions of German civilians in central and Eastern Europe during and following World War II.[1]

The treatment of civilian ethnic Germans — or *Volksdeutsche* — in Yugoslavia may be regarded as a classic case of "ethnic cleansing" on a grand scale.[2] A close look at these mass killings presents a myriad of historical and legal problems, especially when considering modern international law, including The Hague War Crimes Tribunal that has been dealing with war crimes and crimes against humanity in the Balkan wars of 1991–1995. Yet the plight of Yugoslavia's ethnic Germans during and after World War II should be of no lesser concern to historians, not least because an understanding of this chapter of history throws a significant light on the violent breakup of Communist Yugoslavia 45 years later. A better understanding of the fate of Yugoslavia's ethnic Germans should encourage skepticism of just how fairly and justly international law is applied in practice. Why are the sufferings and victimhood of some nations or ethnic groups ignored, while the sufferings of other nations and groups receive fulsome and sympathetic attention from the media and politicians?

At the outbreak of World War II in 1939, more than one and a half million ethnic Germans were living in southeastern Europe, that is, in Yugoslavia, Hungary, and Romania. Because they lived mostly near and along the Danube River, these people were popularly known "Danube

Swabians" or *Donauschwaben*. Most were descendants of settlers who came to this fertile region in the 17th and 18th centuries following the liberation of Hungary from Turkish rule.

For centuries, the Holy Roman Empire and then the Habsburg Empire struggled against Turkish rule in the Balkans, and resisted the "Islamization" of Europe. In this struggle the Danube Germans were viewed as a rampart of Western civilization, and were held in high esteem in the Austrian (and later, Austro-Hungarian) empire for their agricultural productivity and military prowess. Both the Holy Roman and Habsburg empires were multicultural and multinational entities, in which diverse ethnic groups lived for centuries in relative harmony.

After the end of World War I, in 1918, which brought the collapse of the Austro-Hungarian Habsburg Empire, and the imposed Versailles Treaty of 1919, the juridical status of the *Donauschwaben* Germans was in flux. When the National Socialist regime was established in Germany in 1933, the *Donauschwaben* were among the more than twelve million ethnic Germans who lived in central and Eastern Europe outside the borders of the German Reich. Many of these people were brought into the Reich with the incorporation of Austria in 1938, of the Sudetenland region of Czechoslovakia in 1939, and of portions of Poland in late 1939. The "German question", that is, the struggle for self-determination of ethnic Germans outside the borders of the German Reich, was a major factor leading to the outbreak of World War II. Even after 1939, more than three million ethnic Germans remained outside the borders of the expanded Reich, notably in Romania, Yugoslavia, Hungary, and the Soviet Union.

In the first Yugoslavia — a monarchical state created in 1919 largely as a result of efforts of the victorious Allied powers — most of the country's ethnic Germans were concentrated in eastern Croatia and northern Serbia (notably in the Vojvodina region), with some German towns and villages in Slovenia. Other ethnic Germans lived in western Romania and south-eastern Hungary.

This first multiethnic Yugoslav state of 1919–1941 had a population of some 14 million people of diverse cultures and religions. On the eve of World War II it included nearly six million Serbs, about three million Croats, more than a million Slovenes, some two million Bosnian Muslims and ethnic Albanians, approximately half a million ethnic Germans, and another half million ethnic Hungarians. Following the breakup of Yugoslavia in April 1941, accelerated by a rapid German military advance, approximately 200,000 ethnic Germans became citizens of the newly established Independent State of Croatia, a country whose military and civil authorities remained loyally allied with Third Reich Germany until the final week of the war in Europe.[3] Most of the remaining ethnic Germans of former Yugoslavia — approximately 300,000 in the Vojvodina region — came under the jurisdiction of Hungary, which during the war incorporated the region. (After 1945, this region was reattached to the Serbian portion of Yugoslavia.)

The plight of the ethnic Germans became dire during the final months of World War II, and especially after the founding of the second Yugoslavia, a multiethnic Communist state headed by Marshal Josip Broz Tito. In late October 1944, Tito's guerilla forces, aided by the advancing Soviets and lavishly assisted by Western air supplies, took control of Belgrade, the Serb capital that also served as the capital of Yugoslavia. One of the first legal acts of the new regime was the decree of November 21, 1944, on "The decision regarding the transfer of the enemy's property into the property of the state." It declared citizens of German origin as "enemies of the people", and stripped them of civic rights. The decree also ordered the government confiscation of all property, without compensation, of Yugoslavia's ethnic Germans.[4] An additional law, promulgated in Belgrade on February 6, 1945, canceled the Yugoslav citizenship of the country's ethnic Germans.[5]

By late 1944 — when Communist forces had seized control of the eastern Balkans, that is, of Bulgaria, Serbia, and Macedonia — the German-allied state of Croatia still held firm. However, in early 1945, German troops, together with Croatian troops and civilians, began retreating toward southern Austria. During the war's final months, the majority of Yugoslavia's ethnic German civilians also joined this great trek. The refugees' fears of torture and death at Communist hands were well founded, given the horrific treatment by Soviet forces of Germans and others in East Prussia and other parts of Eastern Europe. By the end of the war in May 1945, German authorities had evacuated 220,000 ethnic Germans from Yugoslavia to Germany and Austria. Yet many remained in their war-ravaged ancestral homelands, most likely awaiting a miracle.

After the end of fighting in Europe on May 8, 1945, more than 200,000 ethnic Germans who had remained behind in Yugoslavia effectively became captives of the new Communist regime. Some 63,635 Yugoslav ethnic German civilians (women, men and children) perished under Communist rule between 1945 and 1950 — that is, some 18 percent of the ethnic German civilian population still remaining in the new Yugoslavia. Most died as a result of exhaustion as slave laborers, in "ethnic cleansing", or from disease and malnutrition.[6] Much of the credit for the widely praised "economic miracle" of Titoist Yugoslavia, it should be noted, must go to the tens of thousands of German slave laborers who, during the late 1940s, helped to build the impoverished country.

Property of ethnic Germans in Yugoslavia confiscated in the aftermath of World War II amounted to 97,490 small businesses, factories, shops, farms, and diverse trades. The confiscated real estate and farmland of Yugoslavia's ethnic Germans came to 637,939 hectares (or about one million acres), and became state-owned property. According to a 1982 calculation, the value of the property confiscated from ethnic Germans in Yugoslavia amounted to 15 billion German marks, or about seven billion U.S. dollars. Taking inflation into account, this would today correspond to 12 billion U.S. dollars. From 1948 to 1985, more than 87,000 ethnic Germans who were still residing in Yugoslavia moved to Germany and automatically became German citizens.[7]

All this constitutes a "final solution of the German question" in Yugoslavia.

Numerous survivors have provided detailed and graphic accounts of the grim fate of the ethnic German civilians, particularly women and children, who were held in Communist Yugoslav captivity. One noteworthy witness is the late Father Wendelin Gruber, who served as a chaplain and spiritual leader to many fellow captives.[8] These numerous survivor accounts of torture and death inflicted on German civilians and captured soldiers by Yugoslav authorities add to the chronicle of Communist oppression worldwide.[9]

Of the one and a half million ethnic Germans who lived in the Danube basin in 1939–1941, some 93,000 served during World War II in the armed forces of Hungary, Croatia and Romania — Axis countries that were allied with Germany — or in the regular German armed forces. The ethnic Germans of Hungary, Croatia, and Romania who served in the military formations of those countries remained citizens of those respective states.[10]

In addition, many ethnic Germans of the Danubian region served in the "Prinz Eugen" Waffen S.S. division, which totaled some 10,000 men throughout its existence during the war. (This formation was named in honor of Prince Eugene of Savoy, who had won great victories against Turkish forces in the late 17th and early 18th centuries.)[11] Enlisting in the "Prinz Eugen" division automatically conferred German citizenship on the recruit.

Of the 26,000 ethnic Danubian ethnic Germans serving in various military formations who lost their lives, half perished after the end of the war in Yugoslav camps. Particularly high were the losses of the "Prinz Eugen" division, most of whom surrendered after May 8, 1945. Some 1,700 of these prisoners were killed in the village of Brezice near the Croat-Slovenian border, while the remaining half was worked to death in Yugoslav zinc mines near the town of Bor, in Serbia.[12]

In addition to the "ethnic cleansing" of Danube German civilians and soldiers, some 70,000 Germans who had served in regular Wehrmacht forces perished in Yugoslav captivity. Most of these died as a result of reprisals, or as slave laborers in mines, road construction, shipyards, and so forth. These were mostly troops of "Army Group E" who had surrendered to British military authorities in southern Austria at the time of the armistice of May 8, 1945. British authorities turned over about 150,000 of these German prisoners of war to Communist Yugoslav partisans under pretext of later repatriation to Germany.

Most of these former regular Wehrmacht troops perished in post-war Yugoslavia in three stages: During the first stage more than 7,000 captured German troops died in Communist-organized "atonement marches" (*Sühnemärsche*) stretching 800 miles from the southern border of Austria to the northern border of Greece. During the second phase, in late summer 1945, many German soldiers in captivity were summarily executed or thrown alive into large karst pits along the Dalmatian coast of Croatia. In the third stage, 1945–1955, an additional 50,000 perished as forced laborers due to malnutrition and exhaustion.[13]

The total number of German losses in Yugoslav captivity after the end of the war — including ethnic "Danube German" civilians and soldiers, as well as "Reich" Germans — may therefore be conservatively estimated at 120,000 killed, starved, worked to death, or missing.

What is the importance of these figures? What lessons can be drawn in assessing these post-war German losses?

It is important to stress that the plight of German civilians in the Balkans is only a small portion of the Allied topography of death. Seven to eight million Germans — both military personnel and civilians — died during and after World War II. Half of those perished during the final months of the war, or after Germany's unconditional surrender on May 8, 1945. German casualties, both civilian and military, were arguably higher in "peace" than in "war".

In the months before and after the end of World War II, ethnic Germans were killed, tortured and dispossessed throughout eastern and central Europe, notably in Silesia, East Prussia, Pomerania, the Sudetenland, and the "Wartheland" region. Altogether 12–15 million Germans fled or were driven from their homes in what is perhaps the greatest "ethnic cleansing" in history. Of this number, more than two million were killed or otherwise lost their lives.[14]

The grim events in post-war Yugoslavia are rarely dealt with in the media of the countries that emerged on the ruins of Communist Yugoslavia, even though, remarkably, there is today greater freedom of expression and historical research there than in such western European countries as Germany and France. The elites of Croatia, Serbia, and Bosnia, largely made up of former Communists, seem to share a common interest in repressing their sometimes murky and criminal past with regard to the postwar treatment of German civilians.

The breakup of Yugoslavia in 1990–91, the events leading to it, and the war and atrocities that followed, can only be understood within a larger historical framework. As already noted, "ethnic cleansing" is nothing new. Even if one regards the former Serb-Yugoslav leader Slobodan Milošević and the other defendants being tried by the International War Crimes Tribunal in The Hague as wicked criminals, their crimes are trivial compared to those of Communist Yugoslavia's founder, Josip Broz Tito. Tito carried out "ethnic cleansing" and mass killings on a far greater scale, against Croats, Germans, and Serbs, and with the sanction of the British and American governments. His rule in Yugoslavia (1945–1980), which coincided with the "Cold War" era, was generally supported by the Western powers, which regarded his regime as a factor of stability in this often-unstable region of Europe.[15]

The wartime and post-war plight of Germans in the Balkans also provides lessons about the fate of multi-ethnic and multicultural states. The fate of the two Yugoslavias — 1919–1941 and 1944–1991 — underscores the inherent weakness of multi-ethnic states. Twice in the 20th century, multicultural Yugoslavia fell apart amid needless carnage and a spiral of hatreds among its constituent ethnic groups. One can argue, therefore, that it is better for diverse nations and cultures, let alone different races, to live apart, separated by walls, than to pretend to live in a feigned unity that hides animosities waiting to explode, leaving behind lasting resentments.

Few could foresee the savage inter-ethnic hatred and killings that swept the Balkans following the collapse of Yugoslavia in 1991, and this among peoples of relatively similar anthropological origins, albeit different cultural backgrounds. One can only speculate with foreboding about the future of the United States and Western Europe, where growing inter-racial tensions between the native populations and masses of Third World immigrants portend disaster with far bloodier consequences.

Multicultural Yugoslavia, in both its first and second incarnations, was above all the creation of, respectively, the French, British and American leaders who crafted the Versailles settlement of 1919, and the British, Soviet Russian and American leaders who met at Yalta and Potsdam in 1945. The political figures who created Yugoslavia did not represent the nations in the region, and understood little of the self-perceptions or ethnic-cultural affinities of the region's various peoples.

Although the deaths, suffering and dispossession of the ethnic Germans of the Balkans during and after World War II are well documented by both German authorities and independent scholars, they continue to be largely ignored in the major media of the United States and Europe. Why? One could speculate that if those German losses were more widely discussed and better known, they would likely stimulate an alternative perspective on World War II, and indeed of 20th century history. A greater and more widespread awareness of German civilian losses during and after World War II might well encourage a deeper discussion of the dynamics of contemporary societies. This, in turn, could significantly affect the self-perception of millions of people, forcing many to discard ideas and myths that have fashionably prevailed for more than half a century. An open debate about the causes and consequences of World War II would also tarnish the reputations of many scholars and opinion makers in the United States and Europe. Arguably, a greater awareness of the sufferings of German civilians during and after World War II, and the implications of that, could fundamentally change the policies of the United States and other major powers.

PART IV
LIBERALISM AND DEMOCRACY

DEMOCRACY REVISITED: THE ANCIENTS AND THE MODERNS

by Alain de Benoist

Translated by Tomislav Sunic from the author's book *Démocratie: Le problème* (Paris: Le Labyrinthe, 1985)

"The defenders of every kind of regime claim that it is a democracy," wrote George Orwell.[1] This does not seem to be a recent phenomenon. Guizot remarked in 1849: "So powerful is the sway of the word democracy, that no government and no party dares to live, or thinks it can, without inscribing this word on its banner."[2] This is truer today than ever before. Not everybody is a democrat, but everybody pretends to be one. There is no dictatorship that does not regard itself as a democracy. The former communist countries of Eastern Europe did not merely represent themselves as democratic, as attested by their constitutions;[3] they vaunted themselves as the only real democracies, in contrast to the "formal" democracies of the West.

The near unanimity on democracy as a word, albeit not always a fact, gives the notion of democracy a moral and almost religious content, which, from the very outset, discourages further discussion. Many authors have recognized this problem. Thus, in 1939, T. S. Eliot declared: "When a word acquires a universally sacred character ... as has today the word democracy, I begin to wonder, whether, by all it attempts to mean, it still means anything at all."[4]

Bertrand de Jouvenel was even more explicit: "The discussion on democracy, the arguments in its favor, or against it, point frequently to a degree of intellectual shallowness, because it is not quite clear what this discussion is all about."[5] Giovanni Sartori added in 1962: "In a somewhat paradoxical vein, democracy could be defined as a high-flown name for something which does not exist."[6] Julien Freund also noted, in a somewhat witty tone:

> To claim to be a democrat means little, because one can be a democrat in a contradictory manner — either in the manner of the Americans or the English, or like the East European communists, Congolese, or Cubans. It is perfectly natural that under such circumstances I refuse to be a democrat, because my neighbor might be an adherent of dictatorship while invoking the word democracy.[7]

Thus we can see that the universal propagation of the term democracy does not contribute much to clarifying the meaning of democracy. Undoubtedly, we need to go a step further.

The first idea that needs to be dismissed — an idea still cherished by some — is that democracy is a specific product of the modern era, and that democracy corresponds to a "developed stage" in the history of political regimes.[8] This does not seem to be substantiated by the facts. Democracy is neither more "modern" nor more "evolved" than other forms of governance. Governments with democratic tendencies have appeared throughout history. We note that the linear perspective used in this type of analysis can be particularly deceiving. The idea of progress, when applied to a political regime, appears devoid of meaning. If one subscribes to this type of linear reasoning, it is easy to advance the argument of the "self-evidence" of democracy, which, according to liberals, arises "spontaneously" in the realm of political affairs just as the market "spontaneously" accords with the logic of demand and supply. Jean Baechler notes:

> If we accept the hypothesis that men, as an animal species (sic), aspire spontaneously to a democratic regime that promises them security, prosperity, and liberty, we must then also conclude that, the minute these requirements have

been met, the democratic experience automatically emerges, without ever needing the framework of ideas.⁹

What exactly are these "requirements" that produce democracy, in the same manner as fire causes heat? They need closer examination.

In contrast to the Orient, absolute despotism has always been rare in Europe. Whether in ancient Rome, or in Homer's *Iliad*, Vedantic India, or among the Hittites, one can observe very early the existence of popular assemblies, both military and civilian. In Indo-European societies kings were usually elected; in fact, all ancient monarchies were first elective monarchies. Tacitus relates that among the Germans chieftains were elected on account of their valor, and kings on account of their noble birth (*reges ex nobilitate duces ex virtute sumunt*). In France, for instance, the crown was long both elective and hereditary. It was only with Pippin the Short that the king was chosen from within the same family, and only after Hugh Capet that the principle of primogeniture was adopted. In Scandinavia, the king was elected by a provincial assembly; that election had then to be confirmed by the other national assemblies.

Among the Germanic peoples the practice of "shielding" — or raising the new king on his soldiers' shields — was widespread.¹⁰ The Holy Roman Emperor was also elected, and the importance of the role of the princely electors in the history of Germany should not be neglected. By and large, it was only with the beginning of the twelfth century in Europe that elective monarchy gradually gave way to hereditary monarchy. Until the French Revolution, kings ruled with the aid of parliaments that possessed considerable executive powers. In almost all European communities it was long the status of freeman that conferred political rights on the citizen. "Citizens" were constituent members of free popular communes, which, among other things, possessed their own municipal charters, and sovereign rulers were surrounded by councils in the decision-making process. Moreover, the influence of customary law on juridical practice was an index of popular "participation" in defining the laws. In short, it cannot be stated that Europe's old monarchies were devoid of popular legitimacy.

The oldest parliament in the Western world, the *althing*, the federal assembly of Iceland, whose members gathered yearly in the inspired setting of *Thingvellir*, emerged as early as 930 A. D. Adam von Bremen wrote in 1076: "They have no king, only the laws." The *thing*, or local parliament, designated both a location and the assembly where freemen with equal political rights convened at a fixed date in order to legislate and render justice.[11] In Iceland the freeman enjoyed two inalienable privileges: he had a right to bear arms and to a seat in the thing. "The Icelanders," writes Frederick Durand "created and experienced what one could call by some uncertain yet suggestive analogy a kind of Nordic Hellas, i.e., a community of freemen who participated actively in the affairs of the community. Those communities were surprisingly well cultivated and intellectually productive, and, in addition, were united by bonds based on esteem and respect."[12]

"Scandinavian democracy is very old and one can trace its origins to the Viking era," observes Maurice Gravier.[13] In all of northern Europe this "democratic" tradition was anchored in a very strong communitarian sentiment, a propensity to "live together" (*zusammenleben*), which constantly fostered the primacy of the common interest over that of the individual. Such democracy, typically, included a certain hierarchical structure, which explains why one could describe it as "aristo-democracy." This tradition, based also on the concept of mutual assistance and a sense of common responsibility, remains alive in many countries today, for instance, in Switzerland.

The belief that the people were originally the possessor of power was common throughout the Middle Ages. Whereas the clergy limited itself to the proclamation *omnis potestas a Deo*, other theorists argued that power could emanate from God only through the intercession of the people. The belief of the "power of divine right" should therefore be seen in an indirect form, and not excluding the reality of the people. Thus, Marsilius of Padua did not hesitate to proclaim the concept of popular sovereignty; significantly, he did so in order to defend the supremacy of the emperor (at the time, Ludwig of Bavaria) over the Church. The idea of linking the principle of the people to its leaders was further emphasized in the formula *populus et proceres* (the people and the nobles), which appears frequently in old texts.

Here we should recall the democratic tendencies evident in ancient Rome,[14] the republics of medieval Italy, the French and Flemish communes, the Hanseatic municipalities, and the free Swiss cantons. Let us further note the ancient *boerenvrijheid* ("peasants' freedom") that prevailed in medieval Frisian provinces and whose equivalent could be found along the North Sea, in the Low Lands, in Flanders, Scandinavia, Germany, Austria, and Switzerland. Finally, it is worth mentioning the existence of important communal movements based on free corporate structures, the function of which was to provide mutual help and to pursue economic and political goals. Sometimes these movements clashed with king and Church, which were supported by the burgeoning bourgeoisie. At other times, however, communal movements backed the monarchy in its fight against the feudal lords, thus contributing to the rise of the mercantile bourgeoisie.[15]

In reality, most political regimes throughout history can be qualified as mixed ones. "All ancient democracies," writes François Perroux, "were governed by a de facto or de jure aristocracy, unless they were governed by a monarchical principle."[16] According to Aristotle, Solon's constitution was oligarchic in terms of its Areopagus, aristocratic in terms of its magistrates, and democratic in terms of the make-up of its tribunals. It combined the advantages of each type of government. Similarly, Polybius argues that Rome was, in view of the power of its consuls, an elective monarchy; in regard to the powers of the Senate, an aristocracy; and regarding the rights of the people, a democracy. Cicero, in his *De Republica*, advances a similar view. Monarchy need not exclude democracy, as is shown by the example of contemporary constitutional and parliamentary monarchies today. After all, it was the French monarchy in 1789 that convoked the Estates-General. "[D]emocracy, taken in the broad sense, admits of various forms," observed Pope Pius XII, "and can be realized in monarchies as well as in republics."[17]

Let us add that the experience of modern times demonstrates that neither government nor institutions need play a decisive role in shaping social life. Comparable types of government may disguise different types of societies, whereas different governmental forms may mask identical social realities. (Western societies today have an extremely homogeneous structure even though their institutions and constitutions sometimes offer substantial differences.)

So now the task of defining democracy appears even more difficult. The etymological approach has its limits. According to its original meaning, democracy means "the power of the people". Yet this power can be interpreted in different ways. The most reasonable approach, therefore, seems to be the historical approach — an approach that explains "genuine" democracy as first of all the political system of that ancient people that simultaneously invented the word and the fact.

The notion of democracy did not appear at all in modern political thought until the eighteenth century. Even then its mention was sporadic, frequently with a pejorative connotation. Prior to the French Revolution the most "advanced" philosophers had fantasized about mixed regimes combining the advantages of an "enlightened" monarchy and popular representation. Montesquieu acknowledged that a people could have the right to control, but not the right to rule. Not a single revolutionary constitution claimed to have been inspired by "democratic" principles. Robespierre was, indeed, a rare person for that epoch, who toward the end of his reign, explicitly mentioned democracy (which did not, however, contribute to the strengthening of his popularity in the years to come), a regime that he defined as a representative form of government, i.e., "a state in which the sovereign people, guided by laws that are of their own making, do for themselves all that they can do well, and by their delegates do all that they cannot do themselves."[18]

It was in the United States that the word democracy first became widespread, notably when the notion of "republic" was contrasted to the notion of "democracy". Its usage became current at the beginning of the nineteenth century, especially with the advent of Jacksonian democracy and the subsequent establishment of the Democratic Party. The word, in turn, crossed the Atlantic again and became firmly implanted in Europe — to the profit of the constitutional debates that filled the first half of the nineteenth century. Tocqueville's book *Democracy in America*, the success of which was considerable, made the term a household word.

Despite numerous citations, inspired by Antiquity, that adorned the philosophical and political discourse of the eighteenth century, the genuine legacy drawn from ancient democracy was at that time very weak. The philosophers seemed more enthralled with the example of Sparta than Athens. The debate "Sparta vs. Athens", frequently distorted by bias or ignorance, pitted the partisans of authoritarian egalitarianism against the tenets of moderate liberalism.[19] Rousseau, for instance, who abominated Athens, expressed sentiments that were rigorously pro-Spartiate. In his eyes, Sparta was first and foremost the city of equals (*hómoioi*). By contrast, when Camille Desmoulins thundered against Sparta, it was to denounce its excessive egalitarianism. He attacked the Girondin Brissot, that pro-Lycurgian, "who has rendered his citizens equal just as a tornado renders equal all those who are about to drown." All in all, this type of discourse remained rather shallow. The cult of Antiquity was primarily maintained as a metaphor for social regeneration, as exemplified by Saint-Just's words hurled at the Convention: "The world has been empty since the Romans; their memory can replenish it and it can augur liberty."[20]

If we wish now to continue our study of "genuine" democracy, we must once again turn to Greek democracy rather than to those regimes that the contemporary world designates by the word.

The comparison between ancient democracies and modern democracies has frequently turned into an academic exercise.[21] It is generally emphasized that the former were direct democracies, whereas the latter (due to larger areas and populations) are representative democracies. Moreover, we are frequently reminded that slaves were excluded from the Athenian democracy; consequently, the idea emerged that Athens was not so democratic, after all. These two affirmations fall somewhat short of satisfying answers.

Readied by political and social evolution during the sixth century B.C., as well as by reforms made possible by Solon, Athenian democracy entered its founding stage with the reforms of Cleisthenes, who returned from exile in 508 B.C. Firmly established from 460 B.C., it continued to thrive for the next one hundred and fifty years. Pericles, who succeeded Ephialtes in 461 B.C., gave democracy an extraordinary reputation, which did not at all prevent him from exercising, for more than thirty years, a quasi-royal authority over the city.[22]

For the Greeks democracy was primarily defined by its relationship to two other systems: tyranny and aristocracy.[23] Democracy presupposed three conditions: isonomy (equality before laws); isotimy (equal rights to accede to all public offices); and isegory (liberty of expression). This was direct democracy, known also as "face to face" democracy, since all citizens were allowed to take part in the *ekklesía*, or Assembly. Deliberations were prepared by the *boulé* (Council), although in fact it was the popular assembly that made policy. The popular assembly nominated ambassadors; decided over the issue of war and peace, preparing military expeditions or bringing an end to hostilities; investigated the performance of magistrates; issued decrees; ratified laws; bestowed the rights of citizenship; and deliberated on matters of Athenian security. In short, writes Jacqueline de Romilly, "the people ruled, instead of being ruled by elected individuals." She cites the text of the oath given by the Athenians: "I will kill whoever by word, deed, vote, or hand attempts to destroy democracy … And should somebody else kill him I will hold him in high esteem before the gods and divine powers, as if he had killed a public enemy."[24]

Democracy in Athens meant first and foremost a community of citizens, that is, a community of people gathered in the *ekklesía*. Citizens were classified according to their membership in a *deme* — a grouping that had a territorial, social, and administrative significance. The term *démos*, which is of Doric origin, designates those who live in a given territory, with the territory constituting a place of origin and determining civic status.[25] To some extent *démos* and *ethnos* coincide: democracy could not be conceived in relationship to the individual, but only in the relationship to the polis, that is to say, to the city in its capacity as an organized community. Slaves were excluded from voting not because they were slaves, but because they were not citizens. We seem shocked by this today, yet, after all, which democracy has ever given voting rights to non-citizens?[26]

The notions of citizenship, liberty, or equality of political rights, as well as of popular sovereignty, were intimately interrelated. The most essential element in the notion of citizenship was someone's origin and heritage. Pericles was the "son of Xanthippus from the deme of Cholargus." Beginning in 451 B.C., one had to be born of an Athenian mother and father in order to become a citizen. Defined by his heritage, the citizen (*polítes*) is opposed to *idiótes*, the non-citizen — a designation that quickly took on a pejorative meaning (from the notion of the rootless individual one arrived at the notion of "idiot"). Citizenship, as function, derived thus from the notion of citizenship as status, which was the exclusive prerogative of birth. To be a citizen meant, in the fullest sense of the word, to have a homeland, that is, to have both a homeland and a history. One is born an Athenian — one does not become one (with rare exceptions). Furthermore, the Athenian tradition discouraged mixed marriages. Political equality, established by law, flowed from common origins that sanctioned it as well. Only birth conferred individual *politeía*.[27]

Democracy was rooted in the concept of autochthonous citizenship, which intimately linked its exercise to the origins of those who exercised it. The Athenians in the fifth century celebrated themselves as "the autochthonous people of great Athens," and it was within that founding myth that they placed the pivot of their democracy.[28]

In Greek, as well as in Latin, liberty proceeds from someone's origin. Free man *(e)leudheros* (Greek *eleútheros*), is primarily he who belongs to a certain "stock" (cf. in Latin the word *liberi*, "children"). "To be born of a good stock is to be free," writes Emile Benveniste, "this is one and the same."[29] Similarly, in the German language, the kinship between the words *frei*, "free", and *Freund*, "friend", indicates that in the beginning, liberty sanctioned mutual relationship. The Indo-European root *leudh-*, from which derive simultaneously the Latin *liber* and the Greek *eleútheros*, also served to designate "people" in the sense of a national group (cf. Old Slavonic *ljudú*, "people"; German *Leute*, "people", both of which derive from the root evoking the idea of "growth and development").

The original meaning of the word "liberty" does not suggest at all "liberation" — in a sense of emancipation from collectivity. Instead, it implies inheritance — which alone confers liberty. Thus, when the Greeks spoke of liberty, they did not have in mind the right to break away from the tutelage of the city or the right to rid themselves of the constraints to which each citizen was bound. Rather, what they had in mind was the right, but also the political capability, guaranteed by law, to participate in the life of the city, to vote in the assembly, to elect magistrates, etc. Liberty did not legitimize secession; instead, it sanctioned its very opposite: the bond that tied the person to his city. This was not liberty-autonomy, but a liberty-participation; it was not meant to reach beyond the community, but was practised solely in the framework of the polis. Liberty meant adherence. The "liberty" of an individual without heritage, i.e. of a deracinated individual, was completely devoid of any meaning.

If we therefore assume that liberty was directly linked to the notion of democracy, then it must be added that liberty meant first and foremost the liberty of the people, from which subsequently the liberty of citizens proceeds. In other words, only the liberty of the people (or of the city) can lay the foundations for the equality of political and individual rights, i.e., rights enjoyed by individuals in the capacity of citizens. Liberty presupposes independence as its first condition. Man lives in society, and therefore individual liberty cannot exist without collective liberty. Among the Greeks, individuals were free because (and in so far as) their city was free.

When Aristotle defines man as a "political animal", as a social being, when he asserts that the city precedes the individual and that only within society can the individual achieve his potential (*Politics*, 1253a 19–20), he also suggests that man should not be detached from his role of citizen, a person living in the framework of an organized community, of a *polis*, or a *civitas*. Aristotle's views stand in contrast to the concept of modern liberalism, which posits that the individual precedes society, and that man, in the capacity of a self-sufficient individual, is at once something more than just a citizen.[30]

Hence, in a "community of freemen", individual interests must never prevail over common interests. "All constitutions whose objectives are common interest," writes Aristotle, "are in accordance with absolute justice. By contrast, those whose objective is the personal interest of the governors tend to be defective." (*Politics*, 1279a 17sq). In contrast to what one can see, for instance, in Euripides' works, the city in Aeschylus' tragedies is regularly described as a communal entity. "This sense of community," writes Moses I. Finley, "fortified by the state religion, the myths and traditions, was the essential source of success in Athenian democracy."[31]

In Greece, adds Finley, "liberty meant the rule of law and participation in the decision-making process — and not necessarily the enjoyment of inalienable rights."[32] The law is identified with the genius of the city. "To obey the law meant to be devoted with zeal to the will of the community," observes Paul Veyne.[33] As Cicero wrote, only liberty can pave the way for legality: "*Legum ... servi sumus ut liberi esse possimus*" ("We are the servants of the law in order that we can be free," *Oratio pro Cluentio*, 53.)

In his attempt to show that liberty is the fundamental principle of democracy (*Politics, VII*, 1), Aristotle succeeds in de-emphasizing the factor of equality. For the Greeks equality was only one means to democracy, though it could be an important one. Political equality, however, had to emanate from citizenship, i.e., from belonging to a given people. From this it follows that members of the same people (of the same city), irrespective of their differences, shared the desire to be citizens in the same and equal manner. This equality of rights by no means reflects a belief in natural equality. The equal right of all citizens to participate in the assembly does not mean that men are by nature equal (nor that it would be preferable that they were), but rather that they derive from their common heritage a common capacity to exercise the right of suffrage, which is the privilege of citizens. As the appropriate means to this *téchne*, equality remains exterior to man. This process, as much as it represents the logical consequence of common heritage, is also the condition for common participation. In the eyes of the ancient Greeks it was considered natural that all citizens be associated with political life not by virtue of universal and imprescriptible rights of humans as such, but from the fact of common citizenship. In the last analysis, the crucial notion was not equality but citizenship. Greek democracy was that form of government in which each citizen saw his liberty as firmly founded on an equality that conferred on him the right to civic and political liberties.

The study of ancient democracy has elicited divergent views from contemporary authors. For some, Athenian democracy is an admirable example of civic responsibility (Francesco Nitti); for others it evokes the realm of "activist" political parties (Paul Veyne); for yet others, ancient democracy is essentially totalitarian (Giovanni Sartori).[34] In general, everybody seems to concur that the difference between ancient democracy and modern democracy is considerable. Curiously, it is modern democracy that is used as a criterion for the democratic consistency of the former. This type of reasoning sounds rather odd. As we have observed, it was only belatedly that those modern national governments, today styled "democracies", came to identify themselves with this word. Consequently, after observers began inquiring into ancient democracy, and realized that it was different from modern democracy, they drew the conclusion that ancient democracy was "less democratic" than modern democracy. But, in reality, should we not proceed from the inverse type of reasoning? It must be reiterated that democracy was born in Athens in the fifth century B.C. Therefore, it is Athenian democracy (regardless of one's judgments for or against it) that should be used as an example of a "genuine" type of democracy. Granted that contemporary democratic regimes differ from Athenian democracy, we must then assume that they differ from democracy of any kind. We can see again where this irks most of our contemporaries. Since nowadays everyone boasts of being a perfect democrat, and given the fact that Greek democracy resembles not at all those before our eyes, it is naturally the Greeks who must bear the brunt of being "less democratic"! We thus arrive at the paradox that Greek democracy, in which the people participated daily in the exercise of power, is disqualified on the grounds that it does not fit into the concept of modern democracy, in which the people, at best, participate only indirectly in political life.

There should be no doubt that ancient democracies and modern democracies are systems entirely distinct from each other. Even the parallels that have been sought between them are fallacious. They have only the name in common, since both have resulted from completely different historical processes.

Wherein does this difference lie? It would be wrong to assume that it is related to either the "direct" or "indirect" nature of the decision-making process. Each of them has a different concept of man and a different concept of the world, as well as a different vision of social bonds. The democracy of Antiquity was communitarian and "holist"; modern democracy is primarily individualist. Ancient democracy defined citizenship by a man's origins, and provided him with the opportunity to participate in the life of the city. Modern democracy organizes atomized individuals into citizens viewed through the prism of abstract egalitarianism. Ancient democracy was based on the idea of organic community; modern democracy, heir to Christianity and the philosophy of the Enlightenment, on the individual. In both cases the meaning of the words "city", "people", "nation", and "liberty" are totally changed.

To argue, therefore, within this context, that Greek democracy was a direct democracy only because it encompassed a small number of citizens, falls short of a satisfying answer. Direct democracy need not be associated with a limited number of citizens. It is primarily associated with the notion of a relatively homogeneous people that is conscious of what makes it a people. The effective functioning of both Greek and Icelandic democracy was the result of cultural cohesion and a clear sense of shared heritage. The closer the members of a community are to each other, the more likely they are to have common sentiments, identical values, and the same way of looking at the world, and the easier it is for them to make collective decisions without needing the help of mediators.

In contrast, having ceased to be places of collectively lived meaning, modern societies require a multitude of intermediaries. The aspirations that surface in this type of democracy spring from contradictory value systems that are no longer reconcilable with unified decisions. Ever since Benjamin Constant (*De la liberté des Anciens comparée à celle des Modernes*, 1819), we have been able to measure to what degree, under the impact of individualist and egalitarian ideologies, the notion of liberty has changed. Therefore, to return to a Greek concept of democracy does not mean nurturing a shallow hope of "face to face" social transparency. Rather, it means re-appropriating, as well as adapting to the modern world, the concept of the people and community — concepts that have been eclipsed by two thousand years of egalitarianism, rationalism, and the exaltation of the rootless individual.

LIBERALISM OR DEMOCRACY? CARL SCHMITT AND APOLITICAL DEMOCRACY

"Les temps sont durs; les idées sont molles." François-Bernard Huyghe, *La Soft-Idéologie*, 1987

Growing imprecision in the language of political discourse has turned virtually everyone into a democrat or, at least, an aspiring democrat. East, West, North, South, in all corners of the world, politicians and intellectuals profess the democratic ideal, as if their rhetorical homage to democracy could substitute for the frequently poor showing of their democratic institutions.[1] Does liberal democracy — and this is what we take as our criterion for the "best of all democracies" — mean more political participation or less, and how does one explain that in liberal democracy electoral interests have been declining for years? Judging by voter turnout, almost everywhere in the West the functioning of liberal democracy has been accompanied by political demobilization and a retreat from political participation.² Might it be that consciously or unconsciously, the citizens of liberal democracies realize that their ballot choices can in no substantial manner affect the way their societies are governed, or worse, that the rites of liberal democracy are an elegant smoke screen for the absence of self-government?

Liberal Parenthesis and the End of the Muscled State

This paper will argue both that democracy is not necessarily an accompanying feature of liberalism and that liberal democracy may often be the very opposite of what democracy is supposed to mean. Through the arguments of Carl Schmitt, I shall demonstrate that: 1) democracy can have a different meaning in liberal society than in non-liberal society, 2) the de-politicization of liberal democracy is the direct result of voter mistrust in the liberal political class, and 3) liberal democracy in multi-ethnic countries is likely to face serious challenges in the future.

Over the period of the last fifty years, Western societies have witnessed a rapid eclipse of "hard" politics. Theological fanaticism, ideological ferocity, and politics of power, all of which have until recently rocked European states, have become things of the past. The influence of radical left-wing or right-wing parties and ideologies has waned. "High" politics, as a traditional action and interaction process between the rulers and the ruled, and as a guide for purported national destiny, seems to have become obsolete. With the collapse of Communism in the East, modern liberal democracies in the West appear today as the only alternative forms of government on the barren political and ideological landscape. Moreover, in view of the recent collapse of totalitarian ideologies, liberal democracy seems to have gained even more legitimacy, all the more so as it successfully accommodates differing political views. Western liberal democracy, people believe, can satisfy diverse and disparate opinions, and can continue to function even when these are non-democratic and anti-liberal.

For Schmitt, liberal tolerance towards opposing political views is deceiving. In all of his works, and particularly in *Verfassungslehre* and

Die geistesgeschichtliche Lage des heutigen Parlamentarismus, he points to differences between liberalism and democracy, asserting that liberalism, by its nature, is hostile to all political projects. In liberal democracy, writes Schmitt, "politics, far from being the concern of an elite, has become the despised business of a rather dubious class of persons."[3] One may add that liberal democracy does not appear to be in need of political projects. With its vast technological infrastructure and the free market network, argues Schmitt, liberal democracy has no difficulty in rendering all contending beliefs and opposing ideologies inoffensive, or, at worst, ridiculous.[4]

In liberal democracy, in which most collective projects have already been delegitimatized by belief in individualism and in the private pursuit of economic well-being, "it cannot be required, from any thinkable point of view, that anyone lays down his life, in the interest of the undisturbed functioning [of this society.]"[5] Little by little, liberal democracy makes all political projects unattractive and unpopular, unless they appeal to economic interests. Liberal democracy, writes Schmitt, seems to be fitted for a rational, secularized environment in which the state is reduced to a "night-watchman" supervising economic transactions. The state becomes a sort of inoffensive "mini-state" [*Minimalstaat*] or *stato neutrale.*[6] One could almost argue that the strength of liberal democracy lies not in its aggressive posturing of its liberal ideal, but rather in its renunciation of all political ideals, including its own.

To some extent, this apolitical inertia appears today stronger than ever before, since no valid challenger to liberal democracy appears on the horizon. What a stark contrast to the time prior to World War II, when radical left- and right-wing ideologies managed to draw substantial support from political and intellectual elites! Might it be that the *Entzauberung* of politics has gone so far as to contribute to the strengthening of apolitical liberal democracy? Very revealing, indeed, appears the change in the behavior of modern elites in liberal democracies; left, right, and center barely differ in their public statements or in their political vocabulary. Their styles may differ, but their messages remain virtually the same. The "soft" and apolitical discourse of modern liberal princes, as one French observer recently wrote, prompts the "liberal-socialist" to exclaim: "I will die from loving your beautiful eyes Marquise." And to this the "socialist-liberal" responds: "Marquise, from loving your beautiful eyes, I will die."[7] Left-wing agendas are so often tainted with right-wing rhetoric that they appear to incorporate conservative principles. Conversely, right-wing politicians often sound like disillusioned leftists on many issues of domestic and foreign policy. In liberal democracy, all parties across the political spectrum, regardless of their declaratory differences, seem to be in agreement on one thing: democracy functions best when the political arena is reduced to its minimum and the economic and juridical spheres are expanded to their maximum.

Part of the problem may result from the very nature of liberalism. Schmitt suggests that the notions of liberalism and democracy "have to be distinguished from one another so that the patchwork picture that makes up modern mass democracy can be recognized."[8] As Schmitt notes, democracy is the antithesis of liberalism, because "democracy ... attempts to realize an identity of the governed and the governors, and thus it confronts the parliament as an inconceivable and outmoded institution."[9]

Organic Democracy vs. Apolitical Democracy

True democracy, for Schmitt, means popular sovereignty, whereas liberal democracy and liberal parliament aim at curbing popular power. For Schmitt, if democratic identity is taken seriously, only the people should decide on their political destiny, and not liberal representatives, because "no other constitutional institution can withstand the sole criterion of the people's will, however it is expressed."[10] Liberal democracy, argues Schmitt, is nothing else but a euphemism for a system consecrating the demise of politics and thus destroying true democracy. But a question arises: why, given liberalism's history of tolerance and its propensity to accommodate diverse groups, does Schmitt adamantly reject liberal democracy? Has not liberalism, particularly in the light of recent experiences with "muscled ideologies", proven its superior and humane nature?

The crux of Schmitt's stance lies in his conviction that the concept of "liberal democracy" is semantic nonsense. In its place, Schmitt seems to suggest both a new definition of democracy and a new notion of the political. According to Schmitt, "democracy requires, first homogeneity and second — if the need arises — elimination or eradication of heterogeneity."[11] Homogeneity and the concomitant elimination of heterogeneity are the two pillars of Schmitt's democracy, something that stands in sharp contrast to liberal party systems and the fragmentation of the body politic. Democratic homogeneity, according to Schmitt, presupposes a common historical memory, common roots, and a common vision of the future, all of which can subsist only in a polity where the people speak with one voice. "As long as the people has the will to political existence," writes Schmitt, "it must remain above all formulations and normative beliefs … The most natural way of the direct expression of the people's will is by approvals or disapprovals of the gathered crowd, i.e., the acclamation."[12] To be sure, with his definition of homogeneous democracy that results from the popular will, Schmitt appears to be holding the value of the traditional community above that of civil society that, for the last century, has been the hallmark of liberal democracy.[13] One may therefore wonder to what extent can Schmitt's "organic" democracy be applicable to the highly fractured societies of the West, let alone to an ethnically fragmented America.

Schmitt insists that "the central concept of democracy is the people (*Volk*), not mankind [*Menschheit*]. . . . There can be — if democracy takes a political form — only popular democracy, but not a democracy of mankind [*Es gibt eine Volksdemokratie und keine Menschheitsdemokratie*]."[14] Naturally, this vision of "ethnic" democracy collides with modern liberal democracy, one of the purposes of which, its proponents claim, is to transcend ethnic differences in pluralistic societies. Schmitt's "ethnic" democracy must be seen as the reflection of the uniqueness of a given people who oppose imitations of their democracy by other peoples or races. Since Schmitt's democracy bears a resemblance to ancient Greek democracy, critics must wonder how feasible this democracy can be today. Transplanted into the twentieth century, this democratic anachronism will appear disturbing, not least because it will remind some of both fascist corporate and Third World states with their strict laws on ethnic and cultural homogeneity. Schmitt confirms these misgivings when he states that "a democracy demonstrates its political power by knowing how to refuse or keep at bay something foreign and unequal that threatens its homogeneity [*das Fremde und Ungleiche ... zu beseitigen oder fernzuhalten*]."[15] Any advocate of liberal democracy in modern multicultural societies could complain that Schmitt's democracy excludes those whose birth, race, or simply religious or ideological affiliation is found incompatible with a restricted democracy. Foreign may be a foreign idea that is seen to threaten democracy, and a foreigner may be somebody who is viewed as unfit to participate in the body politic because of his race or creed. In other words, one could easily suspect Schmitt of endorsing the kind of democracy that approximates the "total state."

Nor does Schmitt treat the liberal principles of legality with much sympathy. In his essay *Legalität und Legitimität,* Schmitt argues that each kind of liberal democracy creates the illusion of freedom by according to each political group and opposing opinion a fair amount of freedom of expression as well as a guaranteed legal path to accomplish its goal in a peaceful manner.[16] Such an attitude to legal rights is contrary to the notion of democracy, and eventually leads to anarchy, argues Schmitt, because legality in a true democracy must always be the expression of the popular will and not the expression of factional interests. "Law is the expression of the will of the people (*lex est quod populus jubet*)," writes Schmitt,[17] and in no way can law be a manifestation of an anonymous representative or a parliamentarian who solely looks after interests of his narrow constituency. "Indeed," continues Schmitt, "an ethnically homogeneous and historical people has all the prerequisites to uphold justice and remain democratic, provided it always asserts its will."[18] Of course, one may argue that Schmitt had in mind a form of populist democracy reminiscent of the 1930s' plebiscitary dictatorships that scorned both parliamentary parties and organized elections. In his *Verfassungslehre*, Schmitt attacks free parliamentary elections for creating, through secret balloting, a mechanism that "transforms the citizen (*citoyen*), that is, a specifically democratic and *political* figure, into a private person who only expresses his private opinion and gives his vote."[19] Here Schmitt seems to be consistent with his earlier remarks about ethnic homogeneity. For Schmitt, the much-vaunted "public opinion", that liberals equate with the notion of political tolerance, is actually a contradiction in terms, because a system that is obsessed with privacy inevitably shies away from political openness. True and organic democracy, according to Schmitt, is threatened by liberal secret balloting, and "the result is the sum of private opinions."[20] Schmitt goes on to say that "the methods of today's popular elections [*Volkswahl*] and referendums [*Volksentscheid*] in modern democracy, in no way contain the procedure for genuine popular elections; instead, they organize a procedure for the elections of the individuals based on the total sum of independent ballot papers."[21]

Predictably, Schmitt's view of democratic equality is dependent upon his belief that democracy entails social homogeneity, an idea Schmitt develops more fully in *Verfassungslehre* and *The Crisis of Parliamentary Democracy*.[22, 23] Although liberal democracy upholds the legal equality of individuals, it ignores the equality of rooted citizens. Liberal democracy merely provides for the equality of atomized individuals whose ethnic, cultural, or racial bonds are so weakened or diluted that they can no longer be viewed as equal inheritors of a common cultural memory and a common vision of the future. Undoubtedly, equality and democracy, for Schmitt, are inseparable. Equality in a genuine organic democracy always takes place among "equals of the same kind (*Gleichartigen*)." This corresponds to Schmitt's earlier assertions that "equal rights make good sense where homogeneity exists" (p. 32). Could one infer from these brief descriptions of democratic equality that in an ethnically or ideologically fragmented society equality can never be attained? One might argue that by transferring the *political* discourse of equality to the *juridical* sphere, liberal democracy has elegantly masked glaring inequality in another sphere — that of economics. One could agree with Schmitt that liberal democracy, as much as it heralds "human rights" and legal equality and proudly boasts of "equality of (economic) opportunity", encourages material disparities. Indeed, inequality in liberal democracy has not disappeared, and, in accordance with the Schmitt's observations regarding the shifts in the political sphere, another sphere in which substantial inequality prevails (today, for example the economic sphere), will dominate politics. Small wonder that, in view of its contradictory approach to equality, liberal democracy has been under constant fire from the left and the right.[24]

To sum up, Schmitt rejects liberal democracy on several counts:

1) liberal democracy is not "demokrasia", because it does not foster the identity of the governed and the governors;

2) liberal democracy reduces the political arena, and thus creates an apolitical society, and;

3) in upholding legal equality, and pursuant to its constant search for the wealth that will win it support, liberal democracy results in glaring economic inequality.

The Rule of the People or the Rule of Atomized Individuals?

From the etymological and historical points of view, Schmitt's criticism of liberal democracy merits attention. Democracy signifies the rule of the people, a specific people with a common ethnic background, and not the people construed, after the manner of some liberal democracies, as the atomized agglomeration flowing from a cultural "melting pot." But if one assumes that a new type of homogeneity can develop, e.g., homogeneity caused by technological progress, then one cannot dispute the functionality of a liberal democracy in which the homogenized citizens remain thoroughly apolitical: Hypothetically speaking, political issues in the decades to come may no longer be ethnicity, religions, nation-states, economics, or even technology, but other issues that could "homogenize" citizens. Whether democracy in the twenty-first century will be based on apolitical consensus remains to be seen. Schmitt sincerely feared that the apoliticism of "global liberal democracy" under the aegis of the United States could become a dangerous predicament for all, leading not to global peace but to global servitude.[25] As of today, however, liberal democracy still serves as a normative concept for many countries, but whether this will remain so is an open question.

In view of the increased ethnic fragmentation and continued economic disparities in the world, it seems that Schmitt's analysis may contain a grain of truth. The American experience with liberal democracy has so far been tolerable: that is, the U.S. has shown that it can function as a heterogeneous multi-ethnic society even when, contrary to Schmitt's fears, the level of political and historical consciousness remains very low. Yet, the liberal democratic experiment elsewhere has been less successful. Recent attempts to introduce liberal democracy into the multi-ethnic states of Eastern Europe have paradoxically speeded up their dissolution or, at best, weakened their legitimacy. The cases of the multi-ethnic Soviet Union and the now-defunct Yugoslavia — countries in endless struggles to find lasting legitimacy — are very revealing and confirm Schmitt's predictions that democracy functions best, at least in some places, in ethnically homogeneous societies.[26] In light of the collapse of Communism and Fascism, one is tempted to argue that liberal democracy is the wave of the future. Yet, exported American political ideals will vary according to the countries and the peoples among whom they take root. Even the highly Americanized European countries practice a different brand of liberal democracy from what one encounters in America.

Schmitt observes that liberalism, while focusing on the private rights of individuals, contributes to the weakening of the sense of community. Liberal democracy typifies, for Schmitt, a polity that cripples the sense of responsibility and renders society vulnerable to enemies both from within and without. By contrast, his idea of organic democracy is not designed for individuals who yearn to reduce political activity to the private pursuit of happiness; rather, organic, classical democracy means "the identity of the governors and the governed, of the rulers and the ruled, of those who receive orders and of those who abide by them."[27] In such a polity, laws and even the constitution itself can be changed on a short notice because the people, acting as their own legislators, do not employ parliamentary representatives.

Schmitt's democracy could easily pass for what liberal theorists would identify as a disagreeable dictatorship. Would Schmitt object to that? Hardly. In fact, he does not discount the compatibility of democracy with Communism or even Fascism. "Bolshevism and Fascism," writes Schmitt, "by contrast, are like all dictatorships certainly antiliberal, but not necessarily antidemocratic."[28] Both Communism and Fascism strive towards homogeneity (even if they attempt to be homogeneous by force) by banning all opposition. Communism, for which the resolute anti-Bolshevik Schmitt had no sympathy, can surely be democratic, at least in its normative and utopian stage. The "educational dictatorship" of Communism, remarks Schmitt, may suspend democracy in the name of democracy, "because it shows that dictatorship is not antithetical to democracy."[29] In a true democracy, legitimacy derives not from parliamentary maneuvers, but from acclamation and popular referenda. "There is no democracy and no state without public opinion, and no state without acclamation," writes Schmitt.[30] By contrast, liberal democracy with its main pillars, viz., individual liberty and the separation of powers, opposes public opinion and, thus, must stand forth as the enemy of true democracy. Or, are we dealing here with words that have become equivocal? According to Schmitt, "democratic principles mean that the people as a whole decides and governs as a sovereign."[31] One could argue that democracy must be a form of *kratos*, an exercise, not a limiting, of power. Julien Freund, a French Schmittian, concurs that "democracy is a 'kratos.'" As such it presupposes, just like any other regime, the presence and the validity of an authority."[32] With its separation of powers, the atomization of the body politic, and the neutralization of politics, liberal democracy deviates from this model.

Conclusion: The Liberal "Dictatorship of Well-Being"

If one assumes that Schmitt's "total democracy" excludes those with different views and different ethnic origins, could not one also argue that liberal democracy excludes by virtue of applying an "apolitical" central field? Through apolitical economics and social censure, liberal democracy paradoxically generates a homogeneous consumer culture. Is this not a form of "soft" punishment imposed on those who behave incorrectly? Long ago, in his observations about democracy in America, Tocqueville pointed out the dangers of apolitical "democratic despotism." "If despotism were to be established among the democratic nations of our days, it might assume a different character; it would be more extensive and milder; it would degrade men without tormenting them."[33] Perhaps this "democratic despotism" is already at work in liberal democracies. A person nowadays can be effectively silenced by being attacked as socially insensitive.

Contemporary liberal democracy amply demonstrates the degree to which the economic and spiritual needs of citizens have become homogenized. Citizens act more and more indistinguishably in a new form of "dictatorship of well-being."[34] Certainly, this homogeneity in liberal democracy does not spring from coercion or physical exclusion, but rather from the voter's sense of futility. Official censorship is no longer needed as the ostracism resulting from political incorrectness becomes daily more obvious. Citizens appear more and more apathetic, knowing in all likelihood that, regardless of their participation, the current power structure will remain intact. Moreover, liberal democrats, as much as they complain about the intolerance of others, often appear themselves scornful of those who doubt liberal doctrines, particularly the beliefs in rationalism and economic progress. The French thinker Georges Sorel, who influenced Schmitt, remarked long ago that to protest against the illusion of liberal rationalism means to be immediately branded as the enemy of democracy.[35] One must agree that, irrespective of its relative tolerance in the past, liberal democracy appears to have its own sets of values and normative claims. Its adherents, for example, are supposed to believe that liberal democracy operates entirely by law. Julien Freund detects in liberal legalism "an irenic concept" of law, "a juridical utopia ... which ignores the real effects of political, economic and other relations."[36] No wonder that Schmitt and his followers have difficulty in accepting the liberal vision of the rule of law, or in believing that such a vision can "suspend decisive [ideological] battle through endless discussion."[37] In its quest for a perfect and apolitical society, liberal democracy develops in such a manner that "public discussion [becomes] an empty formality",[38] reduced to shallow discourse in which different opinions are no longer debated. A modern liberal politician increasingly resembles an "entertainer" whose goal is not to persuade the opponent about the validity of his political programs, but primarily to obtain electoral majorities.[39]

In hindsight, it should not appear strange that liberal democracy, which claims to be open to all kinds of technological, economic and sexual "revolutions", remains opposed to anything that would question its apolitical status quo. It comes, therefore, as no surprise that even the word "politics" is increasingly being supplanted by the more anodyne word "policy", just as prime ministers in liberal democracies are increasingly recruited from economists and businessmen.

Schmitt correctly predicted that even the defeat of Fascism and the recent collapse of Communism would not forestall a political crisis in liberal democracy. For Schmitt, this crisis is inherent in the very nature of liberalism, and will keep recurring even if all anti-liberal ideologies disappear. The crisis in liberal parliamentary democracy is the result of the contradiction between liberalism and democracy; it is, in Schmittian language, the crisis of a society that attempts to be both liberal and democratic, universal and legalistic, but at the same time committed to the self-government of peoples.

One does not need to go far in search of fields that may politicize and then polarize modern liberal democracy. Recent events in Eastern Europe, the explosion of nationalisms all around the world, racial clashes in the liberal democratic West — these and other "disruptive" developments demonstrate that the liberal faith may have a stormy future. Liberal democracy may fall prey to its own sense of infallibility if it concludes that nobody is willing to challenge it. This would be a mistake. For neither the demise of Fascism nor the recent collapse of Communism has ushered in a more peaceful epoch. Although Western Europe and America are now enjoying a comfortable respite from power politics, new conflicts have erupted in their societies over multiculturalism and human rights. The end of liberal apolitical democracy and the return of "hard" politics may be taking place within liberal democratic societies.

THE LIBERAL DOUBLE-TALK AND ITS LEXICAL AND LEGAL CONSEQUENCES

Language is a potent weapon for legitimizing any political system. In many instances the language in the liberal West is reminiscent of the communist language of the old Soviet Union, although liberal media and politicians use words and phrases that are less abrasive and less value-loaded than words used by the old Communist officials and their state-run media. In Western academe, media, and public places, a level of communication has been reached that avoids confrontational discourse and that resorts to words devoid of substantive meaning. Generally speaking, the liberal system shuns negative hyperboles and skirts around heavy-headed qualifiers that the state-run media of the Soviet Union once used in fostering its brand of conformity and its version of political correctness. By contrast, the media in the liberal system, very much in line with its ideology of historical optimism and progress, are enamored with the overkill of morally uplifting adjectives and adverbs, often displaying words and expressions such as "free speech", "human rights", "tolerance", and "diversity". There is a wide spread assumption among modern citizens of the West that the concepts behind these flowery words must be taken as something self-evident.

There appears to be a contradiction. If free speech is something "self-evident" in liberal democracies, then the word "self-evidence" does not need to be repeated all the time; it can be uttered only once, or twice at the most. The very adjective "self-evident", so frequent in the parlance of liberal politicians may in fact hide some uncertainties and even some self-doubt on the part of those who employ it. With constant hammering of these words and expressions, particularly words such as "human rights", and "tolerance", the liberal system may be hiding something; hiding, probably, the absence of genuine free speech. To illustrate this point more clearly it may be advisable for an average citizen living in the liberal system to look at the examples of the communist rhetoric that was once saturated with similar freedom-loving terms while, in reality, there was little of freedom and even less free-speech.

Verbal Mendacity

The postmodern liberal discourse has its own arsenal of words that one can dub with the adjective "Orwellian", or better yet "double-talk", or simply call it verbal mendacity. The French use the word "wooden language" (*la langue de bois*) and the German "cement" or "concrete" language (*Betonsprache*) for depicting an arcane bureaucratic and academic lingo that never reflects political reality and whose main purpose is to lead masses to a flawed conceptualisation of political reality. Modern authors, however, tend to avoid the pejorative term "liberal double-talk", preferring instead the arcane label of "the non-cognitive language that is used for manipulative or predictive analyses."[1] Despite its softer and non-abrasive version, liberal double-talk, very similar to the communist "wooden language", has a very poor conceptual universe. Similar to the communist vernacular, it is marked by pathos and attempts to avoid the concrete. On the one hand, it tends to be aggressive and judgemental towards its critics, yet, on the other, it is full of eulogies, especially regarding its multiracial experiments. It resorts to metaphors that are seldom based on real historical analogies and are often taken out of historical context, notably when depicting its opponents with generic "shut-up" words such as "racists", "anti-Semites", or "fascists".

The choice of grammatical embellishers is consistent with the all-prevailing, liberal free market that, as a rule, must employ superlative adjectives for the free commerce of its goods and services. Ironically, there was some advantage of living under the communist linguistic umbrella. Behind the communist semiotics in Eastern Europe, there always loomed popular doubt that greatly helped ordinary citizens to decipher the political lie, and distinguish between friend and foe. The communist metalanguage could best be described as a reflection of a make-belief system in which citizens never really believed and of which everybody, including communist party dignitaries, made fun of in private. Eventually, verbal mendacity spelled the death of Communism both in the Soviet Union and Eastern Europe.

By contrast, in the liberal system, politicians and scholars, let alone the masses, still believe in every written word of the democratic discourse.[2] There seem to be far less heretics, or for that matter dissidents, who dare critically examine the syntax and semantics of the liberal double-talk. Official communication in the West perfectly matches the rule of law and can, therefore, rarely trigger a violent or a negative response among citizens. Surely, the liberal system allows mass protests and public demonstrations; it allows its critics to openly voice their disapproval of some flawed foreign policy decision. Different political and infra-political groups, hostile to the liberal system, often attempt to publicly drum-up public support on behalf or against some issue — be it against American military involvement in the Middle East, or against the fraudulent behavior of a local political representative. But, as an unwritten rule, seldom can one see rallies or mass demonstrations in Australia, America, or in Europe that would challenge the substance of parliamentary democracy and liberalism, let alone discard the ceremonial language of the liberal ruling class. Staging open protests with banners "Down with liberal democracy!", or "Parliamentary democracy sucks!", would hardly be tolerated by the system. These verbal icons represent a "no entry zone" in liberalism.

The shining examples of the double-talk in liberalism are expressions such as "political correctness", "hate speech", "diversity", "market democracy", "ethnic sensitivity training", among many, many others. It is often forgotten, though, that the coinage of these expressions is relatively recent and that their etymology remains of dubious origin. These expressions appeared in the modern liberal dictionary in the late 1970s and early 1980s and their architects are widely ignored. Seldom has a question been raised as to who had coined those words and given them their actual meaning. What strikes the eyes is the abstract nature of these expressions. The expression "political correctness" first appeared in the American language and had no explicit political meaning; it was, rather, a fun-related, derogatory expression designed for somebody who was not trendy, such as a person smoking cigarettes or having views considered not to be "in" or "cool." Gradually, and particularly after the fall of Communism, the conceptualization of political correctness, acquired a very serious and disciplinary meaning.

Examples of political eulogy and political vilification in liberalism are often couched in sentimentalist vs. animalistic words and syllabi, respectively. When the much-vaunted free press in liberalism attempts to glorify some event or some personality that fits into the canons of political rectitude, it will generally use a neutral language with sparse superlatives, with the prime intention not to subvert its readers, such as: "The democratic circles in Ukraine, who have been subject to governmental harassment, are propping up their rank and file to enable them electoral success." Such laudatory statements must be well hidden behind neutral words. By contrast when attempting to silence critics of the system who challenge the foundation of liberal democracy, the ruling elites and their frequently bankrolled journalists will use more direct words — something in the line of old Soviet stylistics, e.g.: "With their ultranationalist agenda and hate-mongering these rowdy individuals on the street of Sydney or Quebec showed once again their parentage in the monstrosity of the Nazi legacy." Clearly, the goal is to disqualify the opponent by using an all pervasive and hyperreal word "Nazism." "A prominent American conservative author

Paul Gottfried writes: "In fact, the European Left, like Canadian and Australian Left, pushes even further the trends adapted from American sources: It insists on criminalizing politically correct speech as an incitement to "fascist excess."[3]

The first conclusion one can draw is that liberalism can better fool the masses than Communism. Due to torrents of meaningless idioms, such as "human rights" and "democracy" on the one hand, and "Nazism" and "Fascism" on the other, the thought control and intellectual repression in liberalism functions far better. Therefore, in the liberal "soft" system, a motive for a would-be heretic to overthrow the system is virtually excluded. The liberal system is posited on historical finitude simply because there is no longer the communist competitor who could come up with its own real or surreal "freedom narrative." Thus, liberalism gives an impression of being the best system — simply because there are no other competing political narratives on the horizon.

What are the political implications of the liberal double-talk? It must be pointed out that liberal language is the reflection of the overall socio-demographic situation in the West. Over the last twenty years all Western states, including Australia, have undergone profound social and demographic changes; they have become "multicultural" systems. ("multicultural" being just a euphemism for a "multiracial" state). As a result of growing racial diversity, the liberal elites are aware that in order to uphold social consensus and prevent the system from possible balkanization and civil war, new words and new syntax have to be invented. It was to be expected that these new words would soon find their way into modern legislations. More and more countries in the West are adopting laws that criminalize free speech and that make political communication difficult. In fact, liberalism, similar to its communist antecedents, it is an extremely fragile system. It excludes strong political beliefs by calling its critics "radicals", which, as a result, inevitably leads to political conformity and intellectual duplicity. Modern public discourse in the West is teeming with abstract and unclear Soviet-style expressions such as "ethnic sensitivity training", "affirmative action", "antifascism", "diversity", and "holocaust studies". In order to disqualify its critics the liberal system is resorting more and more to negative expression such as "anti-Semites", or "neo-Nazi", etc. This is best observed in Western higher education and the media that, over the last thirty years, have transformed themselves into places of high commissariats of political correctness, having on their board diverse "committees on preventing racial perjuries", "ethnic diversity training programs", and in which foreign racial awareness courses have become mandatory for the faculty staff and employees. No longer are professors required to demonstrate extra skills in their subject matters; instead, they must parade with sentimental and self-deprecatory statements that, as a rule, must denigrate the European cultural heritage.

By constantly resorting to the generic word "Nazism" and by using the prefix "anti", the system actually shows its negative legitimacy. One can conclude that even if all anti-Semites and all fascists were to disappear, most likely the system would invent them by creating and recreating these words. These words have become symbols of absolute evil.

The third point about the liberal discourse that needs to be stressed is its constant recourse to the imagery of hyper-reality. By using the referent of "diversity", diverse liberal groups and infrapolitical tribes prove in fact their sameness, making dispassionate observers easily bored and tired. Nowhere is this sign of verbal hyper-reality more visible than in the constant verbal and visual featuring of Jewish Holocaust symbolism that, ironically, is creating the same saturation process among the audience as was once the case with communist victimhood. The rhetoric and imagery of Holocaust no longer function "as a site of annihilation but a medium of dissuasion."[4]

The Legal Trap

Other than as a simple part of daily jargon the expression "hate speech" does not exist in any European or American legislation. Once again, the distinction needs to be made between the legal field and lexical field, as different penal codes of different Western countries are framed in a far more sophisticated language. For instance, criminal codes in continental

Europe have all introduced laws that punish individuals uttering critical remarks against the founding myths of the liberal system. The best example is Germany, a country that often brags it has the most eloquent and most democratic Constitution on Earth. This is at least what the German ruling elites say about their judiciary, and that does not depart much from what Stalin himself said about the Soviet Constitution of 1936. The Constitution of Germany is truly superb, yet in order to get the whole idea of freedom of speech in Germany one needs to examine the country's Criminal Code and its numerous agencies that are in charge of its implementation. Thus, Article 5 of the German Constitution (The Basic Law) guarantees "freedom of speech." However, Germany's Criminal Code, Section 130, and Subsection 3, appear to be in stark contradiction to the German Basic Law. Under Section 130, of the German criminal code a German citizen, but also a non-German citizen, may be convicted, if found guilty, of breaching the law of "agitation of the people" (sedition laws). It is a similar case with Austria. It must be emphasized that there is no mention in the Criminal Code of the Federal Republic of Germany of the Holocaust or the Nazi extermination of the Jews. But based on the context of the Criminal Code this Section can arbitrarily be applied when sentencing somebody who belittles or denies National-Socialist crimes or voices critical views of the modern historiography. Moreover, a critical examination of the role of the Allies during World War may also bring some ardent historian into legal troubles.

The German language is a highly inflected language, as opposed to French and English, which are contextual languages and do not allow deliberate tinkering with prefixes or suffixes, or the creation of arbitrary compound words. By contrast, one can always create new words in the German language, a language often awash with a mass of neologisms. Thus, the title of the Article 130 of the German Criminal Code *Volksverhetzung* is a bizarre neologism and very difficult compound word that is hard to translate into English, and which on top, can be conceptualized in many opposing ways. (Popular taunting, baiting, bullying of the people, public incitement etc.) Its Subsection 3, though is stern and quite explicit and reads in English as follows:

> Whoever publicly or in a meeting approves of, denies, or renders harmless an act committed under the rule of National Socialism... shall be punished with imprisonment for not more than five years, or a fine.

If by contrast the plight of German civilians after World War II is openly discussed by a German academic or simply by some free spirit, he may run the risk of being accused of trivializing the official assumption of sole German guilt during World War II. Depending on a local legislation of some federal state in Germany an academic, although not belittling National Socialist crimes may, by inversion, fall under suspicion of "downplaying" or "trivializing" Nazi crimes — and may be fined or, worse, land in prison. Any speech or article, for instance, that may be related to events surrounding World War may have a negative anticipatory value in the eyes of the liberal inquisitors, that is to say in the eyes of the all prevailing Agency for the protection of the German Constitution (*Verfassungsschutz*). Someone's words, as in the old Soviet system, can be easily misconstrued and interpreted as an indirect belittlement of crimes committed by National Socialists.

Germany is a half-sovereign country still legally at war with the U.S.A and whose Constitution was written under the auspices of the Allies. Yet unlike other countries in the European Union, Germany has something unprecedented. Both on the state and federal levels it has that special government agency in charge of the surveillance of the Constitution, and whose sole purpose is to keep track of journalists, academics and rightwing politicians and observe the purity of their parlance and prose. The famed "Office for the Protection of the Constitution" (*Verfassungsschutz*), as the German legal scholar Josef Schüsselburner writes, "is basically an internal secret service with seventeen branch agencies (one on the level of the federation and sixteen others for each constituent federal state). In the last analysis, this boils down to saying that only the internal secret service is competent to declare a person an internal enemy of the state."[5]

In terms of free speech, contemporary France is not much better. In 1990, a law was passed on the initiative of the socialist deputy Laurent Fabius and the communist deputy Jean-Claude Gayssot. That law made it a criminal offence, punishable by a fine of up to 40,000 euros, or one year in prison, or both, to contest the truth of any of the "crimes against humanity" with which the German National Socialist leaders were charged by the London Agreement of 1945, and that was drafted for the Nuremberg Trials.[6] Similar to the German Criminal Code Section 130, there is no reference to the Holocaust or Jews in this portion of the French legislation. But at least the wording of the French so-called Fabius-Gayssot law is more explicit than the fluid German word *Volksverhetzung*. It clearly states that any Neo-Nazi activity having as a result the belittling of Nazi crimes is a criminal offence. With France and Germany being the main pillars of the European Union these laws have already given extraordinary power to local judges of EU member countries when pronouncing verdicts against anti-liberal heretics.

For fear of being called confrontational or racist, or an anti-Semite, a European politician or academic is more and more forced to exercise self-censorship. The role of intellectual elites in Europe has never been a shining one. However, with the passage of these "hate laws" into the European legislations, the cultural and academic ambiance in Europe has become sterile. Aside from a few individuals, European academics and journalists, let alone politicians, must be the masters of self-censorship and self-delusion, as well as great impresarios of their own postmodern mimicry. As seen in the case of the former communist apparatchiks in Eastern Europe, they are likely to discard their ideas as soon as they cease to be trendy, or when another political double-talk becomes fashionable.

The modern politically correct language, or liberal double-talk, is often used for separating the ignorant grass-roots masses from the upper level classes; it is the superb path to cultural and social ascension. The censorial intellectual climate in the Western media, so similar to the old Soviet propaganda, bears witness that liberal elites, at the beginning of the third millennium, are increasingly worried about the future identity of the countries in which they rule. For sure, the liberal system doesn't yet need truncheons or police force in order to enforce its truth. It can remove rebels, heretics, or simply academics, by using smear campaigns, or accusing them of "guilt by association", and by removing them from important places of decision — be it in academia, the political arena, or the media. Once the spirit of the age changes, the high priests of this new postmodern inquisition will likely be the first to dump their current truths and replace them with other voguish "self-evident" truths. This was the case with the communist ruling class, which after the break down of Communism quickly recycled itself into fervent apostles of liberalism. This will again be the case with modern liberal elites, who will not hesitate to turn into rabid racists and anti-Semites, as soon as new "self evident" truths appear on the horizon.

HISTORICAL DYNAMICS OF LIBERALISM: FROM TOTAL MARKET TO TOTAL STATE

The purpose of this essay is to critically examine the historical dynamics of liberalism and its impact on contemporary Western polities. This essay will argue

a) that liberalism today provides a comfortable ideological "retreat" for members of the intellectual élite and decision makers tired of the theological and ideological disputes that rocked Western politics for centuries;

b) that liberalism can make compromises with various brands of socialism on practically all issues except the freedom of the market place;

c) that liberalism thrives by expanding the economic arena into all aspects of life and all corners of the world, thereby gradually erasing the sense of national and historical community that had formerly provided the individual with a basic sense of identity and psychological security. This essay will also question whether liberalism, despite its remarkable success in the realm of the economy, provides an adequate bulwark against neodemocratic ideologies, or whether under some conditions it may actually stimulate their growth.

In the aftermath of the Second World War, liberalism and Marxism emerged as the two unquestionably dominant ideologies following their military success over their common rival, fascism. This brought them into direct conflict with each other, since each contended, from their own viewpoint, that the only valid political model was their own, denying the validity of their opponent's thesis. Beaud writes that when the liberal and socialist ideas began to emerge, the former quickly cloaked itself in science ("the law of supply and demand", "the iron law of wages"), while the latter had the tendency to degenerate into mysticism and sectarianism.[1]

Some critics of liberalism, such as the French economist François Perroux, pointed out that according to some extreme liberal assumptions, "everything (that) has been happening since the beginning of time (can be attributed to capitalism) as if the modern world was constructed by industrialists and merchants consulting their account books and wishing to reap profits."[2] Similar subjective attitudes, albeit from a different ideological angle, can often be heard among Marxist theorists, who in the analysis of liberal capitalism resort to value judgements colored by Marxian dialectics and accompanied by the rejection of the liberal interpretation of the concept of equality and liberty. "The fact that the dialectical method can be used for each purpose," remarks the Austrian philosopher Alexander Topitsch, "explains its extraordinary attraction and its worldwide dissemination, that can only be compared to the success of the natural rights doctrine of the eighteenth century."[3] Nevertheless, despite their real ideological discord, liberals, neo-liberals, socialists, and "socio-neoliberals", agree, at least in principle, in claiming a common heritage of rationalism, and on the rejection of all non-democratic ideologies, especially racialism. Earlier in this century, Georges Sorel, the French theorist of anarcho-syndicalism, remarked with irony that "to attempt to protest against the illusion of rationalism means to be immediately branded as the enemy of democracy."[4]

The practical conflict between the respective virtues of liberalism and socialism is today seemingly coming to a close, as some of the major Marxist regimes move in the direction of a liberalization of their economies, even though the ideological debate is by no means settled amongst intellectuals. Undoubtedly, the popularity of Marxist socialism is today in global decline amongst those who have to face the problem of making it work. In consequence, despite the fact that support for Marxism amongst Western intellectuals was at its height when repression in Marxist countries was at its peak, liberalism today seems have been accepted as a place of "refuge" by many intellectuals who, disillusioned with the failure of repression in the Marxist countries, nevertheless continue to hold to the socialist principles of universalism and egalitarianism.

As François B. Huyghe comments, welfare state policies accepted by liberals have implemented many of the socialist programs that patently failed in communist countries.[5] Thus, economic liberalism is not only popular among many former left-wing intellectuals (including numbers of East European intellectuals) because it has scored tangible economic results in the Western countries, but also due to the fact that its socialist counterpart has failed in practice, leaving the liberal model as the only uncontested alternative. "The main reason for the victories of economic liberalism," writes Kolm, "are due to the fact that all defective functioning of the non-liberal model of social realization warrants the consideration of the alternative liberal social realization. The examples of such cases abound in the West as in the East; in the North as in the South."[6] In the absence of other successful models, and in the epoch of a pronounced "de-ideologization" process all over Europe and America, modern liberalism has turned out to be a *modus vivendi* for the formerly embattled foes.[7] But are we therefore to conclude that the eclipse of other models and ideologies must spell the end of politics and inaugurate the beginning of the Age of Liberalism?

Long before the miracle of modern liberalism became obvious, a number of writers had observed that liberalism would continue to face a crisis of legitimacy even if its socialist and fascist foes were miraculously to disappear. More recently, Serge-Christophe Kolm has remarked that liberalism and socialism must not be viewed in dialectical opposition, but rather as a fulfilment of each other. Kolm writes that the ideals of liberalism and Marxism "are almost identical given that they are founded on the values of liberty, and coinciding in the applications of almost everything, except on a subject which is logically punctual, yet factually enormous in this world: wage-earning, location of individuals and self."[8] Some have even advanced the hypothesis that liberalism and socialism are the face and the counter-face of the same phenomenon, since contemporary liberalism has managed to achieve, in the long run and in an unrepressive fashion, many of those same goals that Marxian socialism in the short run, employing repressive means, has failed to achieve. Yet differences exist.

Not only do socialist ideologues currently fear that the introduction of free market measures could spell the end of socialism, but socialism and liberalism disagree fundamentally on the definition of equality. Theoretically, both subscribe to constitutional, legal, political and social equality; yet their main difference lies in their opposing views regarding the distribution of economic benefits/rewards, and accordingly, as to their corresponding definition of economic equality. Unlike liberalism, socialism is not satisfied with demanding political and social equality, but insists on equal distribution of economic goods. Marx repeatedly criticized the liberal definition of equal rights, for which he once said that "this equal right is unequal right for unequal labor. This right does not acknowledge class difference because everyone is only a worker like everyone else; but it tacitly recognizes unequal individual talents, and consequently it holds individual skills for natural privileges."[9] Only in a higher stage of Communism, after the present subordination of individuals to capital, that is, after the differences in the rewards of labor have disappeared, will bourgeois rights disappear, and society will write on its banner: "From each according to his capacity, to each according to his needs."[10]

Despite these differences, it may be said that, in general, socialist ideas have always surfaced as unavoidable satellites and pendants of liberalism. As soon as liberal ideas made their inroads into the European feudal scene, the stage for socialist appetites was set — appetites that subsequently proved too large to fulfil. As soon as the early bourgeoisie had secured its position, liquidating guilds and feudal corporations along with the landed aristocracy, it had to face up to critics who accused it of stifling political liberties and economic equality, and of turning the newly enfranchised peasant into a factory slave. In the seventeenth century, remarks Lakoff, the bourgeois ideas of equality and liberty immediately provided the fourth estate with ideological ammunition, which was quickly expressed by numerous proto-socialist revolutionary movements.[11] Under such circumstances of flawed equality, it must not come as a surprise that the heaviest burden for peasants was the hypocrisy of the bourgeoisie, which had hailed the rights of equality as long as it struggled to dislodge the aristocracy from power; yet, the minute it acceded to power, prudently refrained from making any further claims about equality in affluence. David Thomson remarked with irony that "many of those who would defend with their dying breath the rights of liberty and equality (such as many English and American liberals) shrink back in horror from the notion of economic egalitarianism."[12] Also, Sorel pointed out that in general, the abuse of power by an hereditary aristocracy is less harmful to the juridical sentiment of a people than the abuses committed by a plutocratic regime,[13] adding that "nothing would ruin so much the respect for laws as the spectacle of injustices committed by adventurers who, with the complicity of tribunals, have become so rich that they can purchase politicians."[14]

The dynamics of liberal and socialist revolutions gathered steam in the eighteenth and nineteenth century, notably an epoch of great revolutionary ferment in Europe. The liberal 1789 revolution in France rapidly gave way to the socialist Jacobin revolution in 1792; "the liberal" Condorcet was supplanted by the "communist" Babeuf, and the relatively bloodless Girondin coup was followed by the avalanche of bloodshed under the Jacobin terror and the revolt of the "sans-culottes".[15] Similarly, a hundred years later, the February Revolution in Russia was followed by the accelerated October revolution, replacing the social democrat, Kerensky, by the Communist Lenin. Liberalism gobbled up the ancient aristocracy, liquidated the medieval trade corporations, alienated the workers, and then in its turn was frequently supplanted by socialism. It is, therefore, interesting to observe that after its century-long competition with socialism, liberalism is today showing better results in both the economic and ethical domains, whereas the Marxist credo seems to be on the decline. But has liberalism become the only acceptable model for all peoples on earth? How is it that liberalism, as an incarnation of the humanitarian ideal and the democratic spirit, has always created enemies on both the left and the right, albeit for different reasons?

Free Market: The "Religion" of Liberalism

Liberalism can make many ideological "deals" with other ideologies, but one sphere where its remains intransigent is the advocacy of the free market and free exchange of goods and commodities. Undoubtedly, liberalism is not an ideology like other ideologies, and in addition, it has no desire to impose an absolute and exclusive vision of the world rooted in a dualistic cleavage between good and evil, the proletariat and the bourgeoisie, the "chosen and the unchosen ones." Moreover, the liberal ideal lacks that distinctive *telos* so typical of socialist and fascist ideologies. Contrary to other ideologies, liberalism is in general rather sceptical of any concentration of political power, because in the "inflation" of politics, and in ideological fervor, it claims to see signs of authoritarianism and even, as some authors have argued, totalitarianism.[16] Liberalism seems to be best fitted for a secularized polity, which Carl Schmitt alternatively called the "minimal state" (*Minimalstaat*), and *stato neutrale*.[17] It follows that in a society where production has been rationalized and human interaction is subject to constant reification (*Vergegenständlichung*), liberalism cannot (or does not wish to) adopt the same "will to power" that so often characterizes other ideologies. In addition, it is somewhat difficult to envision how such a society can request its citizens to sacrifice their goods and their lives in the interests of some political or religious ideal.[18] The free market is viewed as a "neutral field" (*Neutralgebiet*), allowing only the minimum of ideological conflict, that aims at erasing all political conflicts, positing that all people are rational beings whose quest for happiness is best secured by the peaceful pursuit of economic goals. In a liberal, individualistic society, every political belief is sooner or later reduced to a "private thing" whose ultimate arbiter is the individual himself. The Marxist theoretician Habermas comes to a somewhat similar conclusion, when he argues that modern liberal systems have acquired a negative character: "Politics is oriented to the removal of dysfunctionalities and of risks dangerous to the system; in other words, politics is not oriented to the implementation of practical goals, but to the solution of technological issues."[19] The market may thus be viewed as an ideal social construct whose main purpose is to limit the political arena. Consequently, every imaginable flaw in the market is generally explained by assertions that "there is still too much politics," hampering the free exchange of goods and commodities.[20]

Probably one of the most cynical remarks about liberalism and the liberal "money fetichism", came not from Marx, but from the fascist ideologue Julius Evola, who once wrote: "Before the classical dilemma, your money or your life, the bourgeois will paradoxically be the one to answer: 'Take my life, but spare my money.'"[21] But in spite of its purportedly agnostic and apolitical character, it would be wrong to assert that liberalism does not have "religious roots". In fact, many authors have remarked that the implementation of liberalism has been the most successful in precisely those countries that are known for strong adherence to biblical monotheism. Earlier in this century, the German sociologist Werner Sombart asserted that the liberal postulates of economics and ethics stem from Judeo-Christian legalism, and that liberals conceive of commerce, money and the "holy economicalness" (*heilige Wirtschaftlichkeit*) as the ideal avenue to spiritual salvation.[22] More recently, the French anthropologist Louis Dumont wrote that liberal individualism and economism are the secular transposition of Judeo-Christian beliefs, noting that "just as religion gave birth to politics, politics in turn will be shown to give birth to economics."[23]

Henceforth, writes Dumont in his book *From Mandeville to Marx*, according to the liberal doctrine, man's pursuit of happiness has increasingly come to be associated with the unimpeded pursuit of economic activities. In modern polities, he opines, the substitution of man as an individual for the idea of man as a social being was made possible by Judeo-Christianity: "the transition was thus made possible, from a holistic social order to a political system raised by consent as a superstructure on an ontological given economic basis."[24] In other words, the idea of individual accountability before God, gave birth, over a long period of time, to the individual and to the idea that economic accountability constitutes the linchpin of the liberal social contract — a notion totally absent from organic and traditional nationalistically-organized societies.[25] Thus, Emanuel Rackman argues that Judeo-Christianity played an important role in the development of ethical liberalism in the U.S.A.: "This was the only source on which Thomas Paine could rely in his 'Rights of Man' to support the dogma of the American Declaration of Independence that all men are created equal. And this dogma was basic in Judaism."[26] Similar claims are made by Konvitz in *Judaism and the American Idea*, wherein he argues that modern America owes much to the Jewish Holy Scriptures.[27] Feuerbach, Sombart, Weber, Troeltsch, and others have similarly argued that Judeo-Christianity had a considerable influence on the historical development of liberal capitalism. On the other hand, when one considers the recent economic success of various Asian countries on the Pacific Rim, whose expansionary impetus often overshadows the economic achievements of the countries marked by the Judeo-Christian legacy, one must take care not to equate economic success solely with the Judeo-Christian forms of liberal society.

Equal Economic Opportunity or the Opportunity to Be Unequal?

The strength of liberalism and of free market economics lies in the fact that the liberal ideal enables all people to develop their talents as they best see fit. The free market ignores all hierarchy and social differentiation, except those differences that result from the completion of economic transactions. Liberals argue that all people have the same economic opportunity, and that consequently, each individual, by making best use of his or her talents and entrepreneurship, will alone determine his or her social status. But critics of liberalism often contend that this formula is in itself dependent upon the terms and conditions under which the principles of "economic opportunity" can take place. John Schaar asserts that liberalism has substantially transformed the social arena into the economic field track, and that the formula should read: "equality of opportunity for all to develop those talents which are highly valued by a given people at a given time."[28] According to Schaar's logic, when the whims of the market determine which specific items, commodities or human talents are most in demand, or are more marketable than some others, it will follow that individuals lacking these talents or commodities will experience an acute sense of injustice. "Every society," Schaar continues, "encourages some talents and discourages others. Under the equal opportunity doctrine, the only men who can fulfil themselves and develop their abilities to the fullest are those who are able and eager to do what society demands they do."[29] This means that liberal societies will likely be most content when their members share a homogeneous background and a common culture. Yet modern liberalism seeks to break down national barriers and promote the conversion of hitherto homogeneous nation-states into multi-ethnic and highly heterogeneous political states. Thus, the potential for disputation and dissatisfaction is enhanced by the successful implementation of its economic policies.

It is further arguable that the success of liberalism engenders its own problems. Thus, as Karl Marx was quick to note, in a society where everything becomes an expendable commodity, man gradually comes to see himself as an expendable commodity too. An average individual will be less and less prone to abide by his own internal criteria, values or interests, and instead, he will tenaciously focus on not being left out of the economic battle, always on his guard that his interests are in line with the market. According to Schaar, such an attitude, in the long run, can have catastrophic consequences for the winner as well as the loser: "The winners easily come to think of themselves as being superior to common humanity, while the losers are almost forced to think of themselves as something less than human."[30] Under psychological pressure caused by incessant economic competition, and seized by fear that they may fall out of the game, a considerable number of people, whose interests and sensibilities are not compatible with current demands of the market, may develop feelings of bitterness, jealousness and inferiority. A great many among them will accept the economic game, but many will, little by little, come to the conclusion that the liberal formula "all people are equal", in reality only applies to those who are economically the most successful. Murray Milner, whose analyses parallel Schaar's, observes that under such circumstances, the doctrine of equal opportunity creates psychological insecurity, irrespective of the material affluence of society. "Stressing equality of opportunity necessarily makes the status structure fluid and the position of the individual within it ambiguous and insecure."[31] The endless struggle for riches and security, which seemingly has no limits, can produce negative results, particularly when society is in the throes of sudden economic changes. Antony Flew, in a similar fashion, writes that "a 'competition' in which the success of all contestants is equally probable is a game of chance or lottery, not a genuine competition."[32] For Milner such an economic game is tiring and unpredictable, and if "extended indefinitely, it could lead to exhaustion and collapse."[33]

Many other contemporary authors also argue that the greatest threat to liberalism comes from the constant improvement in general welfare generated by its own economic successes. Recently, two French scholars, Julien Freund and Claude Polin, wrote that the awesome expansion of liberalism, resulting in ever increasing general affluence, inevitably generates new economic and material needs, which constantly cry out for yet another material fulfilment. Consequently, after society has reached an enviable level of material growth, even the slightest economic crisis, resulting in a perceptible drop in living standards, will cause social discord and possibly political upheavals.

Taking a slightly different stance, Polin remarks that liberalism, in accordance with the much-vaunted doctrine of "natural rights", tends, very often, to define man as a final and complete species who no longer needs to evolve, and whose needs can be rationally predicted and finalized. Led by an unquenchable desire that he must exclusively act on his physical environment in order to improve his earthly lot, he is accordingly led by the liberal ideology to think that the only possible way to realize happiness is to place material welfare and individualism above all other goals.[34] In fact, given that the "ideology of needs" has become a tacit criterion of progress in liberalism, it is arguable that the material needs of modern anomic masses must always be "postponed", since they can never be fully satisfied.[35] Moreover, each society that places excessive hopes in a salutary economy will gradually come to view freedom as purely economic freedom and good as purely economic good. Thus, the "merchant civilization" (*civilization marchande*), as Polin calls it, must eventually become a hedonistic civilization in search of pleasure, and self-love. These points are similar to the views held by Julien Freund, who also sees in liberalism a society of impossible needs and insatiable desire. He remarks that "it appears that satiety and overabundance are not the same things as satisfaction, because they provoke new dissatisfaction."[36] Instead of rationally solving all human needs, liberal society always triggers new ones, which in turn constantly create further needs. Everything happens, Freund continues, as if the well-fed needed more than those who live in indigence. In other words, abundance creates a different form of scarcity, as if man needs privation and indigence, "as if he needed some needs."[37] One has almost the impression that liberal society purposely aims at provoking new needs, generally unpredictable, often bizarre. Freund concludes that "the more the rationalization of the means of production brings about an increase in the volume of accessible goods, the more the needs extend to the point of becoming irrational."[38]

Such an argument implies that the dynamics of liberalism, continually begetting new and unpredictable needs, continually threatens the philosophical premises of that same rationalism on which liberal society has built its legitimacy. In this respect, socialist theorists often sound convincing when they in effect argue that if liberalism has not been able to provide equality in affluence, Communism does at least offer equality in frugality!

Conclusion: From Atomistic Society to Totalitarian System

The British imperialist, Cecil Rhodes, once exclaimed: "if I could I would annex the planets!" A very Promethean idea, indeed, and quite worthy of Jack London's rugged individuals or Balzac's entrepreneurs — but can it really work in a world in which the old capitalist guard, as Schumpeter once pointed out, is becoming a vanishing species?[39]

It remains to be seen how liberalism will pursue its odyssey in a society in which those who are successful in the economic arena live side by side with those who lag behind in economic achievement, when its egalitarian principles prohibit the development of any moral system that would justify such hierarchical differences, such as sustained medieval European society. Aside from prophecies about the decline of the West, the truism remains that it is easier to create equality in economic frugality than equality in affluence. Socialist societies can point to a higher degree of equality in frugality. But liberal societies, especially in the last ten years, have constantly been bedevilled by an uneasy choice; on the one hand, their effort to expand the market, in order to create a more competitive economy, has almost invariably caused the marginalization of some social strata. On the other hand, their efforts to create more egalitarian conditions by means of the welfare state brings about, as a rule, sluggish economic performance and a menacing increase in governmental bureaucratic controls. As demonstrated earlier, liberal democracy sets out from the principles that the "neutral state" and free market are the best pillars against radical political ideologies, and that commerce, as Montesquieu once said, "softens up the mores." Further, as a result of the liberal drive to extend markets on a world-wide basis, and consequently, to reduce or eliminate all forms of national protectionism, whether to the flow of merchandise, or of capital, or even of labor, the individual worker finds himself in an incomprehensible, rapidly changing international environment, quite different from the secure local society familiar to him since childhood.

This paradox of liberalism was very well described by a keen German observer, the philosopher Max Scheler, who had an opportunity to observe the liberal erratic development, first in Wilhelmian and then in Weimar Germany. He noted that liberalism is bound to create enemies, both on the right and the left side of the political spectrum: On the left it makes enemies of those who see in liberalism a travesty of the natural rights dogma, and on the right, of those who discern in it the menace to organic and traditional society. "Consequently," writes Scheler, "a huge load of resentment appears in a society, such as ours, in which equal political and other rights, that is, the publicly acknowledged social equality, go hand in hand with large differences in real power, real property and real education. A society in which each has the "right" to compare himself to everybody, yet in which, in reality, he can compare himself to nobody."[40] In traditional societies, as Dumont has written, such types of reasoning could never develop to the same extent because the majority of people were solidly attached to their communal roots and the social status that their community bestowed upon them. India, for example, provides a case study of a country that has significantly preserved a measure of traditional civic community, at least in the smaller towns and villages, despite the adverse impact of its population explosion and the ongoing conflict there between socialism in government and liberalism in the growing industrial sector of the economy. By contrast, in the more highly industrialized West, one could almost argue that the survival of modern liberalism depends on its constant ability to "run ahead of itself" economically.

The need for constant and rapid economic expansion carries in itself the seeds of social and cultural dislocation, and it is this loss of "roots" that provides the seedbed for tempting radical ideologies. In fact, how can unchecked growth ever appease the radical proponents of natural rights, whose standard response is that it is inadmissible for somebody to be a loser and somebody a winner? Faced with a constant expansion of the market, the alienated and uprooted individual in a society in which the chief standard of value has become material wealth, may be tempted to sacrifice freedom for economic security. It does not always appear convincing that liberal societies will always be able to sustain the "social contract" on which they depend for their survival by thrusting people into material interdependence. Economic gain may be a strong bond, but it does not have the affective emotional power for inducing willing self-sacrifice in times of adversity on which the old family-based nation-state could generally rely.

More likely, by placing individuals in purely economic interdependence on each other, and by destroying the more traditional bonds of kinship and national loyalty, modern liberalism may have succeeded in creating a stage where, in times of adversity, the economic individual will seek to outbid, outsmart, and outmaneuver all others, thereby preparing the way for the "terror of all against all", and preparing the ground, once again, for the rise of new totalitarianisms. In other words, the spirit of totalitarianism is born when economic activity obscures all other realms of social existence, and when the "individual has ceased to be a father, a sportsman, a religious man, a friend, a reader, a righteous man — only to become an economic actor."[41] By shrinking the spiritual arena and elevating the status of economic activities, liberalism in fact challenges its own principles of liberty, thus enormously facilitating the rise of totalitarian temptations. One could conclude that as long as economic values remained subordinate to non-economic ideals, the individual had at least some sense of security irrespective of the fact his life was often, economically speaking, more miserable. With the subsequent emergence of the anonymous market, governed by the equally anonymous invisible hand, in the anonymous society, as Hannah Arendt once put it, man has acquired a feeling of uprootedness and existential futility.[42] As pre-industrial and traditional societies demonstrate, poverty is not necessarily the motor behind revolutions. Revolution comes most readily to those in whom poverty is combined with a consciousness of lost identity and a feeling of existential insecurity. For this reason, the modern liberal economies of the West must constantly work to ensure that the economic miracle shall continue. As economic success has been made the ultimate moral value, and national loyalties have been spurned as out of date, economic problems automatically generate deep dissatisfaction amongst those confronted with poverty, who are then likely to fall prone to the sense of "alienation" on which all past Marxist socialist success has been based.

One must therefore not exclude the likelihood that modern liberal society may at some time in the future face serious difficulties should it fail to secure permanent economic growth, especially if, in addition, it relentlessly continues to atomize the family (discouraging marriage, for example, by means of tax systems that favors extreme individualism) and destroys all national units in favor of the emergence of a single worldwide international market, along with its inevitable concomitant, the "international man". While any faltering of the world economy, already under pressure from the Third World population explosion, might conceivably lead to a resurgence of right-wing totalitarianisms in some areas, it is much more likely that in an internationalized society the new totalitarianism of the future will come from the left, in the form of a resurgence of the "socialist experiment", promising economic gain to a population that has been taught that economic values are the only values that matter. Precisely because the "workers of the world" will have come to see themselves as an alienated international proletariat, they will tend to lean toward international socialist totalitarianism, rather than other forms of extreme political ideology.

PART V
MULTICULTURALISM AND COMMUNISM

AMERICA IN THE EYES OF EASTERN EUROPE

While a massive amount of both critical and laudatory literature on America is circulating in Western Europe, only a few critical books on America and the American way of life can be found in today's post-communist Eastern Europe. This essay is my attempt to add to that literature.

Before attempting to tackle this complex subject (an Eastern European account of America), one needs to define terms. People living in the Czech Republic, Hungary, Poland, or Slovenia do not like being called Eastern Europeans; the term "Eastern Europe" has a ring of an insult to their ears. They consider themselves, despite their region's undemocratic past, full-blooded Europeans — as much if not more so than West Europeans. There may be some truth in this semi-complacent attitude. From the ethnic point of view, all post-communist countries in Eastern Europe are highly homogeneous, with only a few non-Europeans living on their soil. By contrast, Western Europe, or what is today part of the fifteen states of the European Union, has a non-European population of approximately 7 percent. Moreover, the population of the United States — which can be thought of as an extension of Western Europe — is well over 25 percent non-European in origin. Ironically, due to the closed nature of its communist past, Eastern Europe has never known a large influx of non-Europeans. The paradox is therefore twofold: the label Eastern Europe is viewed by many as ideologically colored, its derogatory meaning referring to the formerly Soviet-occupied and communist-ruled part of Europe. Second, although claiming to be 100 percent Europeans, all East European nations, and particularly the newborn nation-states in the region, are well aware of their ethnic roots — certainly more so than are West Europeans. For decades, if not centuries, and even during the darkest hours of communism, East Europeans had a strange love for America, while displaying strange resentments toward their next-door European neighbors.

Any American who travels to Budapest, Zagreb, or Warsaw, be it in a public or private capacity, is welcomed. An American backpacker may enjoy passing through Copenhagen or Amsterdam, but he will never be so warmly embraced by West Europeans as he will be by his East European hosts. The communist rule, which lasted well over forty years in Eastern Europe and seventy in Russia, created a mental atmosphere whereby the very term West became synonymous with America, and only to a lesser degree with nearby Western Europe. The West, in the eyes and ears of East Europeans, was not so much the rich and opulent Germany or France, but rather the distant, Hollywood-hazed America.

While one could find scores of Marxist true believers in American academia during the Cold War, most East Europeans privately nurtured strong anticommunist and pro-American feelings. Former Presidents Richard Nixon and Ronald Reagan had more, all be they hidden, true constituents in communized Poland, Hungary, and Albania than on the West or East Coast. It was difficult for many East Europeans, particularly those who physically suffered under Communism, to grasp the motives of young American students during the anti-Vietnam protests in the late sixties. Of course, pro-American and anticommunist sentiments among the wide layers of Eastern European society had to be skillfully hidden. But a great majority of people in Eastern Europe privately applauded the U.S. bombing of Vietnam and the harsh anticommunist rhetoric of Nixon and Reagan. They were all persuaded that, sooner or later, American GIs would liberate their homelands from the red plague. But today East Europeans are beginning to realize that America had other fish to fry than liberating Hungary in 1956 or Poland in 1980.

The Passing of the American Age

After the fall of Communism, the United States is still perceived by many East Europeans as the incarnation of good, a symbol of enormous wealth, and a place of boundless economic opportunity. To some extent, East European attitudes toward America resemble those of West Europeans following World War II. In their eyes, America was a myth that surpassed the often-gloomy American reality. Many East Europeans are now going through similar psychological convulsions and self-induced misperceptions. The first cracks in their imaginary image of America are beginning to appear. On a political level, with the end of the bipolar system and the breakup of the Soviet Union, America has become the only role model in the neighborhood. Whether they like it or not, East European politicians know that entrance into the international community means, first and foremost, obtaining a certificate of good democratic behavior from Uncle Sam, and only much later a passing grade from the fledgling European Union (E.U.). Challenging and opposing U.S. foreign policy in this region is a luxury that no East European ruler can afford, short of paying a hefty price (as Serbia did a half-decade ago).

But contradictions, if not outright hypocrisy, abound on both sides of the Atlantic. Even a self-proclaimed anti-American in Eastern Europe will accept with great mistrust E.U. arbitration of a regional or ethnic dispute or armed conflict. He will always turn his eyes first toward America. Even among America-haters, the unwritten rule is that only America, due to its historical detachment, can be an honest broker. Despite the almost grotesque cravings to join the E.U. exhibited by the entire East European political class, in the back of everybody's mind the quest is to join N.A.T.O. first. The recent entry of Poland, Hungary, and the Czech Republic into N.A.T.O. had far more psychological significance for people in the region than the protractedly scheduled entry into the European Union. Even the most cultivated East European opponent of the American way of life or the harshest critic of U.S. foreign policy does not dispute the fact that America elicits more confidence and sympathy among East Europeans than does the next-door European neighbor, who is traditionally and historically suspected of double deals and treachery.

While Western Europe is often decried and derided by European conservative intellectuals as a protectorate of America or a subject of U.S. cultural imperialism, the fact of the matter is that everybody finds something inexplicably attractive about America. One can rave and rant about its decadence, its highest per-capita prison population, poor educational system, or military overextension, but every citizen in Europe, both west and east, is subconsciously enamored with either the real or surreal image of America.

Even gloomy projections of an apocalyptic end of America must be taken with caution. Many erudite conservative authors depict America as the belated aftershock of the late Roman Empire, with a willful, albeit often dangerous, desire to export global democracy by means of paleo-puritan and neo-liberal messianism. But features of globalism and political messianism were common to all great powers in Europe throughout centuries. The Jacobin and post-Jacobin France at the end of the eighteenth century, for example, was no less a globalist power than America is today. The case was similar with the now-defunct Soviet Union.

Many Europeans, let alone East Europeans, do not realize that America is not just a continent, but a planet with enormous differences in lifestyles and worldviews — despite its often-derided "McDonaldization" or its "Have a nice day" daily discourse. One learns to appreciate the allegedly decadent American system only after great distance in time and space. The supreme paradox is that many ancient and traditional European values were better defended intellectually by the Confederates in 1863 than by conservative Europeans, then and now. But is America still the same country today as it was just a decade ago? Certainly, it has changed dramatically over the past ten years, not just due to a massive influx of non-European immigrants but also to an infusion of new role models and mindsets that they have brought with them. Only fifty years ago the overwhelming majority of American immigrants were Europeans, who saw in their newly adopted homeland an "extension", albeit a distant one, of their unfulfilled European dream. The very geographic distance from Europe made them accept wholeheartedly their new American destiny, yet they continued to honor their old European customs, often better and more colorfully than they had done on the other side of the ocean. This hardly seems to be the case with the new immigrants today. Many of these immigrants, especially those coming from Latin America, do not experience a geographic gap from their abandoned homeland because they live in its close vicinity. What is more, due to the rising tide of globalism, their loyalty is often split between their old homeland and their new American one. They may often experience the American dream as just another passing journey, looking instead to whatever will bring them greater financial and economic success. Early America was grounded in the roots of the Western heritage and had no qualms about displaying the badge of traditional Christian and European values, such as chivalry, honor, and the sense of sacrifice. This seems increasingly difficult to preach to new would-be Americans, whose religious customs, cultural roots, and historical memory often stretch to the different antipodes of the world. Contradictions, paradoxes, and hypocrisies abound.

Probably one of the best early observers of postmodernity, the conservative author and novelist Aldous Huxley, wrote in a little-known essay that America would be the future of the world — even if and when America, as a separate country and jurisdiction, fades into oblivion. The American system of soft ideology — that is, the dictatorship of well-being and the terror of consumerism — makes it globally appealing and yet so self-destructive. As an English sophisticate and aristocratic conservative, Huxley deeply resented the massification of America, in which he foresaw both a blueprint and a carbon copy of softened communist totalitarianism. But was he not a contradictory person himself, despite his visionary predictions? Did he not choose sunny, ahistorical, decadent, and uprooted California as his deathbed, not his own rainy England or somewhere else in rooted Europe? And did he not spend much of his later life on L.S.D.-induced trips?

American vs. Soviet Man

Eastern Europe's distorted image of America, coupled with an often-ludicrous love of the imaginary America, was a logical response to the endless anti-American rhetoric propagated by its former communist masters. Even when communist apparatchiks aired slogans that carried some truth about racial discrimination, poverty, and high crime rates in the United States, the East European masses refused to believe them. This was understandable. How could they believe communist officials, given the fact that the communist system was founded on the big lie and could only function by lying on all wavelengths twenty-four hours a day? Instead, East Europeans opted for their own self-styled vision of America, which real Americans would have found hard to believe in. The gloomier the picture of America presented by the communists, the more East Europeans believed in its opposite pastoral and pristine side.

Ten years after the fall of Communism, Eastern Europeans are gradually toning down their illusions about quick Americanization — that is, a sudden outbreak of affluence — in their countries. Hence another paradox: Ten years ago, communist mendacity, police repression, and economic scarcity prompted them to kick out the red plague, but today it is American-style capitalism that makes them cry out for more communist-style security and economic predictability, saying to themselves, "Who says, after all, that totalitarianism cannot be democratic, and that an individual always knows what is in his own best interests? Sometimes a leader, a strongman, *führer*, *caudillo*, or *vodj*, best knows the answer." The legacy of Communism in Eastern Europe is hard to grasp even for scholars of substantial culture and intellectual probity. Communism created distinct patterns of behavior that will take longer to discard than the ideological or juridical legacy of communist repression. The shrewd traveler to Eastern Europe, whether businessman, politician, or student, will notice that citizens of today's Prague, Bucharest, Budapest, or Zagreb still display behavioral traits of the communist system. The communist culture of social leveling created a peculiar mind-set of base survivalism, visible today even among individuals who brag that they are ardent anticommunists. American businessmen are often amazed with the way the new post-communist political elites conceptualize a free market, forgetting that beneath the style and rhetorical veneer of the new class, the substance of communism was never uprooted. Indeed, from the Balkans to the Baltics, the majority of politicians in Eastern Europe are basically recycled communists, who for obvious geopolitical reasons converted to Americanophile opportunism. It is questionable to what extent they are true democrats now, and to what extent they were true communist democrats twenty years ago. Thus, there are many misunderstandings and misperceptions on both sides of the Atlantic.

The culture of post-communist mediocrity and mendacity cannot be wished away by State Department officials or would-be U.N. Samaritans. Generally speaking, the American attitude toward Eastern Europe is based on pragmatic (albeit too idealistic) models and schemes that foresee a solution, or at least a contingency plan, for every crisis. But formulas or models do not work in post-communist Eastern Europe. An average East European is still prone to irrational emotional outbursts and continues to harbor paranoid conspiracy theories. Given that he sees others, including Americans, as crooks, he will himself continue cheating and pilfering, and do his best to double-cross others. In essence, past communist terror badly weakened what we might call the genetic pool of Eastern Europeans. Therefore, many East Europeans accept the vaunted transition toward democracy — i.e., American-style capitalism — only on a purely rhetorical level. Initiative, commitment, and self-reliance, which are taken for granted by Americans, are nonexistent in Eastern Europe. The imbedded communist practice of double deals presents a formidable barrier in East European — American business or political relationships. Numerous U.S. scholars and politicians think that these barriers will fade away with the brutal implementation of free markets, but they are wrong.

The primitive appeal of Communism abided in the psychological security and economic predictability it provided. Most East Europeans would now like to have it both ways: They would like to retain the economic and political security of Communism, while having all the imagined glitz and glory of projected Americanism. For Eastern Europeans, the American dream basically boils down to transplanting themselves physically into the imaginary yet real soaps of Santa Barbara or Melrose Place. One may argue, as does Jean Baudrillard, a theorist of postmodernity, that America is utopia achieved. This is true in a sense, if we disregard the ever-increasing economic inequalities and growing social anonymity that could spell the end of the American dream. Conversely, Eastern Europe today is a laboratory where different and sometimes obnoxious ideas are officially heralded one day, only to be discarded the next. Americans frequently observe that little can be achieved in this tragic part of Europe by role-modeling or preaching democracy.

Eastern Europe skipped the most important part of its modern history; it never carried out wholesale decommunization, and it never began educating its masses in civility. Consequently, a strong irrational element in human behavior will continue to exist in Eastern Europe. Eastern Europe has already had too much of verbal democracy. What it needs is civility. During the initial post-communist phase, East Europeans became ardent anticommunists who thought that by hollering anticommunist slogans, they would immediately open up the road to rich America. It is no accident that the first governments in post-communist Eastern Europe were made up of radical anticommunist and nationalist spokesmen. Then, during the second phase, which is still in progress, East Europeans, particularly the political class, engaged in a grotesque mimicry of America. Everybody regurgitates the words economic growth, privatization, globalization, and Euro-Atlantic integration without knowing what they stand for. This phase is coming to an end, leaving a dangerous vacuum behind and a minefield of mass anxiety ahead.

The unpredictable nature of the European character is obvious. Who could have foretold the fall of the Berlin Wall, the brutal war between two similar peoples (Croats and Serbs), and the never-ending reshuffling of the E.U.? One may not rule out that after the experiment with "made in the U.S.A."-style ultraliberalism, East Europeans may suddenly, out of defiance, revert to ageless domestic hard-liners. Security comes first;

democracy may be a distant second. The rapid process of Americanization of Eastern Europe, with its self-induced, self-gratifying dreams, may have its nasty drawbacks. If Americans themselves start raising questions about the veracity of their elections and the honesty of their leaders, their poor imitators in Eastern Europe will flock to the large trove of their own strongmen. A parallel could be drawn with former European colonies, which after the end of French and English colonial rule, reverted to their own often-unsavory customs. Moreover, the surplus population they keep sending to open-armed Europe and America bears witness to the decline of the West.

Additional Reading

Jean Baudrillard, *America*, translated by Chris Turner, *America* (New York: Verso, 1989).

Noam Chomsky, *Secrets, Lies and Democracy* (Tucson, AR: Odonian Press, 1994).

Tomislav Sunic, *Against Democracy and Equality: The European New Right* (London: Arktos, 2011).

Alexander Zinoviev, *The Reality of Communism* (London: Victor Gollancz, 1985).

THE DECLINE AND SPLENDOR OF NATIONALISM

No political phenomenon can be so creative and so destructive as nationalism. Nationalism can be a metaphor for the supreme truth but also an allegory for the nostalgia of death. No exotic country, no gold, no woman can trigger such an outpouring of passion as the sacred homeland, and contrary to all Freudians, more people have died defending their homelands than the honor of their women. If we assume that political power is the supreme aphrodisiac, then nationalism must be its ultimate thrill.

To talk about nationalism in Anglo-Saxon countries usually evokes the specter of tribalism, violence, heavy politics, and something that runs counter to the idea of progress. For an American liberal, nationalism is traditionally associated with irrational impulses, with something incalculable that has a nasty habit of messing up a mercantile mindset. A merchant does not like borders and national emblems; his badge of honor is his goods, and his friends are those who make the best offer on the global market. It is no coincidence that during World War II the Merchant preferred the alliance with the Commissar, despite the fact that the Commissar's violence often eclipsed that of the Nationalist. Daniel Bell once wrote that American liberals find it difficult to grasp ethnic infatuation because the American way of thinking is "spatially and temporally suspended." Indeed, to an insular maritime mind, it must appear absolutely idiotic to observe two people quarreling over a small creek or a stretch of land when little economic yield lies in the balance. A politician in America, unlike his rooted European counterpart, is essentially a realtor, and his attitude towards politics amounts to a real estate transaction. It is hard to deny that a person on the move, reared on Jack Kerouac or Dos Passos, is frightened by the ethnic exclusiveness that is today rocking the part of Europe from the Balkans to the Baltics. The mystique of the territorial imperative, with its unpredictable ethnic cauldron, must be a paramount insult to the ideology of the melting pot. Contrary to widespread beliefs, nationalism is not an ideology, because it lacks programmatic dimension and defies categorization. At best, nationalism can be described as a type of earthbound behavior with residues of paganism. Whereas liberalism operates in the rational singular, nationalism always prefers the irrational plural. For the liberal, the individual is the epicenter of politics; for the nationalist, the individual is only a particle in historical community. To visualize different brands of nationalism one could observe a European family camping on the rocky beaches of the French Riviera and contrast it to an American family on the sandy beaches of Santa Barbara. The former meticulously stakes out its turf, keeps its children in fold; the latter nomadically fans out the moment it comes to the beach, with each family member in search of privacy. Incidentally, the word "privacy" does not even exist in continental European languages.

Following World War II, for a European to declare himself a nationalist was tantamount to espousing neofascism. On the ossuary of Auschwitz, few indeed were willing to rave publicly about the romantic ideas of 19th century poets and princes, whose idyllic escapades gave birth, a century later, to an unidyllic slaughterhouse. At Yalta, the idea of a Europe frolicking with the liturgy of blood and soil was considered too dangerous, and both superpowers held high this reminder in the form of their respective strategy of "double containment". After their excursion into the largest civil war in history, Europeans decided not to talk about nationalism or self-determination any longer. Many European intellectuals, and particularly German pundits, preferred instead to recommit their suppressed nationalist energy to far-flung Palestinians, Sandinistas, Cubans, or Congolese instead of to their own ethnic soil. Third World nationalism became for the European mandarins both the esoteric catharsis and the exotic superego; and to theorize about the plight of Xhosa in South Africa, or Ibo in Nigeria, or to stage treks to Cashmere or Katmandu became an elegant way of wallowing in new political romanticism. This vicarious type of meta-nationalism continued to play a role of psychological repository for the dormant and domesticated Europeans who needed time to heal wounds and wait for yet another renaissance.

Has this renaissance already occurred? The liberal parenthesis that lasted for 45 years, and that received its major boost after the recent collapse of its communist alter ego, may indeed be coming to an end. From Iberia to Irkutsk, from Kazakhstan to Croatia, hundreds of different peoples are once again clamoring for their place under the sun. To assume that they are raising their ethnic voices for economic reasons alone is misleading, and liberals are committing a serious mistake when they try to explain away nationalism by virtue of structuralist-functionalist paradigms, or when they shrug it off as a vestige of a traditional ascriptive society. Contrary to popular assumptions, the collapse of communism in Europe and the Soviet Union is a direct spin-off of ethnic frustrations that have for decades lain dormant, but have refused to die away. The paradox apparent at the end of the 20th century is this: while everybody is talking about integration, multiculturalism, ecumenism, and cosmic fraternity, fractures, fissures, and cleavages are appearing everywhere. Paradoxes abound as little Luxembourg preaches sermons to a much larger Slovenia on the utility of staying in the Yugoslav fold; or when Bush, after failing to rescue the Balts, comes to the aid of artificial satrapy in the name of the "self-determination" of its handful of petrocrats; or when Soviet apparatchiks fake concern for the plight of Palestinians only to further crackdown against their Bashkirs and Meshkets.

Nationalism is entering today the third phase of its history, and similar to a heady Hydra and howling Hecuba it is again displaying its unpredictable character. Must it be creative in violence only? Ethnic wars are already raging in Northern Ireland, in the land of Basques, in Corsica, let alone in Yugoslavia, where two opposing nationalisms are tearing Versailles Europe apart and showering the treaty successors with embarrassing and revisionist questions.

There are different nationalisms in different countries and they all have a different meaning. Nationalism can appear on the right; it does, however, appear on the left. It can be reactionary and progressive, but in all cases, it cannot exist unless it has its dialectical Other. German nationalism of the 19th century could not have flourished had Germany not been confronted by the aggressive French Jacobinism; modern English nationalism could not have taken off had it not been haunted by assertive Prussia. Each nationalism must have its *Feindbild*, its image of the evil, because nationalism is by definition the locus of political polarity in which the distinction between the foe and friend, between *hostis* and *amicus*, is brought to its deadly paroxysm. Consequently, it is no small wonder that intra-ethnic, let alone inter-ethnic, wars (like the one raging today between Croats and Serbs) are also the most savage ones, with each side vilifying, demonizing, and praying for the total destruction of the other.

In addition, side by side with its positive founding myths, each nationalism must resort to its negative mythology, which in times of pending national disasters sustains its people in the fight with the enemy. In order to energize younger generations Polish nationalists will resurrect their dead from the Katyn, the Germans their buried from Silesia and Sudetenland; Croats will create their iconography on their postwar mass graveyards, Serbs their hagiography out of their war-camp victims. Body counts, aided by modern statistics and abetted by high-tech earth excavators, will be completed by mundane metaphors that usually tend to inflate one's own victimology and deflate that of the enemy. German nationalists call Poles *Polacks*, and French chauvinists call Germans *Boches*. Who can deny that racial and ethnic slurs are among the most common and picturesque of weapons used by nationalists worldwide?

Nationalism is not a generic concept, and liberal ideologues are often wrong when they reduce European nationalism to one conceptual category. What needs to be underlined is that there are exclusive and inclusive nationalisms, just as there are exclusive and inclusive racisms. Central Europeans, generally, make a very fine distinction between inclusive Jacobin state-determined (*staatsgebunden*) unitary nationalism *vis-à-vis* the soil-culture-blood determined (*volksgebunden*) nationalism of Central and Eastern Europe. Jacobin nationalism is by nature centralistic; it aims at global democracy, and it has found today its valiant, albeit unwitting, standard-bearer in George Bush's ecumenical one-worldism. Ironically, a drive towards unitary French nationalism existed before the Jacobins were even born, and it was the product of a peculiar geopolitical location that subsequently gave birth to the modern French state. Richelieu, or Louis XIV, were as much Jacobins in this sense as their secular successors Saint-Just, Gambetta, or De Gaulle. In France, today, whichever side one looks — left, right, center — the answer is always Jacobinism. In a similar vein, in England, the Tudors and Cromwell acted as unitary nationalists in their liquidations and genocides — *ad majorem Dei gloriam* — of the Cornish and Irish and a host of other ethnic groups. Churchill and other 20th-century English leaders successfully saved Great Britain in 1940 by appealing to unitary nationalism, although their words would have found little appeal today among Scots and Irish.

Contrary to widespread beliefs, the word "nationalism", (*Nazionalismus*) was rarely used in National Socialist Germany. German nationalists in the 1920's and 30's popularized, instead, such derivatives as *Volkstum, Volksheit,* or *Voelkisch,* words that are etymologically affiliated with the word *Deutsch* and that were, during the Nazi rule, synonymously used with the word *rassisch* (racial). The word Volk came into German usage with J. G. Fichte in the early 19th century, when Germany belatedly began to consolidate its state consciousness. The word *Volk* must not be lightly equated with the Latin or English *populus* (people). As an irony of history, even the meaning of the word "people" in the English language is further blurred by its polymorphous significance. People can mean an organic whole, similar to *Volk,* although it has increasingly come to be associated with an aggregate of atomized individuals. Ironically, the German idea of the *Volk* and the Slavic idea of *narodi* have much in common; and indeed, each group can perfectly well understand, often with deadly consequences, each other's national aspirations. It is no small wonder that in the German and Slavic political vocabulary the concept of federalism and democracy will acquire a radically different meaning than in linguistically homogeneous England, France, or America.

By ostensibly putting aside its racist past, yet by pushing its universalist message to the extreme, the West paradoxically shows that it is no less racist today than it was yesterday.

French and English nationalisms lack a solid territorial dimension, and their founding myths lie elsewhere. Over the course of their history, due to their colonial holdings, these countries have acted both as European and non-European nations — which explains, particularly in the light of massive non-European immigration — why their elites find it difficult to argue for their strong ethnic identity. Continental European nationalism, and specifically the German idea of *Volksheit,* is by contrast the product of a set of geographic circumstances unparalleled in France or England. In France and England, the people were created out of the existence of the state. In Germany and Continental Europe, nationalism has manifested itself primarily as a cultural phenomenon of frequently stateless peoples. In Germany, Poland, Romania, etc., poets and writers created the national consciousness of their peoples; in France, princes created state consciousness. Popular figures in Central Europe — like Herder or Father Jahn in Germany, Sandor Petofy in Hungary, Ljudevit Gaj in Croatia, Vuk Karadzic in Serbia, or Taras Shevchenko in the Ukraine — played a crucial role in laying the foundation of the modern state for their respective peoples. Quite different was the story of nationalism in France where *légistes* created the unitary French state by suppressing regionalism in the French Hexagon. Similarly, in England, the role of nation-state builders fell to merchants and to maritime companies, which, aided by buccaneers, brought wealth for the English crown. Interestingly, during the Battle of Britain, Churchill even toyed with the idea of transferring Downing Street and Westminster Palace to the heartland of America — a gesture that in Central Europe would have amounted to national suicide.

Like America, France first became a state, and in turn set the stage for the molding of the French people of different tribes; by contrast, Germans have always been a stateless yet compact people. The history of France is essentially the history of genocide, in which French rulers from the Capétians to the Bourbons, all the way down to modern Jacobins, meticulously carried out destruction of Occitans, Vendeans, Bretons, Franche-Comté, etc. Suppression of regionalism and nativism has been one of the major hallmarks of French acculturation, with the latest attempt being to Frenchify Arabs from the Maghreb countries. Today, France is paying the price for its egalitarian and universalist dreams. On the one hand, it is trying to impose universal values and laws on the masses of Third World immigrants; on the other, it must daily proclaim the principle of self-determination for its multiracial social layers. If one puts things in historical perspective, everything presages that France has become a prime candidate for sparking off racial warfare all over Europe.

Looking at Germany and its East European glacis, a sharp eye immediately discovers a fluid area of levitating borders, "seasonal states", yet strong culturally and historically minded peoples. Central and Eastern European have a long ethnic and historical memory, but their borders fall short of clean-cut ethnographic lines. Germany, for instance, offers a view of an open and poorly defined state yet at the same time it is a closed community. By contrast, Jacobin France, functionalist-minded England, and America are geographically closed states, but open societies. Nationalism in these countries has always been inclusive and has invariably displayed globalist and imperialistic pretensions, notably by spreading its unitary message to disparate peoples worldwide.

Geographic location has also affected the ethnopsychology of European peoples. An average German is essentially a peasant; his psychologic cast and conduct are corporal and telluric. A German displays great courtesy but lacks politeness, and like most peasants he usually exhibits heavy-handed (*schwerfällig*) and frequently awkward approaches to social relations. By contrast, a French-man, irrespective of his ideological stripe and social background, is always a petty bourgeois; he is full of manners and stylishness but also full of pretensions. Unlike a German nationalist, a Frenchman displays a surfeit of manners but lacks courtesy. Even the most ignorant foreign tourist who goes to Germany and France will notice something foggy and unpredictable about Germans, while at the same time he will be gratified by the German sense of professional correctness and absolute honesty. By contrast, the body language and mannerisms of the French, as appealing as they may be, frequently leave one perplexed and disappointed.

In the course of their ethnogeneses, languages gave final veneer to their respective peoples. The German language is an organic language that branches off into eternity; it is also the richest European language. The French language, similar to a great extent to English, is an opaque language spun more by context than by flexion. As idiomatic languages, French and English are ideal for maritime and seaport activities. Over the course of history the French sabir and "pidgin" English proved to be astounding homogenizing agents as well as handy acculturative vectors for the English and French drives toward universalism. Subsequently, English and French became universal languages, in contrast to German, which never spread out beyond the East European marshlands.

The German idea of the *Reich* was for centuries perfectly adapted to the open plains of Europe, which housed diverse and closely knit communities. Neither the Habsburgs nor the Brandenburgs ever attempted to assimilate or annihilate the non-Germanic peoples within their jurisdiction as the French and English did within theirs. The Danube monarchy, despite its shortcomings, was a stable society, proven by its five hundred years of existence. During the First and Second Reich, principalities, towns, and villages within the bounds of the Austrian and Prussian lands had a large amount of self-government that frequently made them vulnerable to French, Swedish, and English imperial ambitions.

German *Volksheit* is an aristocratic as well as a democratic notion, since traditionally the relations between domestic aristocracy and the German people have been organic. Unlike France or England, Germany never experimented with foreign slavery. In Germany, ethnic differences between the local aristocracy and the German people are minimal; by contrast, in France, Spain, and England the aristocracy has usually recruited from the Northern European leadership class and not the masses at large. Incidentally, even now, despite the exactions of the French Revolution, one can see more racial differences between a French aristocrat and an average Frenchman than between a German aristocrat and a German peasant. In Germany, the relationship between the elites and the commoners has always been rooted in the holistic environment, and as a result Germany has remained a society barely in need of an elaborate social contract; it has based social relationships on horizontal hierarchy and corporate structure, buttressed in addition by the idea of "equality among the equals." By contrast, French and English society can be defined as vertically hierarchical and highly stratified; consequently, it should not be surprising that French and English racisms were among the most virulent in the world. It is also worth recalling that the first eugenic and racial laws in this century were not passed in Germany, but in liberal America and England.

Political scientists will one day ponder why the most glaring egalitarian impulses appear in France and America, two countries which, until recently, practiced the most glaring forms of racism. Are we witnessing today a peculiar form of remorse or national-masochism, or simply an egalitarian form of inclusive racism? Inclusive nationalism and racism, that manifest themselves in universalism and globalism, attempt to delete the difference between the foreigner and the native, although in reality the foreigner is always forced to accept the legal superstructure of his now "repented" white masters. By ostensibly putting aside its racist past, yet by pushing its universalist message to the extreme, the West paradoxically shows that it is no less racist today than it was yesterday. An elitist like Vilfredo Pareto wrote that liberal systems in decline seem to worry more about the pedigree of their dogs than the pedigree of their offspring. And a leftist, Serge Latouche, has recently written how liberal racists, while brandishing their ethnic national masochism, force liberal values and liberal legal provisions upon their "decorative coloreds."

Peoples and ethnic groups are like boughs and petals; they grow and decay, but seldom resurrect. France and England may evoke their glorious past, but this past will invariably have to be adjusted to their new ethnically fractured reality. Lithuania was, several centuries ago, a gigantic continental empire; today it is a speck on the map. The obscure Moscow in the 15th century became the center of the future Russian steamroller because other principalities, such as Suzdal or Novgorod, fantasized more about aesthetics than power politics. Great calamities, such as wars and famines, may be harbingers of a nation's collapse, but license and demographic suicide can also determine the outcome of human drama. Post-ideological Europe will soon discover that it cannot forever depend on the whims of technocratic elites who are in search of the chimera of the "common European market." As always, the meaning of carnal soil and precious blood will spring forth from those who best know how to impose their destiny on those who have already decided to relinquish theirs. Or to paraphrase Carl Schmitt, when a people abandons politics, this does not mean the end of politics; it simply means the end of a weaker people.

WOODROW WILSON'S DEFEAT IN YUGOSLAVIA: THE END OF A MULTICULTURAL UTOPIA

Es sollte zugleich die Ansicht wachsen, dass ein dritter Weltkrieg, wenn auch nicht unwahrscheinlich, *so doch nicht unvermeidlich ist.*

— Ernst Jünger, *Über die Linie*, 1950

The violent breakup of Yugoslavia illustrates the growing difficulty of theorizing about the future of multi-ethnic states. Who would have predicted that Yugoslavia, which until recently had been hailed as a "model multi-ethnic socialist state," would come to an end, only seventy-three years after it was created!

Predictably, the much-vaunted liberal models for multi-ethnic states, such as "power sharing", or "consociationalism", will have little attraction in an environment in which different ethnic groups can no longer live together.1 Whether their wish for independence, even when supported by the majority of their ethnic voters, will be welcomed by multi-ethnic America or the multinational United Nations, remains to be seen. Slovenia's, Croatia's, and Bosnia's self-proclaimed and bloody departure from Yugoslavia had little legally binding value, so long as they did not receive the blessing of the U.S.

The American belief that the collapse of Communism in the Soviet Union and Eastern Europe would miraculously bypass the Yalta-drawn borders and bring about the "end of history", needs to be revised. To applaud the end of communism, yet to sermonize about the inviolability of European borders that were drawn in 1919 by Versailles treaty architects, and then in 1945, by their Yalta successors, does not sound very convincing. If America is ready today to adapt itself to a new post-communist reality, it follows that it should also accept a new geopolitical reality. One must not rule out the possibility that American and Atlantic fantasies about multi-ethnic and economic integration may be paralleled by a further Central and East European slide into disintegration, calling into question the security of the entire European continent.

I. Yugoslav Civil War or a Serbian War of Aggression?

Since June 1991 the American administration has viewed the conflict in the former Yugoslavia as a "civil war" pitting secessionist Croatia against the Yugoslav center, Serbia. To call the war in the former Yugoslavia "civil" was quite in line with American globalist rhetoric. In the eyes of the American media, a "civil war" was taking place within the internationally recognized Yugoslav state. American geopolitical concerns also played a role. Washington was not willing to shrug off a country it had helped create in 1919, and that it provided for decades with all the necessary legitimacy and legality. Both as a Serbian-dominated monarchy, and later as Tito's communist non-aligned pseudo-federation, Yugoslavia enjoyed an excellent relationship with America. In addition, Yugoslavia was a full member of various international organizations and regimes, including the United Nations. Also, from the sociological point of view, multi-ethnic America could not dismiss a country that in many instances was a smaller replica of the American melting pot. If Croatia is allowed to walk away, why not tomorrow allow Southern California or Arizona to merge with Mexico? From historical and demographic perspectives, nobody can prevent today's or tomorrow's Mexican Americans from invoking similar "democratic rights to self-determination."

The American view of the war in former Yugoslavia as "civil" was further justified by the fact that whenever a war breaks out in an internationally recognized state — even when a conflict involves two distinct geographic and ethnic components within this state — it is perceived as a "civil war". The U.N. charter explicitly forbids other foreign powers from meddling into the affairs of a country where such "inter-ethnic" conflict may take place.[2] It did not come as a surprise, therefore, when following the Yugo-Serbian armed aggression against Slovenia and Croatia in late June 1991, and against Bosnia in April 1992, America announced that it would provide "good offices", declaring itself willing to be an "honest broker", reassuring repeatedly the Croatian and Bosnian victims, as well as the Serbian aggressor, of American neutrality and impartiality.

Under pressure from America, and under pressure from their own multi-ethnic environments, Spain, England, and France copied the similar American position; that is, the Yugoslav peoples need to "talk with each other", and their federation must somehow be preserved.[3] The fact that the European Community kept inviting both Serbian and Croatian leaders to the negotiating table at the peace conference in The Hague and Brussels, only illustrates the European Community's own fears of a similar "Balkanesque" environment within its own house. Naturally, those conferences only gave Serbia more time and more reason to continue devouring chunks of Croatia and Bosnia. Even today, the idea that the former Yugoslav melting pot could be salvaged as a loose association of independent states, albeit under a different name, prevails in America and the E.U. Must it be recalled that for decades the French and American media portrayed Serbia (and the Serb-run Yugoslavia) as a valiant ally in the First and Second World Wars? With the Serbian invasion of Bosnia in April 1992, the war in the Balkans took a very ugly turn, as it gradually became clear that Serbia, under the pretext of trying to salvage Yugoslavia, was paradoxically destroying it. America began to change its tune. America's decision to swallow the definite break-up of Yugoslavia, as well as its criticism of its pivot, Serbia, was primarily motivated by the world-wide reports of Serbian atrocities, and of Serbian detention camps in Bosnia and Hercegovina.[4]

II. Americanism and Yugoslavism: The Endless Legalism

In contrast to its previous active engagement in the Gulf War, the Bush Administration first took a surprisingly low-key approach to the conflict in former Yugoslavia. The U.S. pledged in July 1991 that it would cede the mediation of the Yugoslav conflict to the European Community, and that it would accept a formula negotiated and approved by the European Community. Yet all European countries continued, and still continue, to have a confusing view of the crisis in former Yugoslavia, and their approaches to solving it range from rhetorical air strikes on Serbian targets to wait-and-see tactics. Only the German government denounced the Serbian aggression — although it prudently refused to commit its own troops to the former Yugoslav republics.

Neither America nor the European Community was willing to see Germany play a stronger card in the Balkans — except, of course, when Germany pays the military cost or takes hundreds of thousands of Balkan refugees. It suffices to recall that when in 1991 the German Minister of Foreign Affairs, Hans D. Genscher, sounded the alarm and accused Serbia of the escalation of violence, the American government cautioned against "German unilateral moves", arguing that such German action could ruin European Community mediation and lead to the spreading of the bloodshed to Kosovo and Macedonia. To some extent, aside from the issue of the recognition or non-recognition of Croatia and Slovenia, the idea still prevails in Washington that the responsibility for the conflict is shared by both Serbia and Croatia, and that the only way the conflict could be resolved is through endless negotiations. When the U.N. peace initiative, headed by the former high-ranking American official Cyrus Vance, got under way in December 1991, one had the impression that this initiative was primarily decided as the American move to block German involvement in the Balkans, rather than as a serious effort to broker a lasting cease-fire.

Other European Community members followed the American lead. On the surface their argument was that with its recognition of the new states, Germany was adding fuel to the fire and reviving the demons of 1941. The real reasons why they failed to act swiftly and together with Germany appear to be more complex. By its recognition of Croatia and Slovenia in December 1991, Germany was effectively showing that it best understood what was going on in the Balkans. Moreover, the German attitude towards the Balkan crisis only exposed the flawed legacy, not only of Yalta, but of Versailles, too. America, France, and England must, ironically, realize today that the country they created *ex nihilo* in 1919, and recreated ex nihilo in 1945, never had any legitimacy, and therefore could never function as a democracy. This time, Yugoslavia is not being destroyed by the proverbial *böser Deutsche*. This time, it is the French and American darling *böses Serbien* that is mercilessly destroying the Versailles architecture and its bizarre multi-ethnic foundations.

Nobody in America is willing to countenance an assertive Germany engaging in unilateral diplomacy and acting in the area of Europe where German involvement is seen by many American politicians, let alone by the Serbian media, as an outright Fourth Reich meddling in Yugoslav affairs. Thus, on the eve of the German recognition of Croatia, American Deputy Secretary Lawrence Eagleburger issued a "stern warning" to the twelve E.C. countries not to follow Germany's example in recognizing Croatia and Slovenia.[5] Some American commentators have suggested that America was opposed to the recognition of Croatia because officials in the Bush administration, like "Lawrence (of Serbia)" Eagleburger, and Brent Scowcroft, had extensive financial ties with Serbian communist circles in former communist Yugoslavia.[6] In view of this possibility, it is wrong to expect America and France to speed up any invasion of "Serboslavia" — a country whose territorial "integrity and unity" America had advocated for a good part of this century.

The Bush Administration's policy towards the Balkans must be seen as neither naïve nor hasty. It was a very well planned and well thought-out policy that refused to divorce itself from Wilsonian moralism or Bush's "new word" ecumenism. The American political indecision, rather than stopping the conflict in the Balkans, encouraged the Yugoslav Army, and its ally Serbia, to go ahead with its aggression against Bosnia. Had America, the E.C., and the U.N. very early on recognized Croatia and Bosnia, or threatened the Yugoslav Army with military strikes, or both, the conflict would probably have never escalated to its later tragic dimensions. As sovereign and internationally recognized states, Croatia and Bosnia would have not been treated as regions in an "ethnic" civil war with another region. In such a new international environment, the Yugoslavia Army would have been deterred from further aggression. Instead, Serbia could interpret the E.C. disagreements, American indecision, and U.N. apoliticism to its advantage — while Croatia and Bosnia saw in it a flagrant rejection of their sovereignty and their newly won independence. American refusal to distinguish clearly between aggressor and victim, between the "Schmittian" *hostis* and *amicus*, rather than slowing down the Serbian aggression, gave green light to future Serbian aggression. The American diplomats made a mistake twice: They clung to the idea of Yugoslavia even when it became clear that Yugoslavia could no longer be held together, and they failed to back up German diplomacy that could have best assessed the new geopolitical tremors in the Balkans and best seen the futility of keeping artificial states together by force. American and European Community blunders seem to have been prompted more by deeply flawed parallels between pre-war Germany and today's Germany, than by any genuine interest in solving the Yugoslav crisis.

III. The Concept of the Political Revisited

The war in Croatia and Bosnia, which has resulted in death and destruction on a scale unparalleled in Europe since World War II, points to the necessity of reassessing the notion of politics and sovereignty. Moreover, it requires a new definition of democracy in a multi-ethnic state. In the post-Cold War world, in a somewhat utopian fashion, the U.S. and the E.C. shrugged off the possibility of war on the European continent. When a war did break out in the former Yugoslavia, it took them months to define it, let alone stop it through resolute military action. Liberal inability to think in terms of classical power politics, and an unwillingness even to assume that Europe may be plagued by the ghost of the past, naturally led to political paralysis. America has lacked a clear vision of how to deal with a post-communist Eastern Europe. America first magnified the importance of preserving Yugoslavia; then, it urged the E.C. to solve the crisis, who with the best intentions could not bring about any cease-fire; and finally, America and the E.C. passed the torch to the apolitical U.N. Paradoxically, the American recognition of Croatia and Slovenia signaled a European and American disengagement from the Yugoslav crisis, precisely at the time when America and Europe should be working towards new security arrangements for all of Europe.[7] Why did Europe and America fail to resolve the conflict quickly when it became clear, a long time ago, that Yugoslavia could no longer be held together? It appears that the long-standing neutral and aloof American attitude towards the Yugoslav crisis has complex geopolitical, economic, and historical roots. Since Yalta both Eastern and Western Europe have played a minor role in foreign politics. "High politics" was the privileged ground of the two superpowers, with their respective policies of double containment. The Soviet Union and America contained each other, but they also contained their own respective allies and satellites. America was not just containing Communism in the East; America was also containing Europe and its main pivot in the West, Germany.[8] It should therefore come as no surprise that during the Cold War, not a single European country was willing or able to engage in "high politics". Neither France, nor Britain, let alone Germany, were in a position to create an all-out European foreign politics and handle crisis spots in Europe or elsewhere. After the end of the Cold War, after the end of bipolarity, and with the Balkan tragedy unfolding, Europe was totally unprepared for the role of a unified arbiter. Be it in the realm of creating European military security, or in developing its common politics towards crisis, Europe has always had to ask for prior American blessing. This ultimately led to European paralysis and to frequent American criticism of unilateral diplomacy, as was seen in the case of American criticism of the German recognition of Croatia. In such a "de-politicized" Europe, it did not take long to understand that European indecision in regard to the war in former Yugoslavia was only asking for a further Serbian war of aggression.

IV. The Return of History

The results of the war in the former Yugoslavia will certainly lead to an unparalleled historical revisionism regarding two world wars in Europe.

Some German observers have pointed out that the Croatian fight for independence indirectly challenged the legacy of Versailles and one of its crucial pillars, Serb-controlled Yugoslavia. Should Serbia lose in the Balkans, then the real winner of World War II, in a retroactive way, becomes Germany.[9] The disappearance of Yugoslavia is already causing different geopolitical shifts in Europe, in which Germany appears as the prime winner and France, America, and Britain as losers. America must be saddened by the dissolution of Yugoslavia. For America, Yugoslavia was a model multi-ethnic state, which aside from being a buffer zone in the East-West condominium, had also had a duty to weaken the natural German plans in Central and Eastern Europe. With the dissolution of Yugoslavia, Woodrow Wilson suffered a serious defeat in Croatia. From the American liberal and mercantile perspective, and according to the liberal belief in economic interdependence and ethnic integration, it makes little sense to discard larger units and encourage the emergence of smaller ones, especially if this results in the disruption of world trade. The behavior of American politicians continues to be motivated by a desire to deal with unitary multi-ethnic states, especially if those states house many intertwined minorities. It is certainly no accident that America was the last country in the West to recognize the futility of the Soviet Union and Yugoslavia. America preferred to deal with Moscow and Belgrade's communist "reformed" leadership, rather than with individual Soviet and Yugoslav anti-communist republics. This static and reactive foreign policy may have been prompted by reasons of international security and stability, but it was also prompted by the fear of Balkanization in America. Integration through economic ties, even at the price of keeping artificial states together, appears worthier in the West than the advocacy of self-determination, especially if the right to self-determination impedes international trade and destroys Wilsonian and President Bush's new world ecumenism. Hence, American reticence to denounce and punish the Serbian aggressor. Oftentimes, when multi-ethnic states begin to breakup, a geopolitical vacuum leads to larger rifts. American fears that the example of Croatia and Bosnia could be followed tomorrow by

Quebec, New Mexico, or California are not groundless at all. The 1992 riots in Los Angeles clearly illustrate that the metaphor of the Balkans and Yugoslavia can surface in America any day and at any time. The imperative of negotiations may be preached to Croats and Bosnians, but negotiations are resolutely rejected by Monroe's and Wilson's grandsons. In April 1992 Bush did not pontificate about sending legal advisors or Bible preachers to pacify Los Angeles rioters. He sent elite soldiers instead. The paradox of the twentieth century is that everybody talks about unity and integration while a little farther to the East — and tomorrow in the West — massive disintegration and ruptures appear everywhere. Secessions and the resurrection of ethnic identities do not bode well for the mercantile new world order and for its main ringleader, America. Although it may be too soon to speculate about the role of the nation-state, judging by the increasing number of states in the U.N. the concept of international law and the concept of sovereignty will urgently require a new *nomos* of the Earth.[10] In conclusion, one may say that the U.S. and the U.N., as much as they like to talk about European unity, may also be happy to see Europe rocked by occasional wars. Would it truly be in America's interest to see a unified Europe become a superpower? Is it truly in America's interest to see Europe politically unified around its main steamroller, Germany? Hardly. Every American politician knows well that a politically (and not economically) united Europe would rule the world. This is the reason why European technocrats, along with their American teachers, are trying today to solve a political crisis in the Balkans with nonpolitical and apolitical means. They are attempting to use mechanisms that, while valid in apolitical America, are totally inappropriate and ineffective in a highly politicized Central and Eastern Europe. Emphasizing "negotiations" and "compromise" in the area of the world where political decision is desperately needed amounts to ignoring the essence of the political as well as the essence of the crisis in the Balkans.[11] The decades-long American belief that Yugoslavia or Czechoslovakia, could be transformed into democratic states proved to be wrong. Yugoslavia could exist only as a Serb-dominated authoritarian or totalitarian country. "Democratic

Yugoslavia" is a contradiction in terms. Aside from the purely "Yugoslav" nature of the war in former Yugoslavia, one can also say that this war is also a European catharsis in which Germany's *Geschichtsbewältigung* is slowly, but definitely, coming to an end. Croatia and Germany have helped each other remove their own terror of history and their historical stigma of "bad guys". It goes without saying that both Croatia and Germany took advantage of each other's diplomatic decisions. By contrast, the indecisiveness of Maastricht-Europe regarding resolution of the Yugoslav crisis only illustrated a growing European fear of any political decision. European "collective security" always depends on a prior blessing from America. The apolitical-economic-Maastrich-market-Europe is dangerously signaling that if a serious crisis begins in Eastern Europe today, and in Western Europe tomorrow, European "high politics" and "high politicians", will not be available. The war in former Yugoslavia, as much as it has eloquently exposed the flaws of Versailles and Yalta, has also demonstrated the dangers of political and social Balkanization, both in Europe and America.

A GLOBAL VILLAGE OR THE RIGHTS OF THE PEOPLES?

The great conflicts of the future will no longer pit left against right, or East against West, but the forces of nationalism and regionalism against the credo of universal democracy. The lofty ideal of the global village seems to be stumbling over the renewed rise of East European separatism, whose aftershocks may soon spill over into the Western hemisphere. Already the dogma of human rights is coming under fire by the proponents of peoples' rights, and the yearning for historical community is making headway into atomized societies deserted by ideologies.

With the collapse of communist internationalism the clock of history has been turned back, and inevitably the words of the 19th-century conservative Joseph de Maistre come to mind: "I have seen Poles, Russians, Italians, but as to man, I declare never to have seen him." Indeed, this paradigmatic universal man, relieved from economic plight and from the burden of history, this man on whom we pattern the ideology of human rights, is nowhere to be seen. He appears all the more nebulous as in day-to-day life we encounter real peoples with specific cultures. If he resides in Brooklyn, his idea of human rights is likely to be different from somebody who lives in the Balkans; if he is a fundamentalist Moslem his sense of civic duty will be different from somebody who is a Catholic. The rise in nationalist sentiments in Eastern Europe should not be seen as only a backlash against communist economic chaos; rather, it is the will of different peoples to retrieve their national memories long suppressed by communism's shallow universalism.

All of Europe seems to be undergoing a paradoxical and almost ludicrous twist of history. On the one hand, Western Europe is becoming more and more an "americano-centric" anational meta-society, while post-communist Eastern Europe threatens to explode into a myriad of mini-states. Conversely, whereas Western Europe is experiencing an unparalleled wave of foreign immigration and the inevitable surge of racism that must follow, the racial homogeneity of East Europeans has made them today more "European" than West Europeans — the East's own multi-ethnic turmoil notwithstanding.

In view of the disintegrating state system in Eastern Europe, Woodrow Wilson's crusades for the right of national self-determination and global democracy must seem contradictory. Home rule as envisioned by the architects of the Treaty of Versailles in 1919 may have suited the demands of Poles, Czechs, and those European peoples who benefited from the collapse of the Austro-Hungarian monarchy, but it had little appeal for those who were forced to exchange one foreign ruler for another. For the Germans stranded in a newly emerged and bloated Poland or Romania in 1919, or for the Slovaks in a hybrid Czechoslovak state, the right to home rule meant nothing less than the creation of their own separate nation-states.

Yugoslavia, too, has owed its relative longevity more to Western liberal well-wishers that to the true consensus of its disparate peoples. For the last seventy years, the Yugoslav experience has been an exercise in civil wars and constant ethnic strife among four of its major ethnic groups. Naturally, in light of the present salvos being exchanged between the Croats and the Serbs, the question that comes to mind is why does the artificial blending of different peoples always lead to instability and ethnic chaos? The answer seems to be rather obvious: that the rights of peoples are incompatible with universalism. Ethnic particularities cannot coexist in a state that places abstract principles of human rights over the real principles of peoples' rights.

It would be impossible to chronicle with precision who is right or wrong in the present ethnic turmoil that besets Yugoslavia. A litany of grievances can be heard today among Croats, Serbs, Slovenes, and ethnic Albanians, of which each group is tirelessly trying to outdo the others with its own impressive victimology. As Yugoslavia demonstrates, in multi-ethnic countries the notion of justice depends solely on the constantly shifting inter-ethnic balance of power, as well as the perception that each ethnic group may have of its neighbor. Both Serbs and Croats, the two largest ethnic groups in Yugoslavia, are today utterly disappointed with their country; the former, on the grounds that Yugoslavia is not centralized enough to allow the consolidation of the Yugoslav state; the latter, on the grounds that Yugoslavia is already too centralized. The lesson to draw today from the Yugoslav experience is that in multi-ethnic states democracy can only function when the national question has been resolved.

Moreover, democracy can take root only within the ethnographic frontiers of various peoples, who will define that word in accordance with their *genius loci* and their own history. Just as it was foolish some time ago to talk about Yugoslav anticommunist dissidence, so it is foolish now to anticipate the emergence of the all-out "Yugoslav" democracy. What seems good for a Croatian democrat today may be seen as a direct threat by somebody who styles himself a Serbian democrat tomorrow. Even America, because of its erratic immigration policy and the declining birthrate among whites, may soon find itself in a similar situation of having to redefine the concept of democracy. The legacy of the Founding Fathers, in the years to come, may be interpreted differently given the changing racial fabric of America. Voting preferences are likely to hinge on skin color, which could lead to a Balkanization worse than the one presently threatening Yugoslavia.

Democracy in any multiethnic state, at least as the global democrats would like to see it, is semantic nonsense; the liberal principle of "one man, one vote" is inapplicable in a country of diverse ethnic groups. Consequently, the genuine democratization of Yugoslavia, or for that matter the multiethnic Soviet Union, would require the disintegration of the country and the establishment of new nation states. The German Holy Empire was an example of a rather stable confederal system that lasted for almost one thousand years, although at one point it was divided into three hundred sovereign principalities.

Paradoxical as it may seem, the ideology of global democracy seems to parallel closely the failed communist Utopia, with one exception: it is presently more successful in the pursuit of its goals. What we are witnessing in the West is a liberal transposition of the Christian ideal of one world into a post-industrial society — a *civitas dei* in an age of cable TV and Michael Jackson. Everything presages, however, that this brand of universalism can be as dangerous for the peoples of Eastern Europe as the now moribund Communism. From the point of view of a globe-trotting merchant a centralized and unified Yugoslavia, or Soviet Union, organized into giant free markets, would be the best solution insofar as that would facilitate the free movement of capital, and thus better ease the strain of ethnic animosity. Indeed, the prospects of having to deal with an additional twenty states on the Euro-Asian continent is a nightmare to a businessman more interested in the free flow of capital than in the self-determination of ethnic groups. The political liberal will surely endorse a global village that includes different ethnic parades — so long as they do not turn into military marches. Such a line of thinking, that "economics determines politics," clearly points to the Marxian morphology inherent in liberalism, confirming, once again, that communism is nothing else but its pesky brainchild.

But will the free bazaar in the global village dissolve ethnic passions? Although the masses in franchised Eastern Europe are today mimicking every move of the West, nothing indicates that their honeymoon with the global village will last long. Ethnic intolerance will only worsen once the peoples of Eastern Europe realize that the global village promises a lot but delivers little.

What makes a people? A people has a common heritage and a will to a common destiny. A people exists despite superficial cleavages such as parties, interest groups, and passing trends in ideologies. As Georges Dumézil, Mircea Eliade, and Carl G. Jung have demonstrated, a people shares a *mythe fondateur* — a communal myth that gives birth to original cultural endeavors. The culture of a people, recalls Alain de Benoist, is its identity card and its mental respiration, and "it is the passport for a future that takes the shape of destiny."

When a people becomes oblivious of its founding myth it is doomed to perish. Worse, it may turn into an aggregate of happy robots whose new dictum of universal human rights could be just another cloak for mindless hedonism. Western Europe is already experiencing this kind of ethnic and cultural oblivion. Paris in August resembles Oran or Marrakesh, and wide stretches of Berlin, at noon, have the distinct flavor of Anatolia. To many foreigners, France is becoming more a synonym for its famous goat cheese and less a symbol of Corneillian heroism, and if one decides to go to Florence it is for a good bottle of Chianti rather than the mystic transcendence experienced through Botticelli's paintings.

Yugoslavia, founded on similar principles of multiculturalism, is a product of the Russian 19th-century pan-Slavism combined with the Wilsonian dream. This experiment has not resulted in perpetual peace. In times of great crises host nations no longer look at aliens as purveyors of exotic folklore, but rather as predators snatching bread from their host's mouth. Peoples are not the same; they never have been and never will be. Ethnic groups can be compared to the inmates of large American prisons, who usually begin to respect each other only when their turf is staked out and when their cells are separated by massive stone walls. Thrown into one cell they are likely to devour each other in a perpetual conflict over "territorial imperative."

The best way, therefore, to resolve the Yugoslavian multiethnic crisis is not by appealing to the spirit of "brotherhood and unity" but rather by dismantling the country into a loose confederal state. Blood and soil will forever determine the life of nations. "Scratch the skin of any globalist, goes the proverb in Croatia, and you will find beneath a passionate Croat, Serb, German, or Jew."

With the end of Communism, the end of history will not follow, as some would wish us to believe. Had the Europeans in the 13th century conjured up the "end of history," the Mongol khananat would have been transferred to the Iberian Peninsula. Had the Germans and the Poles preached the liturgy of affirmative action in 1683, Vienna would shine today as the capital of the Turkish sultans. The endless power game among nations and ethnic groups, the constant shifts in demographic trends, teach us that life goes on in all its "creative" hatred — Hitler, Stalin, or Saddam notwithstanding.

Today, more than ever before in the history of mankind, it is the specificity of peoples that is threatened by the universalist credo. Whether one travels to Warsaw or Sarajevo, or lands in Bucharest or Berlin, the blaring of rock music and the iconography of junk culture have become the new *lingua franca*, of the global village. One could spend days in the Budapest Hilton without ever knowing one had left the suspended bridges of the hotel complex of downtown Atlanta. The new universalism, in order to enforce its creed, no longer needs to resort to genocide and depopulations, to the frigid climate of Kolyma or Katyn, to which Stalin, in the name of a paradigmatic global proletarian, carted off Volga Germans, Kalmuks, and Chechens. The new universalism need only turn to a tepid universe of

Kentucky Fried Chicken, a society in which everybody equals everybody, and where ethnic identities, therefore, mean nothing.

This "cool Stalinism" strips peoples of their souls by creating a *Homo economicus-dollaricus*. The end results of both brands of universalism are pretty much the same, except that the veiled violence of liberal universalism can now be more dangerous than the blunt violence of Communism. It is an irony of history that naked violence often preserves regionalism and ethnic roots; each persecution has its cathartic virtue, and each sacrifice invariably strengthens a peoples' historical memory. Communist violence has triggered a hitherto unseen ethnic pride from the Balkans to the Baltic lands. In an air-conditioned hell of cool universalism, by contrast, regionalism and the love of one's country do not need to be openly crushed; instead, they can be turned into a commodity, and thereby rendered superfluous, if not outright funny. If ever the ethnic pride disappears from Eastern Europe it will not be as a result of communist repression, but rather as the outcome of a new infatuation with capitalist gadgetry. The global village knows how to enslave Ulysses' lotus-eaters without even making them realize the peril that they face.

In a system in which everything has become a commodity, ethnic identity is viewed as an expendable triviality too — a triviality that may at best arouse some culinary interest or a tourist's curiosity. If necessary, universalism will even do good business from the hammer, sickle, and swastika — as long as they sell well. For a globetrotting merchant, home is where he hangs his hat, and where he makes a big buck. Montesquieu was, after all, not wrong when he wrote that commerce is the vocation of equal people.

Until recently, the concepts of egalitarianism and global democracy were strictly limited to Western peoples. Today, in a spasm of masochism, and because of the so-called "white guilt", the West has extended these principles to the antipodes of Earth. The *bon sauvage* has been transformed in our postmodern age into the therapeutic role of white man's superego. Not long ago it was the white man who had to teach the nonwhites the manners of the West. Today the roles are reversed; now it is the non-European, with his pristine innocence, who grafts himself onto the ailing consciousness of the Westerner, pointing out to him the right path to the radiant future.

The very concept of "the West" has been stripped of its original geopolitical and geographical significance, becoming instead a metaphor for a meta-system that encompasses Alaska, the Philippines, South Korea, and any nook or cranny where the idea of the mercantile global village thrives.

With the end of its competing ideology the philosophy of the global village has taken hold in many countries, eulogizing those who support it, vilifying those who don't. What the future holds is not difficult to guess. It may well happen that inter-ethnic troubles will eventually subside in Eastern Europe, but this is not likely to happen in the West, where racial turmoil looms large. We may soon see replicas of the Berlin Wall erected in New York and Philadelphia in order to contain the multiethnic violence of the global village. The lesson of artificial Yugoslavia should not be forgotten. Our "promiscuous altruism", as Garrett Hardin writes, may lead us against our will into a war of all against all.

The cult of the global village appears today as a political response to theological and ideological battles that have rocked the West for more than a century. But it remains to be seen how the singular principle of human rights can be implanted in a world that remains eminently plural. "We invoke human rights," continues Hardin, "to justify interfering in another nation's internal affairs. Thereby we risk making enemies of that nation ... The intentions behind the fiction of 'human rights' may be noble, but insisting on such rights poses grave dangers." Global democracy is the last twilight dream of those who are spiritually homeless and physically uprooted. It is a doctrine that eloquently masks the ethnic and racial reality behind the theology of universalism.

ENDNOTES

Part I: Religion

Marx, Moses, and the Pagans in the Secular City

1. Charles Norris Cochrane, *Christianity and Classical Culture* (New York: Oxford UP, (1957), 254–55, 329.
2. T. R. Glover, *The Conflict of Religion in the Early Roman Empire* (1909; Boston: Beacon, 1960), 242, 254, passim.
3. Friedrich Nietzsche, '*Der Antichrist*', in *Nietzsches Werke* (Salzburg/Stuttgart: Verlag "Das Bergland-Buch", 1952), 983, para. 21.
4. Pierre Gripari, *L'histoire du méchant dieu* (Lausanne: L'Age d'Homme, 1987), 101–2.
5. Michel Marmin, "Les Piegès du folklore", in *La Cause des peuples* (Paris: édition Le Labyrinthe, 1982), 39–44.
6. Nicole Belmont, *Paroles païennes* (Paris: édition Imago, 1986), 160–61.
7. Alain de Benoist, *Noël, Les Cahiers européens* (Paris: Institut de documentations et d'études européens, 1988).
8. Jean Markale, et al., "Mythes et lieux christianisés", *L'Europe païenne* (Paris: Seghers, 1980), 133.
9. About European revolutionary conservatives, see the seminal work by Armin Mohler, *Die Konservative Revolution in Deutschland, 1919–1933* (Darmstadt: Wissenschaftliche Buchgesellschaft, 1972). See also Tomislav Sunic, *Against Democracy and Equality: The European New Right* (London: Arktos, 2011).
10. See notably the works by Alfred Rosenberg, *Der Mythus des 20. Jahrhunderts* (München: Hoheneichen Verlag, 1933). Also worth noting is the name of Wilhelm Hauer, *Deutscher Gottschau* (Stuttgart: Karl Gutbrod, 1934), who significantly

popularized Indo-European mythology among National Socialists; on pages 240–54 Hauer discusses the difference between Judeo-Christian Semitic beliefs and European paganism.

11. Jean Markale, "Aujourd'hui, l'esprit païen?" in *L'Europe païenne* (Paris: Seghers, 1980), 15. The book contains pieces on Slavic, Celtic, Latin, and Greco-Roman paganism.

12. Milton Konvitz, *Judaism and the American Idea* (Ithaca: Cornell UP, 1978), 71. Jerol S. Auerbach, "Liberalism and the Hebrew Prophets", in *Commentary* 84:2 (1987):58. Compare with Ben Zion Bokser in "Democratic Aspirations in Talmudic Judaism", in *Judaism and Human Rights,* ed. Milton Konvitz (New York: Norton, 1972): "The Talmud ordained with great emphasis that every person charged with the violation of some law be given a fair trial and before the law all were to be scrupulously equal, whether a king or a pauper" (146). Ernst Troeltsch, *Die Soziallehren der christlichen Kirchen and Gruppen* (1922; Aalen: Scientia Verlag, 1965), 768; also the passage "Naturrechtlicher and liberaler Character des freikirchlichen Neu-calvinismus", (762–72). Compare with Georg Jellinek, *Die Erklärung der Menschen-und Bürgerrechte* (Leipzig: Duncker and Humblot, 1904): "(t)he idea to establish legally the unalienable, inherent and sacred rights of individuals, is not of political, but religious origins" (46). Also Werner Sombart, *Die Juden and das Wirtschaftsleben* (Leipzig: Verlag Duncker and Humblot, 1911): "Americanism is to a great extent distilled Judaism ('geronnenes Judentum')" (44).

13. David Miller, *The New Polytheism* (New York: Harper and Row, 1974), 7, passim.

14. Serge Latouche, *L'occidentalisation du monde* (Paris: La Découverte, 1988).

15. Thomas Molnar, "La tentation païenne", *Contrepoint* 38 (1981), 53.

16. Alain de Benoist, *Comment peut-on etre païen?* (Paris: Albin Michel, 1981), 25.

17. Alain de Benoist, *L'éclipse du sacré* (Paris: La Table ronde, 1986), 233; see also the chapter, "De la sécularisation", 198–207. Also, Carl Schmitt, *Die politische Theologie* (München and Leipzig: Duncker und Humblot, 1922), 35–46: "(a)ll salient concepts in modern political science are secularized theological concepts" (36).

18. Gèrard Walter, *Les origines du communisme* (Paris: Payot, 1931): "Les sources judaiques de la doctrine communiste chrétienne" (13–65). Compare with Vilfredo Pareto, *Les systèmes socialistes* (Paris: Marcel Girard, 1926): "Les systèmes métaphysiques-communistes" (2:2–45). Louis Rougier, *La mystique démocratique, ses origines ses illusions* (Paris: éd. Albatros, 1983), 184. See in its entirety the passage, "Le judaisme et la révolution sociale", 184–187.

19. Louis Rougier, *Celse contre les chrétiens* (Paris: Copernic, 1977), 67, 89. Also, Sanford Lakoff, "Christianity and Equality", in *Equality*, ed. J. Roland Pennock and John W. Chapaman (New York: Atherton, 1967), 128–30.

20. Alain de Benoist, "L'Eglise, L'Europe et le Sacré", in *Pour une renaissance culturelle* (Paris: Copernic, 1979), 202.

21. Louis Rougier, *Celse*, 88.

22. *Comment peut-on être païen?*, 170, 26. De Benoist has been at odds with the so-called neo-conservative "nouveaux philosophes", who attacked his paganism on the grounds that it was a tool of intellectual anti-Semitism, racism, and totalitarianism. In his response, de Benoist levels the same criticism against the "nouveaux philosophes." See "Monothéisme-polythéisme: le grand debat", *Le Figaro Magazine*, 28 April 1979, 83: "Like Horkheimer, like Ernest Bloch, like Levinas, like René Girard, what B. H. Lévy desires is less 'audacity,' less ideal, less politics, less power, less of the State, less of history. What he expects is the accomplishment of history, the end of all adversity (the adversity to which corresponds the Hegelian *Gegenständlichkeit*), disincarnate justice, the universal peace, the disappearance of frontiers, the birth of a homogenous society..."

23. Ernest Renan, *Histoire générale des langues sémitiques* (Paris: Imprimerie Impériale, 1853), 6.

24. Mircae Eliade, *Histoire des croyances et des idées religieuses* (Paris: Payot, 1976), 1:369, passim.

25. Jean-Marie Domenach, *Le retour du tragique* (Paris: édition du Seuil, 1967), 44–45.

26. Jean Haudry, *Les Indo-Européens* (Paris: PUF, 1981), 68.

27. Hans. K. Günther, *The Religious Attitude of Indo-Europeans*, trans. Vivian Bird and Roger Pearson (London: Clair Press, 1966), 21.

28. Alain de Benoist and Pierre Vial, *La Mort* (Paris: ed. Le Labyrinthe, 1983), 15.

29. Giorgio Locchi, "L'histoire", *Nouvelle Ecole* 27/28 (1975):183–90.

30. Sigrid Hunke, *La vraie religion de l'Europe*, trans. Claudine Glot and Jean-Louis Pesteil (Paris: Le Labyrinthe, 1985), 253, 274. The book was first published under the title *Europas eigene Religion: Der Glaube der Ketzer* (Bergisch Gladbach: Gustav Lubbe, 1980).

31. Mircae Eliade, *The Myth of the Eternal Return or, Cosmos and History*, trans. Willard R. Trask (Princeton: Princeton UP, 1965), 106–7.

32. Pierre Chaunu, *Histoire et foi* (Paris: Edition France-Empire, 1980), quoted by de Benoist, *Comment peut-on être païen?* 109.

33. Michel Maffesoli, *La violence totalitaire* (Paris: PUF, 1979), 228–29.
34. See Paul Tillich, *The Eternal Now* (New York: Scribner's, 1963), 41, passim. "Shrug of eternity" are the last words Arthur Koestler uses in his novel *Darkness at Noon* (New York: Modern Library, 1941), 267.
35. Georgio Locchi, et al., "Über den Sinn der Geschichte", *Das unvergängliche Erbe* (Tübingen: Grabert Verlag, 1981), 223.
36. Walter Scott, *A New Look at Biblical Crime* (New York: Dorset Press, 1979), 59.
37. *Comment peut-on être païen?* 157–58.
38. Mircea Eliade, *Histoire des croyances*, 1:194.

Part II: Cultural Pessimism

History and Decadence: Spengler's Cultural Pessimism Today

1. In the case of the European "New Right", see Jean Cau, *Discours de la décadence* (Paris: Copernic, 1978), Julien Freund, *La décadence: histoire sociologique et philosophique d'une expérience humaine* (Paris: Sirey, 1984*)*, and Pierre Chaunu, *Histoire et décadence* (Paris: Perrin, 1981). In the case of authors of "leftist sensibility", see Jean Baudrillard's virulent attack against simulacra and hyperreality in America: *Amérique* (Paris: Grasset, 1986); in English, *America*, trans. Chris Turner (New York, London: Verso, 1988) and Jean-François Huyghe, *La soft-idéologie* (Paris: Laffont, 1987). There is a certain Spenglerian whiff in Christopher Lasch, *The Culture of Narcissism* (New York: Warner Books, 1979), and probably in Richard Lamm, *Megatraumas: America at the Year 2000* (Boston: Houghton Mifflin, 1985). About European cultural conservatives see my *Against Democracy and Equality: The European New Right* (London: Arktos Media Ltd, 2011).

2. See Spengler's critic and admirer Heinrich Scholz, *Zum "Untergang des Abendlandes"* (Berlin: von Reuther and Reichard, 1920). Scholz conceives of history as polycentric occurrences concentrated in creative archetypes. (117). My trans.

3. Oswald Spengler, *The Decline of the West*, trans. Charles Francis Atkinson, 2 vols. (1926; New York: Knopf, 1976), 1:21. My text, however, contains my own translations from *Der Untergang des Abendlandes* (München: Beck, 1923), 1:28–29. Citations hereafter are in the text, in parentheses, giving references to these two editions, respectively.

4. Vilfredo Pareto, "Dangers of Socialism", in *The Other Pareto*, ed. Placido Bucolo, trans. Gillian and Placido Bucolo, pre. Ronald Fletcher (New York: St. Martin's, 1980). Pareto writes: "There are some people who imagine that they can disarm the enemy by complacent flattery. They are wrong. The world has always belonged to the stronger and will belong to them for many years to come. Men only respect those who make themselves respected. Whoever becomes a lamb will find a wolf to eat him" (125). In a similar vein, Gustave le Bon, *Psychologie politique* (1911; Paris: Les Amis de G. L. Bon, 1984), writes: "Wars among nations have, by the way, always been the source of the most important progress. Which pacifist people has ever played any role in history?" (79). My trans.

5. John Lukacs, *The Passing of the Modern Age* (New York: Harper, 1970), 10, 9.

6. Claude Polin, *L'esprit totalitaire* (Paris: Sirey, 1977), 111. My trans.

7. Claude Polin, *Le totalitarisme* (Paris: Presses Universitaires Françaises, 1982) argues that egalitarianism, universalism and economism are the three pivots of totalitarianism: "Totalitarian power is first and foremost the power of all against all; the tyranny of all against all. Totalitarian society is not constructed from the top down to the bottom, but from the bottom up to the top" (117). My trans.

8. "Is World Peace Possible" in *Selected Essays*, trans. Donald O. White (1936: Chicago: Henry Regnery, 1967), 207.

9. Serge Latouche, *L'occidentalisation du monde* (Paris: La Découverte, 1989), 9. My trans. About Westerners' self-hate and self-denial, see Alain de Benoist, *Europe, Tiers monde même combat* (Paris: Laffont, 1986): "And whereas Christian universalism had once contributed to the justification of colonization, Christian pastoralism today inspires decolonization. This 'mobilization of consciences' crystallizes itself around the notion of culpability." The colonized is no longer "a primitive" who ought to be "led to civilization." Rather, he is a living indictment, indeed, an example of an immaculate morality from whom the "civilized" has much to learn (62). See also Pascal Bruckner, *Le sanglot de l'homme blanc; Tiers monde, culpabilité, haine de soi* (Paris: Seuil, 1983), 13: for the bleeding-heart liberal Westerner "the birth of the Third world gave birth to this new category; expiatory militantism." My trans.

10. Spengler, "Pessimismus", *Reden and Aufsätze* (München: Beck, 1937), 70; in English, "Pessimism?" in *Selected Essays*, 143.

11. Konrad Lorenz, *The Waning of Humaneness* (Boston: Little, Brown, 1987), 58–59.

12. It would be impossible to enumerate all cultural pessimists who usually identify themselves as heroic pessimists, often as conservative revolutionaries, or aristocratic nihilists. Poets and novelists of great talent such as Gottfried Benn, Louis F. Céline,

Ezra Pound, and others, were very much inspired by Oswald Spengler. See Gottfried Benn, "Pessimismus", in *Essays und Aufsätze* (Wiesbaden: Limes, 1959): "Man is not alone, thinking is alone. Thinking is self-bound and solitary" (357). See also the apocalyptic prose of Ernst Jünger, *An der Zeitmauer* (Werke) (Stuttgart: Klett, 1959): "It seems that cyclical system corresponds to our spirit. We make round-shaped watches, although there is no logical compulsion behind it. And even catastrophes are viewed as recurrent, as for example floods and drought, fire-age and ice-age" (460–61). My trans.

13. Friedrich Sieburg, *Die Lust am Untergang* (Hamburg: Rowohlt, 1954), 54. My trans.

Emile Cioran and the Culture of Death

1. Emile Cioran, *Syllogismes de l'amertume* (Paris: Gallimard, 1952), p. 72 (my trans.).
2. *De l'inconvénient d'etre né* (Paris: Gallimard, 1973), p. 161–162. (my trans.) (*The Trouble with Being Born*, translated by Richard Howard: Seaver Bks., 1981).
3. Cioran, *Le mauvais démiurge* (Paris: Gallimard, 1969), p. 63. (my trans.).
4. *Syllogismes de l'amertume*, p. 87 (my trans.). 5. Ibid., p. 176.
6. *De l'inconvénient d'etre né*, p. 11 (my trans.). 7. Ibid., p. 29.
8. Ibid., p. 23.
9. Ibid., p. 141.
10. *Syllogismes de l'amertume*, p. 61 (my trans.).
11. *La tentation d'exister*, (Paris: Gallimard, 1956), p. 37–38 (my trans.) (*The Temptation to Exist*, translated by Richard Howard; Seaver Bks., 1986).
12. *Syllogismes de l'amertume*, p. 151 (my trans.). 13. Ibid., p. 156.
14. Ibid., p. 158.
15. *Histoire et utopie* (Paris: Gallimard, 1960), p. 59. (my trans.) (*History and Utopia*, trans. by Richard Howard, Seaver Bks., 1987).
16. *Syllogismes de l'amertume*, p. 154 (my trans.)
17. Ibid., p. 86.
18. *De l'inconvénient d'etre né*, p. 154 (my trans.).
19. Ibid. p. 155.
20. *Syllogismes de l'amertume*, p. 109.
21. *Histoire et utopie* (Paris: Gallimard, 1960), p. 14 (my trans.).

Part III: Race / The Third Reich

The Destruction of Ethnic Germans and German Prisoners of War in Yugoslavia, 1945–1953

1. Mads Ole Balling, *Von Reval bis Bukarest* (Copenhagen: Hermann-Niermann-Stiftung, 1991), vol. I and vol. II.

2. L. Barwich, F. Binder, M. Eisele, F. Hoffmann, F. Kühbauch, E. Lung, V. Oberkersch, J. Pertschi, H. Rakusch, M. Reinsprecht, I. Senz, H. Sonnleitner, G. Tscherny, R. Vetter, G. Wildmann, and others, *Weissbuch der Deutschen aus Jugoslawien: Erlebnisberichte 1944–48* (Munich: Universitäts Verlag, Donauschwäbische Kulturstiftung, 1992, 1993), vol. I, vol. II.

3. On Croatia's armed forces during World War II, and its destruction after 1945 by the Yugoslav Communists, see, Christophe Dolbeau, *Les Forces armées croates, 1941–1945* (Lyon [BP 5005, 69245 Lyon cedex 05, France]: 2002). On the often critical attitude of German military and diplomatic officials toward the allied Ustasha regime of the Independent State of Croatia ("NDH"), see Klaus Schmider, *Partisanenkrieg in Jugoslawien 1941–1944* (Hamburg: Verlag E. S. Mittler & Sohn, 2002). This book includes an impressive bibliography, and cites hitherto unpublished German documents. Unfortunately, the author does not provide precise data as to the number of German troops (including Croat civilians and troops) who surrendered to British forces in southern Austria, and who were subsequently handed over to the Yugoslav Communist authorities. The number of Croat captives who perished after 1945 in Communist Yugoslavia remains an emotion-laden topic in Croatia, with important implications for the country's domestic and foreign policy.

4. Anton Scherer, Manfred Straka, *Kratka povijest podunavskih Nijemaca/ Abriss zur Geschichte der Donauschwaben* (Graz: Leopold Stocker Verlag/ Zagreb: Pan Liber, 1999), esp. p. 131; Georg Wildmann, and others, *Genocide of the Ethnic Germans in Yugoslavia 1944–1948* (Santa Ana, Calif.: Danube Swabian Association of the U.S.A., 2001), p. 31.

5. A. Scherer, M. Straka, *Kratka povijest podunavskih Nijemaca/ Abriss zur Geschichte der Donauschwaben* (1999), pp. 132–140.

6. Georg Wildmann, and others, *Verbrechen an den Deutschen in Jugoslawien, 1944–48* (Munich: Donauschwäbische Kulturstiftung, 1998), esp. pp. 312–313. Based on this is the English-language work: *Georg Wildmann, and others, Genocide of the Ethnic Germans in Yugoslavia 1944–1948* (Santa Ana, Calif.: Danube Swabian Association of the U.S.A., 2001).

7. G. Wildmann, and others, *Verbrechen an den Deutschen in Jugoslawien, 1944–48*, esp. p. 274.

8. Wendelin Gruber, *In the Claws of the Red Dragon: Ten Years Under Tito's Heel* (Toronto: St. Michaelswerk, 1988). Translated from German by Frank Schmidt. In 1993, the ailing Fr. Gruber returned to Croatia from exile in Paraguay, to spend his final years in a Jesuit monastery in Zagreb. I spoke with him shortly before his death on August 14, 2002, at the age of 89.

9. Stéphane Courtois, and others, *The Black Book of Communism: Crimes, Terror, Repression* (Cambridge: Harvard Univ. Press, 1999).

10. G. Wildmann, and others, *Verbrechen an den Deutschen in Jugoslawien* (cited above), p. 22.

11. Armin Preuss, *Prinz Eugen: Der edle Ritter* (Berlin: Grundlagen Verlag, 1996).

12. Otto Kumm, *Geschichte der 7. S.S.-Freiwilligen Gebirgs-Division "Prinz Eugen"* (Coburg: Nation Europa, 1995).

13. Roland Kaltenegger, *Titos Kriegsgefangene: Folterlager, Hungermärsche und Schauprozesse* (Graz : Leopold Stocker Verlag, 2001).

14. Alfred-Maurice de Zayas, *Nemesis at Potsdam: The Expulsion of the Germans from the East* (Lincoln: Univ. of Nebraska, 1989 [3rd rev. ed.]); Alfred-Maurice de Zayas, *The German Expellees: Victims in War and Peace* (New York: St. Martin's Press, 1993); Alfred-Maurice de Zayas, *A Terrible Revenge: The "Ethnic Cleansing" of the East European Germans, 1944–1950* (New York: St. Martin's Press, 1994); Ralph F. Keeling, *Gruesome Harvest: The Allies' Postwar War Against the German People* (Institute for Historical Review, 1992).

15. Tomislav Sunic, *Titoism and Dissidence: Studies in the History and Dissolution of Communist Yugoslavia* (Frankfurt, New York: Peter Lang, 1995).

Part IV: Liberalism and Democracy

Democracy Revisited: The Ancients and the Moderns

1. George Orwell, *Selected Essays* (Baltimore: Johns Hopkins University Press, 1957), p. 149.

2. François Guizot, *De la démocratie en France* (Paris: Masson, 1849), p. 9.

3. Georges Burdeau observes that judging by appearances, in terms of their federal organization, the institutions of the Soviet Union are similar to those of the United

States, and in terms of its governmental system the Soviet Union is similar to England. *La démocratie* (Paris : Seuil, 1966), p. 141.

4. T. S. Eliot, *The Idea of a Christian Society* (London: Faber & Faber, 1939).
5. Bertrand de Jouvenel, *Du pouvoir* (Geneva : Cheval ailé, 1945), p. 411.
6. Giovanni Sartori, *Democratic Theory* (Westport, CT: Greenwood, 1962), p. 3.
7. "Les démocrates ombrageux", *Contrepoint* (December 1976), p. 111.
8. Other authors have held exactly the opposite opinion. For Schleiermacher, democracy is a "primitive" political form in contrast to monarchy, which is thought to correspond to the demands of the modern state.
9. "Le pouvoir des idées en démocratie", *Pouvoir* (May 1983), p. 145.
10. Significantly, it was with the beginning of the inquiry into the origins of the French monarchy that the nobility, under Louis XIV, began to challenge the principles of monarchy.
11. The word "thing", which designated the parliament, derives from the Germanic word that connoted originally "everything that is gathered together." The same word gave birth to the English "thing" (German *Ding*: same meaning). It seems that this word designated the assembly in which public matters, then affairs of a general nature, and finally "things" were discussed.
12. "Les fondements de l'État libre d'Icelande: trois siècles de démocratie médiévale", in *Nouvelle Ecole* 25–26 (Winter 1974–75), pp. 68–73.
13. *Les Scandinaves* (Paris: Lidis [Brepols], 1984), p. 613.
14. Cf. P. M. Martin, *L'idée de royauté à Rome. De la Rome royale au consensus républicain* (Clermont-Ferrand: Adosa, 1983).
15. Here "democracy", as in the case of peasants' freedoms as well, already included social demands, although not "class struggle" — a concept ignored by ancient democracy. In the Middle Ages the purpose of such demands was to give voice to those who were excluded from power. But it often happened that "democracy" could be used against the people. In medieval Florence, social strife between the *popolo grosso* and the *popolo minuto* was particularly brisk. On this Francesco Nitti writes: "The reason the working classes of Florence proved lukewarm in defense of their liberty and sympathized instead with the Medicis was because they remained opposed to democracy, which they viewed as a concept of the rich bourgeoisie." Francesco Nitti, *La démocratie*, vol. 1 (Paris: Felix Alcan, 1933, p. 57).
16. This opinion is shared by the majority of students of ancient democracies. Thus, Victor Ehrenberg sees in Greek democracy a "form of enlarged aristocracy." Victor Ehrenberg, *L'état grec* (Paris: Maspéro, 1976), p. 94.

17. Pius XII, 1944 Christmas Message: http://www.ewtn.com/library/PAPALDOC/P12XMAS.HTM.
18. M. Robespierre, "On Political Morality", speech to the Convention, February 5, 1794: http://chnm.gmu.edu/revolution/d/413/
19. On this debate, see the essay by Luciano Guerci, "Liberta degli antichi e liberta dei moderni", in *Sparta, Atene e i 'philosophes' nella Francia del Setecento* (Naples: Guido, 1979).
20. Camille Desmoulins, speech to the Convention, March 31, 1794. It is significant that contemporary democrats appear to be more inclined to favor Athens. Sparta, in contrast, is denounced for its "war-like spirit." This change in discourse deserves a profound analysis.
21. Cf., for example, the essay by Moses Finley, *Démocratie antique et démocratie moderne* (Paris: Payot, 1976), which is both an erudite study and a pamphlet of great contemporary relevance. The study is prefaced by Pierre Vidal-Naquet, who, among other errors, attributes to Julien Freund (see n. 7, above) positions that are exactly the very opposite of those stated in the preface.
22. To cite Thucydides: "Thanks to his untainted character, the depth of his vision, and boundless disinterestedness, Pericles exerted on Athens an incontestable influence…. Since he owed his prestige only to honest means, he did not have to truckle to popular passions…. In a word, democracy supplied the name; but in reality, it was the government of the first citizen." (*Peloponnesian War II*, 65)
23. One of the best works on this topic is Jacqueline de Romilly's essay *Problèmes de la démocratie grecque* (Paris: Hermann, 1975).
24. Romilly, *Problèmes de la démocratie grecque*.
25. The word *démos* is opposed to the word *laós*, a term employed in Greece to designate the people, but with the express meaning of "the community of warriors."
26. In France, the right to vote was implemented only in stages. In 1791, the distinction was still made between "active citizens" and "passive citizens." Subsequently, the electorate was expanded to include all qualified citizens able to pay a specified minimum of taxes. Although universal suffrage was proclaimed in 1848, it was limited to males until 1945.
27. On the evolution of that notion, see Jacqueline Bordes, *'Politeia' dans la pensée grecque jusqu'à Aristote* (Paris: Belles Lettres, 1982).
28. Nicole Loraux interprets the Athenian notion of citizenship as a result of the "imaginary belonging to an autochthonous people" (*Les enfants d'Athéna. Idées athéniennes sur la citoyenneté et la divison des sexes* [Paris: Maspéro, 1981]). The myth of Erichthonios (or Erechtheus) explains in fact the autochthonous character and

the origins of the masculine democracy, at the same time as it grafts the Athenian ideology of citizenship onto immemorial foundations.

29. Emile Benveniste, *Le vocabulaire des institutions indo-européennes*, vol. 1 (Paris : Minuit, 1969), p. 321.

30. On the work of Aristotle and his relationship with the Athenian constitution, see James Day and Mortimer Chambers, *Aristotle, History of Athenian Democracy* (Berkeley, CA: University of California Press, 1962).

31. Finley, *Démocratie antique et démocratie moderne*, p. 80.

32. Finley, *Démocratie antique et démocratie moderne*, p. 141.

33. Veyne adds: "Bourgeois liberalism organizes cruising ships in which each passenger must take care of himself as best as he can, the crew being there only to provide for the common goods and services. By contrast, the Greek city was a ship where the passengers made up the crew." Paul Veyne, "Les Grecs ont-ils connu la démocratie?" *Diogène*, October-December 1983, p. 9.

34. For the liberal critique of Greek democracy, see Paul Veyne, "Les Grecs ontils connu la démocratie?" and Giovanni Sartori, *Democratic Theory* (see n. 6 above).

Liberalism or Democracy: Carl Schmitt and Apolitical Democracy

1. See Giovanni Sartori, *Democratic Theory* (Detroit: Wayne State University Press, 1962), 3. "In a somewhat paradoxical vein, democracy could be defined as a high-flown name for something which does not exist." See, for instance, the book by French "Schmittian" Alain de Benoist, *Démocratie: Le problème* (Paris: Le Labyrinthe, 1985), 8. "Democracy is neither more 'modern' nor more 'evolved' than other forms of governance: Governments with democratic tendencies have appeared throughout history. We can observe how the linear perspective used in this type of analysis can be particularly deceiving." Against the communist theory of democracy, see Julien Freund, considered today as a foremost expert on Schmitt, in *Politique et impolitique* (Paris: Sirey, 1987), 203. "It is precisely in the name of democracy, designed as genuine and ideal and always put off for tomorrow that non-democrats conduct their campaign of propaganda against real and existing democracies." For an interesting critique of democratic theory, see Louis Rougier, *La Mystique démocratique* (Paris: Albatros, 1983). Rougier was inspired by Vilfredo Pareto and his elitist anti-democratic theory of the state.

2. See, for instance, an analysis of U.S. "post-electoral politics", which seems to be characterized by the governmental incapacity to put a stop to increasing appeals to

the judiciary, in Benjamin Ginsberg and Martin Shefter, *Politics by other Means: The Declining Importance of Election in America* (New York: Basic Books, Inc., 1990).

3. Carl Schmitt, *The Crisis of Parliamentary Democracy*, trans. Ellen Kennedy (Cambridge: MIT, 1985), 4.

4. The views held by some leftist scholars concerning liberalism closely parallel those of Schmitt, particularly the charge of "soft" repression. See, for instance, Jürgen Habermas, *Technik und Wissenschaft als Ideologie* (Frankfurt: Suhrkamp, 1968). See also Régis Debray, *Le Scribe: Genèse du politique* (Paris: Grasset, 1980).

5. Carl Schmitt, *Der Begriff des Politischen* (München und Leipzig: Duncker und Humblot, 1932), 36. Recently, Schmitt's major works have become available in English. These include: *The Concept of the Political*, trans. G. Schwab (New Brunswick: Rutgers University Press, 1976); *Political Romanticism*, trans. G. Oakes (Cambridge: MIT Press, 1986); and *Political Theology*, trans. G. Schwab (Cambridge: MIT Press; 1985). There may be some differences between my translations and the translations in the English version.

6. Schmitt, *Der Begriff*, 76.

7. François-Bernard Huyghe, *La soft-idéologie* (Paris: Robert Laffont, 1987), 43.

8. Schmitt, *The Crisis of Parliamentary Democracy*, 8.

9. Schmitt, *The Crisis of Parliamentary Democracy*, 15.

10. Schmitt, *The Crisis of Parliamentary Democracy*, 15.

11. Schmitt, *The Crisis of Parliamentary Democracy*, 9.

12. Carl Schmitt, *Verfassungslehre* (München und Leipzig: Verlag von Duncker und Humblot, 1928), 83.

13. See Ferdinand Tönnies, *Community and Society (Gemeinschaft und Gesellschaft)*, trans. and ed. Charles P. Loomis (New York: Harper & Row, 1963). Tönnies distinguishes between hierarchy in modern and traditional society. His views are similar to those of Louis Dumont, *Homo Hierarchicus, The Caste System and its Implications*, trans. Mark Sainsbury and L. Dumont (Chicago: University of Chicago Press, 1980). Dumont draws attention to "vertical" vs. "horizontal" inequality among social groups.

14. Schmitt, *Verfassungslehre*, 234.

15. Schmitt, *The Crisis of Parliamentary Democracy*, 9.

16. Carl Schmitt, *Du Politique*, trans. William Gueydan (Puiseaux: Pardès, 1990), 46. *Legalität und Legitimität* appears in French translation, with a preface by Alain de Benoist, as *Légalité et légitimité*.

17. Schmitt, *Du Politique*, 57.

18. Schmitt, *Du Politique*, 58. See also Schmitt's *Verfassungslehre*, 87–91:
19. Schmitt, *Verfassungslehre*, 245.
20. Schmitt, *Verfassungslehre*, 246.
21. Schmitt, *Verfassungslehre*, 245.
22. Schmitt, *The Crisis of Parliamentary Democracy*, 10.
23. Schmitt, *The Crisis of Parliamentary Democracy*, 13.
24. See, for instance, the conservative revolutionary, Arthur Moeller van den Bruck, *Das Dritte Reich* (1923) whose criticism of liberal democracy often parallels Carl Schmitt's, and echoes Karl Marx, *The Critique of the Gotha Program*, (New York: International Publishers, 1938), 9. "Hence equal rights here (in liberalism) means in principle bourgeois rights. The equal right is an unequal right for unequal labor." See also Schmitt's contemporary Othmar Spann with a similar analysis, *Der wahre Staat* (Leipzig: Verlag von Qnelle und Meyer, 1921).
25. See Carl Schmitt, "L'unité du monde", trans. Philippe Baillet in *Du Politique*, 237–49.
26. In some multi-ethnic states, liberal democracy has difficulty taking root. For instance, the liberalisation of Yugoslavia has led to its collapse into its ethnic parts. This could bring some comfort to Schmitt's thesis that democracy requires a homogeneous *Volk* within its ethnographic borders and state. See Tomislav Sunic, "Yugoslavia, the End of Communism the Return of Nationalism", *America* (April 20, 1991), 438–440.
27. Schmitt, *Verfassungslehre*, 234. See for a detailed treatment of this subject the concluding chapter of Paul Gottfried, *Carl Schmitt: Politics and Theory* (Westport and New York: Greenwood Press, 1990).
28. Schmitt, *The Crisis of Parliamentary Democracy*, 16.
29. Schmitt, *The Crisis of Parliamentary Democracy*, 28.
30. Schmitt, *Verfassungslehre*, 247.
31. Carl Schmitt; "L'état de droit bourgeois", in *Du Politique*, 35.
32. Freund, *Politique et impolitique*, 204.
33. Alexis de Tocqueville, *Democracy in America* (New York: Alfred Knopf, 1966), vol. 2, book fourth, Ch. 6.
34. There is a flurry of books criticizing the "surreal" and "vicarious" nature of modern liberal society. See Jean Baudrillard, *Les stratégies fatales* ("Figures du transpolitique") (Paris: Grasset, 1983). Also, Christopher Lasch, *The Culture of Narcissism* (New York: Warner Books, 1979).
35. Georges Sorel, *Les illusions du progrès* (Paris: M. Rivière, 1947), 50.
36. Freund, *Politique et impolitique*, 305.

37. Carl Schmitt, *Politische Theologie* (München und Leipzig: Verlag von Duncker und Humblot, 1934), 80.
38. Schmitt, *The Crisis of Parliamentary Democracy*, 6.
39. Schmitt, *The Crisis of Parliamentary Democracy*, 7.

The Liberal Double-Talk and Its Lexical Legal Consequences

1. A. James Gregor, *Metascience and Politics* (1971 London: Transaction, 2004), 318.
2. Alan Charles Kors, "Thought Reform: The Orwellian Implications of Today's College Orientation", in *Reasononline*, (March 2000). See the link: http://reason.com/0003/fe.ak.thought.shtml.
3. Paul Gottfried, *The Strange Death of Marxism* (Columbia and London: University of Missouri Press, 2005), 13.
4. Jean Baudrillard, *The Evil Demons of Images* (University of Sydney: The Power Inst. of Fine Arts, 1988), 24.
5. Josef Schüsslburner, *Demokratie-Sonderweg Bundesrepublik* (Lindenblatt Media Verlag: Künzlau, 2004), 233.
6. See *Journal officiel de la République française*, 14 juillet 1990 page 8333loi n° 90-615.

Historical Dynamics of Liberalism: From Total Market to Total State

1. Michael Beaud, *A History of Capitalism 1500-1980* (Paris: New York: Monthly Review Press, 1983), 80.
2. François Perroux, *Le capitalisme* (Paris: PUF, 1960), 31.
3. Ernst Topitsch, "Dialektik — politische Wunderwaffe?", *Die Grundlage des Spätmarxismus*, edited by E. Topitsch, Rüdiger Proske, Hans Eysenck et al., (Stuttgart: Verlag Bonn Aktuell GMBH), 74.
4. Georges Sorel, *Les illusions du progrès* (Paris: Marcel Rivière, 1947), 50.
5. François-Bernard Huyghe, *La Soft-idéologie* (Paris: Laffont, 1988). See also, Jean Baudrillard, *La Gauche divine* (Paris: Laffont, 1985). For an interesting polemics concerning the "treason of former socialists clerics who converted to liberalism", see Guy Hocquenghem, *Lettre ouverte à ceux qui sont passés du col Mao au Rotary* (Paris: Albin Michel, 1986).
6. Serge-Christophe Kolm. *Le libéralisme moderne* (Paris: PUF, 1984), 11.
7. Carl Schmitt, *Die geistegeschichtliche Lage des heutigen Parlametatarismus* (München and Leipzig: Verlag von Duncker and Humblot, 1926), 23.

8. Kolm, op. cit., 96.
9. Karl Marx, *Kritik des Gothaer Programms* (Zürich: Ring Verlag A.G., 1934), 10.
10. Ibid., 11.
11. Sanford Lakoff, "Christianity and Equality", *Equality*, edited by J. Roland Pennock and J. W. Chapmann, (New York: Atherton Press, 1967), 128–130.
12. David Thomson, *Equality* (Cambridge: University Press, 1949), p. 79.
13. Sorel, op. cit., 97.
14. Loc. cit.
15. Theodore von Sosnosky, *Die rote Dreifältikeit* (Einsiedeln: Verlaganstalt Benziger and Co., 1931).
16. Cf. Raymond Aron, *Democracy and Totalitarianism* (New York: Frederick Praeger Publishers, 1969), 194 and passim.
17. Carl Schmitt, *Der Begriff des Politischen* (München and Leipzig: Verlag von Duncker and Humblot, 1932), 76 and passim.
18. Ibid., 36.
19. Jürgen Habermas, *Technik and Wissenschaft als Ideologie* (Frankfurt: Suhrkamp Verlag, 1968), 77.
20. Alain de Benoist, *Die entscheidenden Jahre, "In der kaufmännisch-merkantilen Gesellschaftsform geht das Politische ein"* (Tübingen: Grabert Verlag, 1982), 34.
21. Julius Evola, "Procès de la bourgeoisie", *Essais politiques* (Paris: édition Pardès, 1988), 212. First published in *La vita italiana*, "Processo alla borghesia", XXVıII, nr. 324 (March 1940): 259–268.
22. Werner Sombart, *Der Bourgeois*, cf. "Die heilige Wirtschaftlichkeit"; (München and Leipzig: Verlag von Duncker and Humblot, 1923), 137–160.
23. Louis Dumont, *From Mandeville to Marx; The Genesis and Triumph of Economic Ideology* (Chicago: The University of Chicago Press, 1977), 16.
24. Ibid., 59.
25. Cf. L. Dumont, *Essays on Individualism* (Chicago: The University of Chicago Press, 1986).
26. Emanuel Rackman, "Judaism and Equality" in *Equality*, edited by J. Roland Pennock and John W. Chapman (New York: Atherton Press, 1967), 155.
27. Milton Konvitz, *Judaism and the American Idea* (Ithaca and London: Cornell University Press, 1978). Also, German jurist Georg Jellinek argues in *Die Erklärung der Menschen-und Bürgerrechte* (Leipzig: Duncker and Humbolt, 1904), 46, that "the idea to establish legally the unalienable, inherent, and sacred rights of individuals, is not of political but religious origin."

28. John Schaar, "Equality of Opportunity and Beyond", in *Equality*, op. cit., 230.
29. Ibid., 236.
30. Ibid., 235.
31. Murray Milner, *The Illusion of Equality* (Washington and London: Jossey-Bass Inc. Publishers, 1972), 10.
32. Antony Flew, *The Politics of Procrustes* (New York: Promethean Books, 1981), 111.
33. Milner, op. cit., 11.
34. Claude Polin, *Le libéralisme, espoir ou péril* (Paris: Table ronde, 1984), 211.
35. Ibid. 213.
36. Julien Freund, *Politique, Impolitique* (Paris: ed. Sirey, 1987), 336. Also in its entirety, "Théorie des besoins", 319–353.
37. Loc. cit.
38. Ibid., 336–337.
39. Joseph Schumpeter, *Capitalism, Socialism and Democracy* (New York: Harper and Row, 1975), 165 and passim.
40. Max Scheler, *Das Ressentiment im Aufbau der Moralen (Abhandlungen and Aufsäzte)* (Leipzig: Verlag der weissen Bücher, 1915), 58.
41. Claude Polin, *Le totalitarisme* (Paris: PUF, 1982), 123. See also Guillaume Faye, *Contre l'économisme* (Paris: ed. le Labyrinthe, 1982).
42. Hannah Arendt, *The Origins of Totalitarianism* (New York: Meridian Book, 1958), 478.

Part V: Multiculturalism and Communism

Woodrow Wilson's Defeat in Yugoslavia: The End of a Multicultural Utopia

1. Arend Lijphart, "The Power-Sharing Approach," in V. Montville, ed., *Conflict and Peacemaking in Multiethnic Societies* (Lexington, Mass.: D.C. Heath, 1990). Tomislav Sunic is assistant professor of political science at Juniata College in Pennsylvania. He is currently working in the Department of Culture at the Croatian Ministry of Foreign Affairs in Zagreb.
2. *United Nations Charter*, Articles 2(4) and 2(7). See also R. J. Vincent, *Non-intervention and International Order* (Princeton: Princeton University Press, 1974), 233–77.

3. "Yugoslavia Country Report," published by *The Economist Intelligence Unit*, no. 3, 1991, 7.
4. "Not Quite Belsen," *The Economist*, August 15–21, 1992.
5. "U.N. Fights Bonn's Embrace of Croatia," *New York Times*, December 14, 1991.
6. Patrick Glynn, "Yugoblunder"; and "Lawrence of Serbia," *New Republic*, February 24, 1992.
7. Jonathan Eyal, "E.C. Baptism Turns to Debacle," *The Guardian*, January 16, 1992.
8. Wolfram Hanrieder, *Germany, America, Europe: Forty Years of German Foreign Policy* (New Haven: Yale University Press, 1989).
9. Viktor Meier, "Im Hintergrund Amerika, Die westliche Feindseligkeit gegen Kroatien und Slowenien," *Frankfurter Allgemeine Zeitung*, January 2, 1992.
10. From the liberal perspective see, Morton Halperin and David Scheffer, "What Recognition of New Nations Really Means," *The Christian Science Monitor*, January 31, 1991. From an entirely different perspective, see Alain de Benoist's approach to "multi-ethnicism." "L'Idée d'Empire," in *Nation et Empire* (Paris: Acts of XXIV colloquium of the GRECE, 1991).
11. For a theoretical approach to understanding political decision and "apolitical decision" within the European Community and the United Nations in regard to the Yugoslav crisis, one could still draw lessons from the classic by Carl Schmitt, *Der Begriff des Politischen* (Berlin: Duncker und Humblot, 1932).

INDEX

0–9
1968 62, 208–211

A
Abraham 13–22, 77
A.D.L. 73
Aeschylus 122
Africa 10, 36–42, 61, 73–83, 172
African Americans 72
Age of Liberalism 148
Alain de Benoist 5–21, 42–50, 112, 193–213
Alaska 196
Albania 163
Albanian Muslims 94
Albanians 93–105, 191
Albingensians 93
Algeria 94
Alliance of Sinai 13
Alpine 74–80
America xiv, 31–34, 62–93, 118–213
American Declaration of Independence 80, 153
Americanophile 168
Americans ix, 71–72, 90–96, 113, 166–181
Ammianus Marcellinus 26
Amsterdam 163
anarchy 44, 130
antiquity 3, 71
anti-Semite 3, 28, 145
anti-Semites 67–77, 139–146
Antony Flew 155, 212
Appler, Hans 91
Arabs 42, 74, 93, 176

Arendt, Hannah 160, 212
Aristotle 116–122, 207
Aryans 71–76
Ataturk, Kemal Pasha 74
atheists 5
Augustinčić, Antun 97
Auschwitz 36, 172
Australia 139–141
Austria 81–83, 104–116, 143, 203
Austro-Hungarian Empire 81
Axis of Evil 88

B
Babeuf, François-Noël 150
Bacque, James 83
Badinski, Curt 80
Baechler, Jean 113
Balkan wars 103
Balkans 57, 82–92, 104–110, 168–195
Balzac, Honoré de 157
barbarians 3, 55
Barbarians 82
Basques 173
Battle of Britain 176
Baudelaire, Charles 5, 62
Bayerlein, Fritz 94
Beach, Daniel A. 67
Beaud, Michel 147, 210
Bedouins 76
Belgium 74
Bell, Daniel 171
Bendersky, Joseph 85
Benn, Gottfried 65, 201–202

Benoist, Alain de 5-23, 42-50, 112, 193-213
Berbers 42
Berlin 65-79, 169, 193-213
Beutner, Johannes 102
Bible, the 6, 22-25, 88, 188
Biblical message 5
Blot, Jean 28
Bob Dylan 62
Bogumils 54, 93
Bolshevik 3, 17, 134
Bolshevik Revolution 17
Bolshevism 80, 134
Bolshevik 3, 17, 134
Bolsheviks 3
Bolzano 82
Bor 107
Bosnia 109, 180-187
Bosnia and Hercegovina 182
Bosnian Muslims 93-105
Bourbons 176
Brave New World Revisited 64
Breker, Arno 71-72, 99-100
Bremen 88, 115
Bretons 176
Brissot, Girondin 118
Britain 174-187
Brossat, Alain 93
Brussels 182
Bucharest 167, 194
Budapest 163-167, 194
Bulgaria 105
Bush Administration 182-184
Bush, George W. 88, 173-188

C

Caesarism 35-36
California xiii, 64-92, 166, 181-188, 207
Caligula 2
Canaris, Wilhelm 80
Cape Verde 95
Capet, Hugh 114
Capétians 176
Carl Gustav Jung 5
Carthage 19
Cashmere 172
Castoriadis, Cornelius 48
Cathars 54, 93
Catholic 4-13, 92-94, 190
Catholic Church 4, 93
Catholicism 4-13
Catholic liturgy 4
Céline, Louis-Ferdinand 100, 201
Celsus 3
Celts 5, 82
censorship 34, 101, 135-145
centaurs 23, 69
central Europe xii, 94, 108
Cézanne, Paul 101
Chaffar, Sakah 91
Chaunu, Pierre 17, 199-200
Chechens 194
Christianity 2-28, 51, 92, 124, 153, 197-199, 211
anti-Christian 4
Christ 4, 18-27, 52
Christian authorities 2
Christian Churches 4
Christian fanaticism 3
Christian saints 4
Christian sects 3
Christian texts 2
Christian violence 2
Churchill, Winston 174-176
Cicero 116-122
Cioran, Emile xiv, 50-60, 202
classicism xi, 71-72, 99
Clauss, Ludwig Ferdinand 75-76
Cleisthenes 119
Cocaine 63
Cocteau, Jean 62
Cold War 81, 109, 163, 185-186
Cologne 88
Communism ix-x, 22, 63, 91-102, 126-212
Communist 9, 81, 103-109, 137, 151, 195-204

Communist Yugoslavia 103–109, 203–204
Constant, Benjamin 125
Constantine 2
Copenhagen 163, 203
Cornish 174
Corsica 173
Courbet, Gustave 101
Croatia ix, 4, 81–84, 104–109, 172–213
Croats 82–109, 169–174, 188–191
Cro-Magnon 82
Czech Republic 162–164
Czechoslovakia 84, 104, 188
Czechs 190

D

Daemling, Joachim 91
Dali, Salvador 100
Danube 82, 103–108, 178, 203
Danube Swabians 103
Darwin, Charles 21
Darwinism 35
David, Jacques Louis 7, 24, 88–98, 150, 198, 211–213
De Gaulle 174
de Jouvenel, Bertrand 113, 205
De Quincey, Thomas 62
death penalty 2
Debray, Régis 45–46, 208
Dedek, Emil 80
degenerate artists 96
democracy 11–41, 57–63, 87–93, 112–209
Denmark 65
Descartes, René 47
Désirée, Norbert 91
Desmoulins, Camille 118, 206
Deuteronomy 24, 88
Dickens, Charles 63
Die Brücke or Neue Sachligkeit 101
Dier, Amadeus 102
Dinaric 75
Diocletian 2
Dolbeau, Christopher 80–90, 203
Domansky, Heinrich 80

Downing Street 176
Dresden xii, 88
Dubrovnik 56, 82
Dufy, Raoul 64
Dumézil, Georges 5, 193
Dumont, Louis 152–158, 208–211
Durand, Gilbert 29, 115
Dybilasz, Walter 80

E

Eagleburger, Lawrence 184
Eastern Europe xii–xiv, 3, 58, 83, 103–112, 133–145, 162–196
egalitarianism 10–11, 34, 46, 118–125, 148–150, 195–201
Egypt 91
Ehrenburg, Ilya Grigoryevich 85–86
Eighteenth century 2, 73–82, 117–118, 147, 165
Eisenhower, Dwight 83–87
El Hadj 91
Eliade, Mircea 5–20, 51, 193–200
Encyclopaedists, the 47
England 91, 166–184, 205
Enlightenment 22, 80, 124
Enthoven, J. P. 45
Entine, Jon 77
Ephialtes 119
ethnic Albanians 105, 191
Euro Americans 71
Europe ix–xiv, 2–118, 133–150, 162–201, 213
European colonies 170
European Community 182–185, 213
European Union 92, 144–145, 162–164
Europeans xi–xiii, 7–23, 37–38, 69–75, 92, 162–174, 190–199
Evola, Julius 9, 152, 211
Expressionism 101

F

Fabius-Gayssot law 145
February Revolution 151
Federal Republic of Germany 71, 96, 143
Fichte, Johann Gottlieb 29, 175

Flanders 116
Flew, Antony 155, 212
Founding Fathers 192
Fox, Vicente 73
France 4–5, 51–114, 145–150, 163–206
France la Doulce 58
Franche-Comté 176
Franz Joseph II 82
Frederick the Great 80
French Hexagon 176
French Revolution 28, 56–58, 114–117, 178
Freudo-Boasians 78
Freund, Julien 113–120, 134–136, 155–156, 200–212
Friuli 90
Frum, David 88

G

Gaj in, Ljudevit 176
Gambetta 174
Genscher, Hans 183
George Orwell 112, 204
German Reich 104
Germans xii–xiv, 5, 31, 71–114, 174–177, 190–204
Germany x, 5, 31, 64–116, 143–145, 158–189, 213
Germans xii–xiv, 5, 31, 71–114, 174–177, 190–204
Germany Must Perish! 85
Gestapo 80–81
Gillabert, Emile 25
Giorgio Locchi 14, 199
Girondin coup 150
Globocnik, Odilo 81
Glodkowski, Erich 80
Gnosticism 26
Goebbels, Josef 64, 79, 98–99
Goethe, Johann Wolfgang von 39
Gomorrah 88
Gospel, the 2–5, 19–26, 93
Goths 82
Gottfried, Paul 65, 141, 201–210
Gravier, Maurice 115

Great Britain 174
Greece 22, 71, 99–108, 122, 206
Greeks 5, 19, 51–70, 119–123
Grey Eminence 64
Gripari, Pierre 20, 197
Grohnert, Reinhard 69
Gruber, Wendelin 107, 204
Guarani 93
Guderian, Heinz 80
Guizot, François 112, 204
Gulag 36, 63
Gulf War 182

H

Habermas, Jürgen 152, 208–211
Habsburg Empire 104
Habsburgs 178
Hague War Crimes Tribunal, The 103
Hamburg 88, 202–203
Hardin, Garrett 77, 196
Hassan II 100
Haudry, Jean 20, 199
Haus der Deutschen Kunst 98–99
Hebrews 19–24
Hegel, Georg Wilhelm Friedrich 29
Heidegger, Martin 5, 21, 50
Heidelberg 87
Heiden, Ludwig 91
Heim, Aribert 91
Heinemann, Manfred 69
Hellmich, Hans 80
Heraclitus 5, 50
Herder, J. G. 47, 176
hillbilly 82
Hilz, Sepp 102
Hindus 92
Hitler, Adolf 64, 81–99, 194
Hittites 74, 114
holism 47
Holland 63–65
Hollywood 76, 163
Homer 61–69, 114
Homo Americanus 88

Huguenots 80
Hungarians 105
Hungary 84–107, 162–164, 176
Hunke, Sigrid 14, 199
Hutus 73
Huxley, Aldous 64, 166
Huyghe, François B. 125, 148, 200–210

I

Iberia 172
Ibo 172
Iceland 115
Illyrian 74, 94
Inquart, Arthur Seyss 81
Ionesco, Eugene 51
IQ 67–74, 94
Irish 174
Irkutsk 172
Islam 91–93
Israel xii, 15–27, 90–93
Israelites 19–27
Istanbul 74
Italians 72, 190
Italy 21, 51, 71, 90, 102, 116

J

Jacobinism 173–174
Jacobins 97, 174–176
Jahn, Friedrich Ludwig 176
janissaries 94
Jellyby, Ms. 63
Jena 56
Jews xii–xiii, 3–28, 76–94, 143–145
Joachim-Eugène, Louis 91
Joshua 24–25
Judaism 10–27, 92, 153, 198, 211
Jewish God 3
Jung, Carl Gustav 5, 193
Jünger, Ernst 49, 64–65, 180, 202

K

Kaiser Wilhelm Institut für Anthropologie 69
Kalmuks 194
Kaltenbrunner, Ernst 81

Karadzic, Vuk 176
Karst 84
Katmandu 172
Katyn 174, 194
Kaufman, Theodore 85
Kazakhstan 172
Kerensky, Alexander 151
Khaldun, Ibn 42
King Achish 24
Klimsch, Fritz 71, 100
Koestler, Arthur 18, 200
Kohl, Helmut 64
Kolm, Serge-Christophe 148–149, 210
Konvitz, Milton 153, 198, 211
Kunst dem Volke 98–99
Kunstkammer 99
Kusić, Grgo 82
Kwazulus 73

L

La Rochelle, Pierre Drieu 63–64
Latin 67–70, 92–93, 120, 166–175, 198
Latin America 92–93, 166
Latinos 92
Leibniz, G. W. 47
Lenin, Vladimir 151
Lepzig 89
Levantine 69
liberalism 8–23, 43–49, 61–63, 118–159, 171, 193, 207–210
libertarianism 44
Lithuania 179
Locchi, Giorgio 14–18, 199–200
London Agreement 145
London, Jack 61, 145, 157, 170, 197–212
Lorenz, Konrad 39–40, 201
Los Angeles 188
Louis XIV 174, 205
L.S.D. 64, 166
Ludwig of Bavaria 115
Lukacs, John 34, 201
Lupasco, Stephen 51
Luxembourg 173

M

Macedonia 105, 183
Machiavelli, Nicolo 59
Maffesoli, Michel 17, 29, 200
Maghreb 176
Maillol, Aristide 100
Manet, Edouard 101
Marcus Aurelius 55–56, 82
Marx, Karl xiv, 2–5, 18, 32–43, 149–154, 197, 209–211
Marxism 11–28, 43, 147–149, 210
Marxists 10–18, 43–49
Maschke, Günther 89
Mauscheljude 77
McDonaldization 165
Mediterranean, the 61, 73–80
mescaline 64
Messianism 17
Mexican Americans 72, 181
Michael Jackson 74, 192
Michelangelo 71, 99
Middle Ages 70, 93, 115, 205
Middle East 73, 92, 139
Mierzinsky, Kurt 80
Mikulicz, Adalbert 80
Milch, Erhard 94
Milner, Murray 155, 212
Milošević, Slobodan 109
Mischlinge 77
Mitterrand, François 64
Molnar 8–9, 198
Mondrian, Piet 71, 96
Mongoloid 74
monotheism 5–28, 152
Montesquieu 117, 158, 195
Montesquieu, Charles-Louis de Secondat, baron de La Brède et de 117, 158, 195
Morgenthau Jr., Henry xii, 85
Morin, Edgar 46
Mosaic law 19
Moscow 56, 82, 179–187
Moses xiv, 2, 17–25, 122, 197–206
Moslem 190

Mozambique 4
multiculturalism ix, 137, 173, 193
Munich 88–99, 203
Mustafa, Ibrahim 91

N

Napoleon 39, 82
National Socialism x–xi, 68–79, 95–102, 144
National Socialist Germany 78, 90–101, 175
National Socialist regime 71, 96–104
nationalism 7–12, 45, 89, 170–189
nationalist extremism 3
Nationalist Socialist 75
Nationalists 47
N.A.T.O. 164
Nazi 64–81, 95, 140–145, 175
Naziism 5
Ndebele 73
neo-Nazis 67
Nero 2
New Mexico 188
New York 170, 196–213
New Zealand 95
Nietzsche, Friedrich 3–37, 54, 197
nihilism 41–52
Nixon, Richard 163
Nolte, Ernst 91
Nordic xii, 70–82, 115
Novalis (a.k.a. Georg Philipp Friedrich Freiherr von Hardenberg) 61
Novgorod 179
N.S.D.A.P. 71, 96–100

O

Occidental Observer, The xiv, 78
Occitans 176
October revolution 151
Odysseus 61
Old Testament 19, 88–92
Olympic Games 26
Ordnung 89
Ortung 89

Ottoman 93–94
Ottoman empire 94

P
paganism 2–23, 171, 198–199
pagain idols 2–12
pagan cults 4, 26
pagan deities 2
pagan Europe 2–4
pagan spirit 4
pagan temples 2–4
pagan thinkers 5–14
pagans 2–26, 38
paganism 2–23, 171, 198–199
pagans 2–26, 38
Paine, Thomas 153
Pakistan 73
Paleozoic era, the 53
Palestinians 172–173
Panonia 55
pan-Slavism 193
Paraguay 93, 204
Pareto, Vilfredo 5–10, 179, 198–207
Paris 56–58, 82, 112, 193–213
Patagonia 78, 95
Pavelić, Ante 94–97
Pawel, Bronislaw 80
Pericles 119–120, 206
Perroux, François 116, 147, 210
Petofy, Sandor 176
Philadelphia 196
Philippines 92, 196
Pierre Chaunu 17, 199–200
Pius XII 116, 206
Poland 104, 162–164, 176, 190
rural Poles 4
Poles 4, 174, 190–194
Polin, Claude 35–36, 155–156, 201–212
Pollock, Jackson 71, 96
polytheism 3–29
Pomerania 108
Pope Innocent IX 55
Portugal 4

postmodern 7, 87, 138–146, 195
postmodernity 62, 78, 90, 166–169
Potsdam 84, 110, 204
Pound, Ezra 5, 202
Prague 167
Praxiteles 71, 99
Prince Eugene of Savoy 107
Princess Helena 82
Promethean 14, 65, 157, 212
propaganda 72–99, 145, 207
Prussia 80, 106–108, 173
Punjab 73

Q
Quebec 140, 188

R
Rabin, Yitzhak 77
race ix–xii, 11, 67–95, 130
racial hygiene 69
Rackman, Emanuel 153, 211
Radisch, Hans 80
Radziej, Georg 80
Reagan, Ronald 163
Renaissance 4, 21, 71, 99
Rhine 79–83
Rhodes, Cecil 157
Richelieu 174
Rigg, Bryan Mark 94
right-wingers 67
Robespierre, Maximilien 117, 206
Rodin, Auguste 97
Rolling Stones 62
Romania 51, 103–107, 176, 190
Romans 19–27, 61–70, 118
Romanticism 4, 61, 98, 208
Rome 2–10, 33, 70, 92, 114–116, 205
Christian Rome 2
Roman Emperor 2, 82, 114
Romilly, Jacqueline de 119, 206
Roper, Allen G. 70
Rougier 10, 198–207
Rousseau, Jean-Jacques 118
Russia 3, 81–90, 151, 163

Russians 190
Rwanda 73
S
Sahara 73
Saint Paul 26
Saint-Just 29, 118, 174
San Antonio 74
Sarajevo 194
Sarmatian 51
Sartori, Giovanni 113–123, 205–207
satyrs 23, 69
Schaar, John 154–155, 211
Scheler, Max 158, 212
Schmitt, Carl xiv, 10, 79–88, 125–136, 151, 179, 198–213
Schopenhauer, Arthur 50
Schwarzenegger, Arnold 82
Scythian 51
Sehnsucht nach dem Tode 61
Seidler, Franz W. 83
Seneca 21, 70
Serbia 104–109, 164, 176–187, 213
Serbs 105–109, 169–174, 191
Seurat, Georges-Pierre 64
Shevchenko, Taras 176
Sigrid Hunke 14, 199
Sikhs 73
Skorzeny, Otto 81
Slavic deities 4
Slavs xii, 5, 79–82
slaves 73, 118–120
Slavic 4, 74–80, 93, 175, 198
Slavs xii, 5, 79–82
Slovakia 81
Slovaks 190
Slovenia 104, 162–186
socialism 8–20, 61, 146–158
Solon 70, 116–119
Sombart, Werner 152–153, 198, 211
Sontag, Susan 76
Sophocles 50
Sorel, Georges 135, 147–150, 209–211

South Korea 196
South Tyrol 81–82
Soviet Union xi–xii, 10, 100–104, 133–139, 164–192, 204–205
Spain 178–182
Sparta 9, 118, 206
Spartan 70–71
Spengler, Oswald xiv, 5–9, 31–41, 55, 200–202
St. Paul 52
Stalin, Josef 29, 63, 143, 194
Stalinism 5, 195
Stimson, Henry L. 85
Stockholm 74
Sudetenland 104–108, 174
Sulpicius Severus 26
Suzdal 179
Switzerland 115–116
T
T. S. Eliot 112, 205
Tacitus 5, 21, 114
Tarek Hussein Farid 91
Television 21, 51, 65, 103, 192, 212
Thal 82
The Hague 103–109, 182
The Morgenthau Plan 85
The Third Reich 66, 203
Theodosius 2
Theophilus of Sarapeum 26
Third Reich xii–xiv, 66–79, 91–105, 203
Third World 7, 38, 110, 130, 160, 172–176
Thomson, David 150, 211
Thorak, Josef 71–72, 99–100
Tillich, Paul 18, 200
Tito, Josip Broz 97–109, 181, 204
Titoist Yugoslavia 106
Tocqueville, Alexis de 118, 135, 209
Tönnies, Ferdinand 42–44, 208
Topitsch, Alexander 147, 210
Transcaucasia 63–73
Tresmontant, Claude 27
Trigano, Shmuel 27–28
Troeltsch, Ernst 153, 198

Troy 19
Turkey 73–74, 91
Turkmenistan 73
Turks 74, 93
Tutsis 73
Twentieth century ix–xi, 5, 32–33, 62–67, 97–110, 129, 173, 188

U
Ukraine 81, 140, 176
United Nations (UN) 180–181, 212–213
United States (USA) xii–xiii, 71, 87–117, 133, 162–167, 204
universalism 10–38, 148, 177–201
universalist 3–12, 32, 175–179, 194
U.S.S.R. 69, 95
Utley, Freda 87

V
Valverde, J. 52
Vance, Cyrus 183
Vatican 75, 93
Vendeans 176
Venona documents 85
Vermeer, Jan 64
Versailles 104–110, 173–190
Versailles Treaty of 1919 104
Veyne, Paul 122–123, 207
Vico, Gianbattista 32, 55
Victor Emmanuel III 82
Vienna 79–82, 194
Vietnam 163
völkisch 102
Volkswagen 98
von Brauchitsch, Walter 80
von Dombrowski, Ernst 102
von Manstein, Erich 94
von Notzing, Caspar Schrenk 88
von Rendulic, Lothar 81
von Verschuer, Otmar 77

W
Waffen SS xii
War Crimes Tribunal in The Hague 109
Warsaw 81, 163, 194

Weber, Max 79, 153
Wehrmacht xii, 80–94, 107–108
Weimar Republic 64, 158
West, the x–xiii, 27–89, 112, 125–200
Westminster Palace 176
White Americans 72
White Europeans 70–72
White nationalists 67–78, 92
Whites xi–xiii, 72–77, 94
Wilson, Woodrow xiv, 180–190, 212
World War I 31, 104
World War II ix–xiii, 40, 85, 97–110, 127, 144, 164–172, 185–187, 203
Wotan 21

X
Xhosa 73, 172

Y
Yalta 84, 110, 172–189
Yemen 94
Yugoslavia xiv, 84, 97–110, 133, 173–212
Yule 4

Z
Zagreb 94, 163–167, 203–212
Zednicek, Franz 80
Zeus 21
Zulus 73

OTHER BOOKS PUBLISHED BY ARKTOS

Sri Dharma Pravartaka Acharya	*The Dharma Manifesto*
Alain de Benoist	*Beyond Human Rights*
	Carl Schmitt Today
	The Indo-Europeans
	Manifesto for a European Renaissance
	On the Brink of the Abyss
	The Problem of Democracy
	View from the Right (vol. 1–3)
Arthur Moeller van den Bruck	*Germany's Third Empire*
Matt Battaglioli	*The Consequences of Equality*
Kerry Bolton	*Revolution from Above*
	Yockey: A Fascist Odyssey
Isac Boman	*Money Power*
Ricardo Duchesne	*Faustian Man in a Multicultural Age*
Alexander Dugin	*Eurasian Mission: An Introduction to Neo-Eurasianism*
	The Fourth Political Theory
	Last War of the World-Island
	Putin vs Putin
	The Rise of the Fourth Political Theory
Koenraad Elst	*Return of the Swastika*
Julius Evola	*Fascism Viewed from the Right*
	A Handbook for Right-Wing Youth
	Metaphysics of War
	Notes on the Third Reich
	The Path of Cinnabar
	Recognitions
	A Traditionalist Confronts Fascism
Guillaume Faye	*Archeofuturism*
	Archeofuturism 2.0
	The Colonisation of Europe
	Convergence of Catastrophes
	A Global Coup
	Sex and Deviance
	Understanding Islam
	Why We Fight
Daniel S. Forrest	*Suprahumanism*
Andrew Fraser	*Dissident Dispatches*
	The WASP Question

OTHER BOOKS PUBLISHED BY ARKTOS

Génération Identitaire	*We are Generation Identity*
Paul Gottfried	*War and Democracy*
Porus Homi Havewala	*The Saga of the Aryan Race*
Rachel Haywire	*The New Reaction*
Lars Holger Holm	*Hiding in Broad Daylight*
	Homo Maximus
	Incidents of Travel in Latin America
	The Owls of Afrasiab
Alexander Jacob	*De Naturae Natura*
Jason Reza Jorjani	*Prometheus and Atlas*
	World State of Emergency
Roderick Kaine	*Smart and SeXy*
Lance Kennedy	*Supranational Union and New Medievalism*
Peter King	*Here and Now*
	Keeping Things Close
Ludwig Klages	*The Biocentric Worldview*
	Cosmogonic Reflections
Pierre Krebs	*Fighting for the Essence*
Stephen Pax Leonard	*Travels in Cultural Nihilism*
Pentti Linkola	*Can Life Prevail?*
H. P. Lovecraft	*The Conservative*
Charles Maurras	*The Future of the Intelligentsia & For a French Awakening*
Michael O'Meara	*Guillaume Faye and the Battle of Europe*
	New Culture, New Right
Brian Anse Patrick	*The NRA and the Media*
	Rise of the Anti-Media
	The Ten Commandments of Propaganda
	Zombology
Tito Perdue	*Morning Crafts*
	Philip
	William's House (vol. 1–4)
Raido	*A Handbook of Traditional Living*

OTHER BOOKS PUBLISHED BY ARKTOS

STEVEN J. ROSEN — *The Agni and the Ecstasy*
The Jedi in the Lotus

RICHARD RUDGLEY — *Barbarians*
Essential Substances
Wildest Dreams

ERNST VON SALOMON — *It Cannot Be Stormed*
The Outlaws

SRI SRI RAVI SHANKAR — *Celebrating Silence*
Know Your Child
Management Mantras
Patanjali Yoga Sutras
Secrets of Relationships

TROY SOUTHGATE — *Tradition & Revolution*

OSWALD SPENGLER — *Man and Technics*

TOMISLAV SUNIC — *Against Democracy and Equality*
Titans are in Town

HANS-JÜRGEN SYBERBERG — *On the Fortunes and Misfortunes of Art in Post-War Germany*

ABIR TAHA — *Defining Terrorism: The End of Double Standards*
The Epic of Arya (2nd ed.)
Nietzsche's Coming God, or the Redemption of the Divine
Verses of Light

BAL GANGADHAR TILAK — *The Arctic Home in the Vedas*

DOMINIQUE VENNER — *For a Positive Critique*
The Shock of History

MARKUS WILLINGER — *A Europe of Nations*
Generation Identity

DAVID J. WINGFIELD (ED.) — *The Initiate: Journal of Traditional Studies*